UNAPOLOGETICALLY BAPTIST

UNAPOLOGETICALLY BAPTIST

A BIBLICAL EXPOSITION FOR NEW AND LONGTIME BAPTIST

by

JEREMY W. ODOM

iPREACH
PUBLICATIONS

© 2024

UNAPOLOGETICALLY BAPTIST:
A BIBLICAL EXPOSITION FOR NEW AND LONGTIME BAPTISTS

Copyright © 2024 by Jeremy W Odom

ISBN 979-8-9914-9850-0

Library of Congress Control Number: 2024919480

Printed in the United States of America

DEDICATION

To the Damascus Missionary Baptist Church, Lena, Louisiana, where I was baptized and nurtured in my early faith; to the First Baptist Church-Amulet Street, Natchitoches, Louisiana, where I began my ministry as a young man in 2002; to the Bright Morning Star Missionary Baptist Church, Marco, Louisiana, where I embarked on my first pastorate in 2008; to the Louisiana Home and Foreign Missions Baptist Convention, whose officers have guided and inspired me to embrace the Baptist faith with conviction; and to the Saint Rest Baptist Church, Frierson, Louisiana, my current pastorate, where I continue to serve and grow in ministry—this book is prayerfully and affectionately dedicated.

May it stand as a testament to the enduring faith and shared mission that unite us in the work of our Lord and Savior.

Dr. Jeremy W. Odom
2024

CONTENTS

Acknowledgements i

Preface ii

Introduction iii

PART I. OUR HISTORY

1   An Overview of the Baptist Church 3

2   Pioneers and Founders 11

3   Theological Innovators and Modern Leaders 17

4   Milestones and Movements in Baptist History 25

PART II. THE FAITH CONTRACT

5   Introduction of the Church Covenant 33

6   A Profound Pronouncement 39

7   A Commitment to Church Advancement 45

8   A Commitment to Personal Faith 51

9   A Commitment to the Community of Faith 57

10   A Commitment to Continual Fellowship 63

11   The Covenant in Worship and Life 69

PART III. THE GUIDING PRINCIPLES

12   The Declaration of Faith 79

13   The Scriptures 87

14   The True God 91

15   The Fall of Man 95

16   The Way of Salvation 99

17   Justification 105

18   The Freeness of Salvation 111

19	Grace in Regeneration	117
20	Repentance and Faith	123
21	God's Purpose of Grace	129
22	Sanctification	135
23	The Perseverance of Saints	141
24	The Harmony of the Law and the Gospel	147
25	A Gospel Church	153
26	Baptism and the Lord's Supper	157
27	The Christian Sabbath	161
28	Civil Government	165
29	The Righteous and the Wicked	169
30	Christian Education	173
31	Social Service	177
32	Stewardship	183
33	Evangelism and Missions	187
34	The Resurrection	191
35	The Return of the Lord	195
36	The World to Come	199

PART IV. GOVERNANCE

37	Introduction to Church Governance	205
38	Church Composition	209
39	Church Officers	213
40	Key Responsibilities of Church Boards	217
41	Church Discipline	223
42	Developing and Implementing Effective Policies for Church Auxiliaries	227

43 Church Governance and Decision Making 233

44 Financial Management and Oversight 237

45 Legal and Ethical Considerations 241

46 Relation to Other Bodies 245

47 Future Trends in Church Governance 249

PART V. ORDINANCES OF THE CHURCH

48 The Role of Ordinances in Baptist Identity 257

49 Administration of the Ordinances 263

50 Baptism 269

51 The Lord's Supper 275

PART VI. A JOB FOR EVERYONE

52 Introduction to Church Committees and Auxiliaries 283

53 Understanding Church Committees 287

54 Understanding Church Auxiliaries 291

55 Key Responsibilities of Church Auxiliaries 297

56 Effective Management and Coordination of Church
    Auxiliaries 303

57 Challenges and Solutions in Managing Church Auxiliaries 309

58 Evaluating and Improving the Effectiveness of Church
    Auxiliaries 313

59 Case Studies and Best Practices in Church Management 319

60 Future Trends and Innovations in Church Management 323

PART VII. KEY OBSERVANCES AND TRADITIONS

61 The Rich Tradition of Baptist Observances 329

62 Church Anniversary 337

63 Pastor Anniversary 343

64   Musician Appreciation 349

65   Choir Anniversary 353

66   Church Picnic 359

67   Family and Friends Day 363

68   Homecoming Service 367

69   Men's and Women's Day 371

70   Installation of Church Officers 375

71   Missionary Day 379

72   Minister Ordination 383

73   Deacon Ordination 389

74   Pastoral Installation 395

75   Revivals 401

76   Youth and Children's Day 409

77   Easter Sunrise Service 413

78   Watch Night 417

APPENDICES

List of National Baptist Conventions Additional Resources 425

Additional Resources 429

Glossary of Baptist Terminology 433

Bibliography 439

ACKNOWLEDGMENTS

The journey of writing *Unapologetically Baptist* has been one of profound reflection, discovery, and collaboration. This book would not have been possible without the support, guidance, and encouragement of many individuals to whom I owe a great debt of gratitude.

First and foremost, I give thanks to God, whose grace and wisdom have guided me throughout this process. His Word has been a constant source of inspiration and clarity, and it is my prayer that this book will honor Him and serve His purposes in the lives of its readers.

I am deeply grateful to my family for their unwavering support and encouragement. Your love and understanding have been a pillar of strength throughout the writing of this book. Thank you for believing in me and for your patience as I devoted countless hours to this project.

A special acknowledgment goes to my Pastor and cousin, Rev. Frank "Doug" Randle, Jr. Your guidance, prayers, and support have been a source of immense encouragement. Your leadership and wisdom have profoundly impacted my ministry and have been instrumental in shaping my approach to this work.

I also want to express my gratitude to the members of Saint Rest Baptist Church in Frierson, Louisiana. Your prayers, encouragement, and willingness to engage in thoughtful discussions have enriched this book in ways I could not have imagined. To my fellow pastors and ministers, particularly those who have walked alongside me in ministry, your insights and fellowship have been invaluable.

I am also indebted to the many scholars, historians, and theologians whose work has informed and influenced this book.

Their contributions to the study of Baptist history and doctrine have provided a solid foundation upon which this book is built.

To my mentors, both past and present, who have nurtured my faith and ministry, I am forever grateful. Your wisdom, guidance, and example have left an indelible mark on my life, and I am honored to carry forward the legacy of faithful Baptist witness that you have entrusted to me.

Finally, to my readers—whether you are a longtime Baptist, new to the faith, or simply exploring what it means to be Baptist—thank you for allowing me the privilege of sharing this journey with you. It is my hope that this book will deepen your understanding, strengthen your faith, and inspire you to live out your Baptist identity with conviction and joy.

To all who have played a part in the creation of this book, whether mentioned by name or not, please know that your contributions have not gone unnoticed. This book is as much yours as it is mine, and I am deeply thankful for your support.

With heartfelt gratitude,

Dr. Jeremy W. Odom

PREFACE

Reflecting on my journey from the baptismal waters of Damascus Missionary Baptist Church in Lena, Louisiana, to my current pastorate at Saint Rest Baptist Church in Frierson, Louisiana, I am reminded of the deep roots and profound impact of the Baptist faith. "Unapologetically Baptist: A Biblical Exposition for New and Longtime Baptists" is a labor of love, born from my appreciation for our tradition and a desire to share its rich history, guiding principles, and vibrant practices.

In recent years, we've witnessed a significant shift away from Baptist beliefs, influenced by rapid technological advancements and a perceived erosion of foundational structure within many "so-called Baptists." It's crucial to remember that the Baptist tradition is deeply anchored in Scripture, with doctrines firmly rooted in biblical teaching. Yet, as our faith faces challenges, it's essential to reaffirm our commitment to these core principles.

I recall my own experiences growing up in a Baptist church where tradition sometimes overshadowed genuine belief. Many attended out of habit, treating the church more as a family legacy than a source of spiritual truth. This personal reflection underscores the urgency of revisiting and reaffirming the foundational principles of Baptist faith.

This book emerges from a need to keep these foundational precepts fresh and relevant. Over the past two years, I have conducted rigorous study and research to ensure that this work presents accurate and relevant material. I have selected sources based on their verifiable reputations and carefully scrutinized each assertion to maintain credibility.

Special attention has been given to exploring the origins of the Baptist Church in America, identifying key figures who have shaped its history, and examining its core beliefs and observances. By addressing both historical and contemporary challenges, I aim to provide readers with a comprehensive understanding of our faith and its significance.

In preparing this book, I have also anticipated potential criticisms of the current state of Baptist beliefs. Recognizing that there are diverse perspectives within our community, I encourage readers to engage with the material critically and thoughtfully. Reflect on how these principles apply to your own life and church community and consider how you can actively contribute to the preservation and vitality of our tradition.

I invite you to join me on this journey of exploration and reaffirmation. May "Unapologetically Baptist" serve as a guide to understanding Baptist beliefs and as a call to action, inspiring you to embrace and live out the core tenets of our faith with renewed passion and clarity.

Thank you for embarking on this journey with me. Let us reaffirm the strength and beauty of our Baptist heritage and actively engage in shaping its future.

In Christ's service,

Dr. Jeremy W. Odom

INTRODUCTION

In a world where denominational lines often blur, and religious identities are increasingly questioned, the importance of understanding and affirming one's faith tradition cannot be overstated. For Baptists, this is particularly crucial. Rooted in a rich history of theological conviction and ecclesiastical practice, the Baptist faith represents a distinct and vital expression of Christianity that has influenced millions of lives across generations.

Unapologetically Baptist is more than just a guide; it is a declaration of commitment to the foundational principles that have defined Baptist belief and practice for centuries. Whether you are a new believer, a lifelong Baptist, or simply someone interested in the Baptist tradition, this book is designed to deepen your understanding, strengthen your faith, and equip you to live out your convictions with clarity and confidence.

In the chapters that follow, we will journey through the heart of Baptist identity, exploring everything from our historical roots to the doctrines that shape our daily lives. We will examine the covenant that binds us as a community of believers and delve into the guiding principles—our Articles of Faith—that articulate what we believe and why. We will also look at the governance structures that ensure order and accountability within our churches, and we will consider the ordinances that serve as outward expressions of our inward faith.

But this book is not just about understanding; it is about application. The Baptist tradition is one of active engagement—within our churches, our communities, and the world at large. That is why this book also includes practical insights into church committees, auxiliaries, and other ministries that allow every member of the congregation to contribute meaningfully to the mission of the church.

Throughout this journey, we will remain anchored in Scripture, the ultimate authority for all Baptist belief and practice. By grounding our exploration in the Word of God, we ensure that our understanding of what it means to be Baptist is not only historically informed but also biblically sound.

As you read through these pages, my hope is that you will find not only knowledge but also inspiration—an encouragement to embrace your Baptist identity with renewed vigor and a deeper appreciation for the faith we hold dear. In a time when many are drifting away from denominational distinctives, *Unapologetically Baptist* calls us to stand firm in our convictions, unapologetically embracing the faith that has been passed down to us through the generations.

Thank you for joining me on this journey. Together, let us rediscover the beauty, depth, and relevance of being Baptist in today's world.

PART I. OUR HISTORY

CHAPTER ONE
AN OVERVIEW OF THE BAPTIST CHURCH

Introduction

The Baptist Church is a distinct and vibrant tradition within Christianity, characterized by its unique beliefs, practices, and organizational structures. This chapter provides an in-depth overview of the Baptist Church, exploring its historical origins, core doctrines, ecclesiology, and the practical aspects of Baptist life. By understanding these foundational elements, readers can gain a comprehensive appreciation of what defines the Baptist tradition and how it functions within the broader Christian context.

Historical Origins

Early Beginnings and Anabaptist Influence

The Baptist tradition finds its roots in the broader Reformation movement of the 16th century. The Anabaptists, who emerged during this period, played a pivotal role in shaping early Baptist thought. Leaders like Conrad Grebel and Felix Manz rejected infant baptism, advocating instead for believer's baptism based on personal faith and conviction. Their emphasis on voluntary church membership and the separation of church and state influenced early

Baptist leaders, who sought to establish a new tradition centered on these principles.

The Founding of the First Baptist Churches

The formal beginning of the Baptist Church is often traced to John Smyth and his congregation in Amsterdam in 1609. Smyth, an English Separatist, established a church that practiced believer's baptism, marking the inception of the Baptist tradition. His congregation's emphasis on voluntary association and local church autonomy became foundational principles for Baptists.

In 1612, Thomas Helwys, a former member of Smyth's congregation, returned to England and founded the first Baptist church on English soil. Helwys' church emphasized religious liberty and the separation of church and state, principles that would become central to Baptist identity. This early church model laid the groundwork for the development of Baptist congregations and their distinctive practices.

Core Doctrines and Beliefs

Believer's Baptism

One of the hallmark beliefs of the Baptist tradition is believer's baptism. Baptists hold that baptism should be reserved for those who can personally profess their faith in Jesus Christ, as opposed to infant baptism. This practice reflects the Baptist emphasis on individual faith and conscious commitment to Christ. Believer's baptism is typically administered by full immersion, symbolizing the believer's identification with the death, burial, and resurrection of Christ.

Congregational Autonomy

Another core principle of the Baptist Church is congregational autonomy. Baptists believe that each local church is a self-governing body, responsible for its own affairs and decisions. This autonomy means that individual congregations are free to govern themselves without interference from external authorities or denominational hierarchies. Congregational autonomy underscores the Baptist commitment to the independence and authority of the local church.

The Priesthood of All Believers

The doctrine of the priesthood of all believers is a fundamental Baptist belief. This principle asserts that every Christian has direct access to God and is responsible for their own spiritual growth and ministry. Unlike traditions that emphasize a distinct clerical hierarchy, Baptists believe that all members of the church are called to minister to one another and contribute to the church's mission. This belief fosters a sense of shared responsibility and equality within the Baptist community.

The Separation of Church and State

The Baptist tradition has a strong historical commitment to the separation of church and state. Early Baptists, influenced by figures like Roger Williams, advocated for religious liberty and the protection of the church from government interference. This principle is rooted in the belief that faith and worship should be voluntary and free from coercion. The separation of church and state remains a significant aspect of Baptist identity and advocacy.

Church Structure and Governance

Local Church Governance

Baptist churches are characterized by their congregational governance structure. Each local church operates as an autonomous entity, with its own elected leaders and decision-making processes. Key leadership roles typically include the pastor, deacons, and various ministry leaders. The pastor is responsible for preaching, teaching, and providing spiritual leadership, while deacons assist with practical matters and support the pastor's ministry.

The congregation plays an active role in church decision-making, including the selection of leaders, approval of budgets, and the establishment of policies. This participatory approach reflects the Baptist commitment to democratic and accountable governance within the local church.

Baptist Associations and Conventions

While local churches maintain autonomy, many Baptists participate in associations and conventions for fellowship, mutual support, and cooperative ministry. Associations are regional gatherings of Baptist churches that work together on common projects and initiatives. Conventions, such as the Southern Baptist Convention, serve a similar purpose but operate on a larger scale, often including churches from multiple regions or nations.

These associations and conventions provide opportunities for Baptists to collaborate on mission work, educational programs, and social services. They also offer a platform for addressing shared concerns and promoting Baptist values on a broader scale. However, it is important to note that while these bodies provide support and coordination, they do not exercise authority over individual churches.

Worship and Practices

Worship Style and Elements

Baptist worship varies widely among congregations but generally emphasizes the centrality of preaching and the proclamation of Scripture. Services often include singing hymns and contemporary worship songs, reading from the Bible, and prayer. The sermon, delivered by the pastor or a guest preacher, is a focal point of Baptist worship and is intended to provide biblical teaching and application.

Baptist worship services may also incorporate other elements such as Lord's Supper (Communion) and baptism. The observance of the Lord's Supper is a significant practice that commemorates the death and resurrection of Jesus Christ. Baptists typically celebrate the Lord's Supper quarterly or on a regular basis, depending on the church's tradition.

The Lord's Supper and Baptism

The Lord's Supper, or Communion, is a central ordinance in Baptist worship. Baptists believe in the symbolic nature of the elements— the bread and the cup—as a means of remembering Christ's sacrifice. The observance of the Lord's Supper is typically conducted in a solemn and reflective manner, with an emphasis on the spiritual significance of the act.

Baptism, as previously noted, is practiced by full immersion and is seen as an outward sign of an inward change. It is typically administered to individuals who have made a personal confession of faith and are joining the church. Baptism is a key aspect of Baptist identity and is considered an important step in the believer's spiritual journey.

Key Doctrinal Issues and Contemporary Debates

Theology and Doctrine

Baptist theology is grounded in a commitment to Scripture as the ultimate authority in matters of faith and practice. Baptists uphold the inerrancy and sufficiency of the Bible, viewing it as the inspired Word of God. This belief shapes Baptist doctrine and practice, influencing everything from preaching and teaching to personal conduct and church governance.

Contemporary debates within the Baptist tradition often center around issues such as gender roles, LGBTQ+ inclusion, and social justice. These debates reflect broader societal discussions and highlight the diversity of thought within the Baptist community. While some Baptist congregations and denominations take progressive stances on these issues, others adhere to more conservative positions. The ongoing dialogue within the Baptist tradition underscores the dynamic nature of Baptist theology and practice.

Social Justice and Ethics

The Baptist tradition has a complex relationship with social justice issues. Historically, Baptists have been involved in advocating for various social causes, including civil rights and humanitarian efforts. Figures like Martin Luther King Jr. exemplify the Baptist commitment to social justice and equality.

However, there are also varying perspectives within the Baptist community on issues related to social justice and ethics. Some Baptist churches and leaders are actively engaged in social justice initiatives, while others emphasize personal piety and evangelism as primary concerns. This diversity of perspectives reflects the broader spectrum of Baptist thought and practice.

Conclusion

The Baptist Church is a diverse and dynamic tradition with a rich history and distinctive beliefs. From its early origins in the Reformation to its contemporary global presence, Baptists have navigated various historical and theological developments. Understanding the core doctrines, church structure, and practices of the Baptist tradition provides valuable insight into its identity and significance within the broader Christian context.

By exploring the foundational principles and contemporary issues facing Baptists, readers can gain a deeper appreciation for the complexities and contributions of the Baptist tradition. As Baptists continue to engage with evolving societal and theological challenges, their commitment to core beliefs and practices remains central to their identity and mission.

CHAPTER TWO
PIONEERS AND FOUNDERS

Introduction

The Baptist tradition is deeply rooted in the contributions of early pioneers and founders who shaped its core principles and practices. This chapter explores the lives and legacies of key figures from the early days of the Baptist movement, highlighting their foundational roles in establishing and defining Baptist beliefs. Their pioneering efforts laid the groundwork for the vibrant and diverse Baptist tradition we know today.

John Smyth

Early Life and Ministry John Smyth (circa 1566-1612) was a pivotal figure in the early Baptist movement. Born in England, Smyth studied at Cambridge University, where he was influenced by Puritan ideas. His journey towards Baptist beliefs began with a growing dissatisfaction with the Anglican Church and its practices.

Founding of the First Baptist Church In 1609, Smyth and a group of separatists formed the first Baptist congregation in Amsterdam. This church, often referred to as the "Amsterdam Baptist Church," was significant for its commitment to believer's baptism and the rejection of infant baptism. Smyth's theological shift marked a crucial departure from traditional practices and laid the foundation for future Baptist beliefs.

Theological Contributions Smyth's work emphasized the importance of a believer's personal faith in baptism, contrasting sharply with the infant baptism practiced by many other Christian traditions. His writings, including *The Differences of the Churches of the Separatists from the Church of England*, provided a theological framework for understanding and practicing believer's baptism.

Impact and Legacy John Smyth's contributions to Baptist theology and church practice were profound. His emphasis on believer's baptism and congregational autonomy influenced subsequent Baptist leaders and helped to establish the foundational principles of Baptist identity.

Thomas Helwys

Early Life and Departure Thomas Helwys (circa 1575-1616) was another key figure in the early Baptist movement. A contemporary and associate of John Smyth, Helwys played a crucial role in the development of Baptist beliefs and practices. Born in England, he initially shared Smyth's separatist views but later diverged in significant ways.

Establishment of the First Baptist Church in England Upon returning to England, Helwys established the first Baptist church in England in 1612. This congregation was marked by its commitment to religious liberty and separation from the state church. Helwys's church emphasized the importance of voluntary association and believer's baptism, setting a precedent for future Baptist churches.

Advocacy for Religious Liberty Helwys was a strong advocate for religious freedom, a stance that was radical for his time. In his work

A Short Declaration of the Mystery of Iniquity, Helwys argued for the separation of church and state and the right of individuals to worship according to their conscience. His advocacy for religious liberty was a significant departure from the prevailing norms and laid the groundwork for future debates on religious freedom.

Impact and Legacy Thomas Helwys's contributions to Baptist theology and religious liberty were foundational. His emphasis on voluntary church membership and separation of church and state influenced subsequent Baptist thought and practice, establishing important principles for the Baptist tradition.

Roger Williams

Early Life and Settlement in America Roger Williams (circa 1603-1683) was a prominent figure in the early American Baptist movement. Born in England, Williams immigrated to the Massachusetts Bay Colony, where he became a vocal critic of the Puritan establishment. His disagreements with the colonial authorities led him to seek a new path for religious practice.

Founding of Rhode Island and the First Baptist Church In 1636, Williams founded the Rhode Island Colony, establishing a haven for religious dissenters. The First Baptist Church of Providence, organized by Williams in 1638, was notable for its commitment to religious freedom and the separation of church and state. Williams's efforts in Rhode Island created a model for religious tolerance and self-governance.

Contributions to Religious Freedom and Native American Relations Williams's commitment to religious freedom and fair treatment of Native Americans set him apart as a forward-thinking leader. His writings, including *The Bloudy Tenent of Persecution*, argued for the separation of church and state and the importance of religious liberty. Williams also engaged in efforts to negotiate peaceful relations with Native American tribes, demonstrating his commitment to justice and equity.

Impact and Legacy Roger Williams's legacy is marked by his pioneering work in religious freedom and the establishment of a model for religious tolerance. His contributions to the Baptist movement and his advocacy for the separation of church and state continue to influence American religious and political thought.

William Carey

Early Life and Missionary Work William Carey (1761-1834) was a key figure in the development of modern Baptist missions. Born in England, Carey was a self-taught scholar and a passionate advocate for global missions. His early work focused on translating the Bible into multiple languages and establishing mission stations in India.

Missionary Contributions in India Carey's work in India included the establishment of educational institutions and the translation of the Bible into several Indian languages. His efforts in founding the Baptist Missionary Society and his work in education and social reform had a profound impact on the spread of Christianity in India. Carey's approach to missions was characterized by a focus on both evangelism and social transformation.

Legacy and Influence on Modern Baptist Missions William Carey's contributions to Baptist missions are widely recognized and celebrated. His emphasis on translating Scripture and establishing educational institutions laid the groundwork for modern missionary efforts. Carey's legacy endures through the continued work of missionary organizations and his influence on contemporary Baptist missions.

George Lisle (George Liele)

Early Life and Ministry George Lisle (circa 1750-1820), also known as George Liele, was a pioneering African American missionary and preacher. Born into slavery in Georgia, Liele's conversion to Christianity led him to become a prominent preacher and missionary. His work had a significant impact on the Baptist movement in the Caribbean.

Missionary Work in Jamaica In 1783, Liele moved to Jamaica, where he established the first Baptist church on the island. His efforts in Jamaica included evangelism, church planting, and social reform. Liele's work was instrumental in spreading Baptist beliefs in the Caribbean and laying the foundation for future missionary efforts in the region.

Impact on African American Baptist History George Lisle's contributions to the Baptist movement are particularly notable for his role as an African American missionary. His work in Jamaica and his commitment to evangelism and social reform reflect his dedication to spreading the gospel and improving the lives of those he served.

Legacy George Lisle's legacy is marked by his pioneering missionary work and his role in spreading Baptist beliefs in the Caribbean. His contributions to African American Baptist history and his impact on global missions continue to be recognized and celebrated.

Crispus Attucks

Early Life and Role in the American Revolution Crispus Attucks (circa 1723-1770) was an African American who played a significant role in the American Revolution. Born in Massachusetts, Attucks was a sailor and laborer who became a symbol of resistance against British oppression. His involvement in the Boston Massacre and his subsequent death made him a martyr for the cause of American independence.

Symbolism of Attucks's Resistance Attucks's resistance against British troops and his role in the Boston Massacre are significant for their symbolic representation of the struggle for liberty and justice.

His actions have been remembered as a powerful example of courage and resistance against tyranny.

Connection to Baptist Tradition While Attucks was not directly involved in the Baptist movement, his legacy of resistance and the quest for justice resonate with Baptist principles of freedom and equality. His story highlights the broader context of struggle for religious and political freedom, which aligns with Baptist values.

Legacy Crispus Attucks's legacy extends beyond his role in the American Revolution. His story serves as a powerful reminder of the struggle for liberty and justice, values that are deeply embedded in the Baptist tradition.

Conclusion

The pioneers and founders of the Baptist movement played crucial roles in shaping its doctrines, practices, and identity. From John Smyth and Thomas Helwys to William Carey and George Lisle, their contributions laid the foundation for the Baptist tradition. The impact of these early figures continues to be felt in contemporary Baptist practice, reflecting their enduring legacy in the evolution of the Baptist faith.

CHAPTER THREE
THEOLOGICAL INNOVATORS AND
MODERN LEADERS

Introduction

The evolution of Baptist thought and practice is marked by the contributions of significant theological innovators and contemporary leaders who have shaped the direction of the tradition. This chapter explores the lives and legacies of pivotal figures from the 19th century to the present, highlighting their contributions to Baptist theology, education, and leadership. Their influence extends from foundational doctrines to modern practices, reflecting the dynamic nature of the Baptist movement.

John Newton Brown

John Newton Brown (1803-1868) was a key figure in the development of Baptist polity and doctrine in the 19th century. His most notable contribution, the *Baptist Church Manual*, has had a lasting impact on Baptist churches across America.

Early Life and Education John Newton Brown was born in New Hampshire and educated at Brown University. His early pastoral ministry was marked by a commitment to systematic theology and church governance, which would later influence his work on the *Baptist Church Manual*.

Contributions to Baptist Theology Brown's *Baptist Church Manual* was first published in 1853 and has since become a standard reference for Baptist churches. The manual addressed church organization, membership, and disciplinary procedures, reflecting a careful balance of theological precision and practical application. It provided a comprehensive guide for Baptist church life, influencing how churches handle internal matters and interact with the broader community.

Influence on Baptist Polity Brown's work was instrumental in shaping Baptist polity, providing a framework for church governance that emphasized congregational autonomy and democratic decision-making. His manual has been adopted and adapted by numerous Baptist congregations, highlighting his enduring influence on Baptist church structure and practice.

Legacy John Newton Brown's contributions extend beyond his writings; his impact on Baptist polity and church life remains evident in contemporary Baptist practice. His emphasis on organized church governance and his approach to theological issues continue to inform Baptist thought and practice.

Francis Wayland

Francis Wayland (1796-1865) was a leading theologian and educator whose work had a profound impact on Baptist education and moral philosophy. His contributions to Baptist thought are still relevant today.

Life and Academic Career Wayland was born in New York and graduated from Brown University. He became a professor and later the president of Brown University, where he was influential in shaping the institution's approach to education and theology.

Theological Contributions Wayland's writings on moral philosophy and Christian ethics were groundbreaking. His work emphasized the integration of faith and reason, advocating for a rational approach to theology that respected both Scripture and human experience. His book, *The Elements of Moral Science*, was widely influential, shaping Baptist thought on ethics and morality.

Educational Reforms As president of Brown University, Wayland implemented reforms that emphasized a liberal arts education, integrating moral and religious instruction with academic studies. His vision for higher education influenced Baptist institutions and contributed to the development of a more comprehensive approach to theological education.

Legacy Francis Wayland's impact on Baptist education and moral philosophy is evident in the continued emphasis on ethical considerations within Baptist thought. His contributions to both academic and religious spheres reflect his commitment to integrating faith with intellectual inquiry.

B.H. Carroll

B.H. Carroll (1843-1914) was a seminal figure in Baptist education, founding Southwestern Baptist Theological Seminary and shaping Baptist theological education in the American South.

Founding of Southwestern Baptist Theological Seminary
Carroll's vision for a Southern Baptist seminary became a reality with the establishment of Southwestern Baptist Theological Seminary in 1908. His leadership in founding the seminary provided a critical resource for training Baptist ministers and educators in the region.

Theological Contributions Carroll's approach to theology was characterized by a commitment to traditional Baptist doctrines, including inerrancy and the autonomy of the local church. His emphasis on rigorous theological education and his contributions to Baptist scholarship helped to shape the theological landscape of the Southern Baptist Convention.

Influence and Legacy B.H. Carroll's impact on Baptist education is reflected in the ongoing prominence of Southwestern Baptist Theological Seminary as a leading institution for Baptist training. His legacy endures through the continued influence of his theological and educational work on Baptist ministry and scholarship.

J.D. Greear

J.D. Greear (born 1973) is a contemporary Baptist leader known for his dynamic approach to evangelism, church planting, and cultural engagement. His leadership has shaped the direction of the Southern Baptist Convention in recent years.

Early Life and Ministry Greear was born in North Carolina and graduated from the University of North Carolina at Chapel Hill before earning his seminary degree from Southeastern Baptist Theological Seminary. His early ministry was marked by a focus on church planting and reaching unchurched populations.

Leadership within the Southern Baptist Convention As president of the Southern Baptist Convention from 2018 to 2021, Greear emphasized a vision of church multiplication and cultural engagement. His leadership was characterized by efforts to address social justice issues and foster unity within the convention.

Focus on Evangelism and Church Planting Greear's approach to ministry includes a strong emphasis on evangelism and church planting. His work at The Summit Church, where he serves as pastor, has been notable for its focus on reaching new communities and expanding the reach of the gospel.

Legacy J.D. Greear's influence on the Southern Baptist Convention and contemporary Baptist practice is significant. His focus on practical evangelism and church planting continues to shape the direction of Baptist ministry and reflects a commitment to addressing current challenges facing the church.

Samuel C. Tolbert, Jr.

Samuel C. Tolbert, Jr. (born 1955) is a prominent Baptist leader whose work has had a significant impact on both the Louisiana Home and Foreign Missions Baptist Convention, Inc. and the National Baptist Convention of America International, Inc.

Presidency of the Louisiana Home and Foreign Missions Baptist Convention, Inc. Before becoming president of the National Baptist Convention, Tolbert served as president of the Louisiana Home and Foreign Missions Baptist Convention, Inc. His leadership in this role was marked by efforts to strengthen mission work and support local congregations in Louisiana.

Role as President of the National Baptist Convention of America International, Inc. Tolbert's presidency of the National Baptist Convention has been characterized by a focus on social justice, educational advancement, and institutional support. His leadership has been influential in shaping the direction of the convention and addressing contemporary issues within the Baptist community.

Contributions to Baptist Leadership and Social Justice
Tolbert's work in advocating for social justice and educational initiatives reflects his commitment to applying Baptist principles in practical ways. His efforts to promote unity and address the needs of marginalized communities highlight his dedication to both faith and social action.

Legacy Samuel C. Tolbert, Jr.'s impact on Baptist leadership and social justice is significant. His contributions to the National Baptist Convention and his focus on practical ministry issues continue to influence contemporary Baptist practice and thought.

Elias Keach and Benjamin Keach

Elias Keach (circa 1640-1701) and Benjamin Keach (1640-1704) were influential figures in early Baptist evangelism and theology, contributing to the development of Baptist doctrine and practice in the 17th century.

Elias Keach Elias Keach, known for his evangelistic efforts, played a crucial role in spreading Baptist beliefs in the American colonies. His work included preaching and organizing Baptist churches, which contributed to the growth of the Baptist movement in the New World.

Benjamin Keach Benjamin Keach was a prominent Baptist preacher and theologian known for his contributions to Baptist doctrine and hymnody. His writings on Baptist beliefs and his promotion of hymns within Baptist worship were influential in shaping Baptist practice.

Contributions to Baptist Doctrine and Hymnody Benjamin Keach's work on Baptist doctrine and his role in promoting hymns reflected his commitment to theological precision and vibrant worship. His contributions to Baptist hymnody helped to enrich Baptist worship practices and foster a deeper theological understanding within the tradition.

Legacy The contributions of Elias and Benjamin Keach to Baptist evangelism, doctrine, and worship continue to be recognized in Baptist history. Their influence on early Baptist practices and their role in shaping the development of the Baptist movement highlight their enduring legacy.

Conclusion

The theological innovators and modern leaders covered in this chapter have made significant contributions to the Baptist tradition, shaping its development from the 19th century to the present. Their work reflects a dynamic interplay of doctrine, education, and practical ministry, highlighting the ongoing evolution of Baptist thought and practice. The legacies of these figures underscore the depth and breadth of Baptist influence, illustrating how past and present leaders have shaped the movement's trajectory.

CHAPTER FOUR
MILESTONES AND MOVEMENTS IN
BAPTIST HISTORY

Introduction

The Baptist tradition has been shaped by a series of significant milestones and movements that have influenced its development and identity. This chapter delves into key historical events, movements, and transformations that have defined the Baptist Church. By examining these milestones, readers can better understand the evolution of Baptist beliefs, practices, and institutions over time.

Early Influences and Foundations

The Anabaptist Movement (16th Century)

The Anabaptist movement, emerging in the early 16th century, played a crucial role in shaping Baptist principles. The Anabaptists, including figures such as Conrad Grebel and Felix Manz, advocated for believer's baptism and a separation from state-controlled churches. Their insistence on voluntary membership and adult baptism set the stage for Baptist theology.

The Anabaptists faced severe persecution from both Protestant and Catholic authorities due to their radical reforms and rejection of infant baptism. Their emphasis on a church composed solely of believers, rather than infants and adults, deeply influenced the development of Baptist identity. Although distinct from Baptists, the Anabaptists' principles of believers' baptism and church autonomy were foundational for early Baptists.

The Formation of the First Baptist Churches (1609-1612)

The Baptist tradition formally began with John Smyth and his congregation in Amsterdam in 1609. Smyth, an English Separatist, founded a church that practiced believer's baptism and rejected infant baptism. This marked the official emergence of the Baptist movement, characterized by a commitment to voluntary church membership and autonomy.

Smyth's church soon faced internal disagreements, leading to the formation of a separate congregation under Thomas Helwys in England in 1612. Helwys' church, established in Spitalfields, London, became the first Baptist church on English soil. Helwys' commitment to religious liberty and the separation of church and state was a defining feature of this early Baptist congregation. His work laid the groundwork for the Baptist movement in England and beyond.

Expansion and Development in America

The Establishment of the First Baptist Church in America (1638)

Roger Williams, a Puritan minister and advocate for religious freedom, founded the First Baptist Church in America in Providence, Rhode Island, in 1638. Williams' church was established on the principles of voluntary association and believer's baptism, reflecting a commitment to religious liberty and the separation of church and state.

Williams' efforts in Providence represented a significant shift from the established religious practices of the time, as he emphasized the importance of individual conscience and religious freedom. His church became a model for Baptist practice in the American colonies, showcasing the Baptist commitment to personal faith and local church autonomy.

The Great Awakening (1730s-1740s)

The Great Awakening, a series of religious revivals in the American colonies during the 1730s and 1740s, had a profound impact on the Baptist movement. Evangelists like George Whitefield and Jonathan Edwards sparked a wave of religious fervor that led to a significant increase in Baptist congregations.

The revivals associated with the Great Awakening emphasized personal piety and a direct relationship with God, which resonated with Baptist principles. The movement's emphasis on individual conversion and spiritual renewal reinforced Baptist beliefs and contributed to the growth of Baptist churches across the American colonies. The Great Awakening also influenced Baptist preaching and worship practices, highlighting the importance of heartfelt and passionate ministry.

Civil War and Its Impact

The Formation of the Southern Baptist Convention (1845)

The formation of the Southern Baptist Convention (SBC) in 1845 marked a pivotal moment in Baptist history. This split from the Triennial Convention arose from disagreements over missions and the issue of slavery. The SBC was established as a response to the desire for greater autonomy among Southern Baptist churches and reflected regional differences within the American Baptist movement.

The SBC's formation highlighted the complex relationship between Baptists and societal issues, such as slavery. The Convention's establishment underscored the Baptist commitment to local church governance while also revealing deep-seated divisions within the denomination. The SBC became a significant force within American Baptists, influencing theology, missions, and social issues.

The Abolitionist Movement and Baptist Involvement

During the 19th century, Baptists played varied roles in the abolitionist movement. Figures such as George Lisle, an African American Baptist preacher and missionary, and Nat Turner, who led a rebellion, illustrate the diverse responses among Baptists to the issue of slavery.

Some Baptist leaders and churches were actively involved in advocating for abolition, while others were aligned with pro-slavery positions. This period reflected broader societal conflicts and showcased the complex role of Baptists in the fight against slavery. The divergent responses to abolition within the Baptist community highlighted the tension between religious convictions and societal norms.

The 20th Century and Modern Transformations

The Landmark Movement (1850s)

The Landmark Movement, led by figures such as J.R. Graves and James M. Pendleton, emerged in the 1850s and emphasized the autonomy of local Baptist churches and adherence to strict Baptist distinctives. The movement's focus on "Landmarkism" posited that true Baptist churches followed a specific New Testament pattern of church polity and practice.

The Landmark Movement had a lasting impact on Baptist ecclesiology, influencing debates on church authority and practice. Landmarkism's emphasis on historical continuity and adherence to

Baptist distinctives contributed to shaping Baptist identity and governance. The movement's legacy can be seen in various Baptist groups that continue to adhere to Landmark principles.

The Civil Rights Movement (1950s-1960s)

The Civil Rights Movement of the 1950s and 1960s was a defining period for American Baptists, notably through the leadership of Martin Luther King Jr., a Baptist minister and civil rights leader. King's advocacy for racial equality and justice resonated with Baptist principles of social justice and equality.

King's involvement in the Civil Rights Movement highlighted the Baptist commitment to addressing contemporary social issues and promoting justice. His leadership and activism influenced both the broader American society and the Baptist community, shaping Baptist responses to racial and social justice issues. The Civil Rights Movement marked a significant moment in the ongoing struggle for equality and justice within the Baptist tradition.

Global Expansion and Contemporary Issues

The Rise of the Global Baptist Movement

In the 20th and 21st centuries, Baptists experienced significant global expansion. The rise of Baptist conventions and churches across Africa, Asia, and Latin America reflects a growing international presence. Key figures such as William Carey, known as the father of modern missions, played a crucial role in advancing Baptist missions worldwide.

The global expansion of Baptist churches underscores the tradition's adaptability and commitment to spreading the Gospel across diverse cultural contexts. The international growth of Baptists has led to a rich tapestry of Baptist expressions, reflecting the tradition's relevance and impact on a global scale.

Contemporary Debates and Challenges

Today, Baptists face a range of contemporary issues, including debates on theology, social justice, and denominational unity. Discussions on topics such as gender roles, LGBTQ+ inclusion, and the impact of digital technology on church life reflect the dynamic nature of the Baptist tradition.

The ongoing dialogue within the Baptist community highlights the diversity of thought and practice within the tradition. As Baptists navigate these modern challenges, they continue to engage with evolving societal and theological issues while maintaining their core beliefs and values.

Conclusion

The history of the Baptist tradition is marked by significant milestones and movements that have shaped its identity and impact. From its early roots in the Anabaptist movement to its contemporary global presence, Baptists have navigated periods of profound change and development. Understanding these historical milestones provides valuable context for appreciating the depth and diversity of the Baptist tradition and its ongoing relevance in the modern world.

By exploring the key events, movements, and transformations within Baptist history, readers gain insight into the complex and dynamic nature of the Baptist tradition. The history of Baptists reflects both a commitment to core principles and an ability to adapt and respond to changing societal and theological landscapes.

PART II. THE FAITH CONTRACT

CHAPTER FIVE
INTRODUCTION TO THE CHURCH
COVENANT

T he Church Covenant holds a pivotal role in the life of Baptist congregations, serving as a formal and communal declaration of faith and commitment. It provides a framework for understanding the collective responsibilities and spiritual aspirations of church members. This chapter will explore the historical development, purpose, and significance of the Church Covenant, with a specific focus on the version found in J. Newton Brown's "A Declaration of Faith" (1853).

Historical Overview

Church Covenants have a long history within Baptist tradition, originating as a means to formalize the shared commitments of church members. These documents emerged to define the relationship between individuals and their church community, establishing guidelines for mutual support, accountability, and spiritual growth. Historically, Church Covenants varied widely in wording and emphasis, reflecting the diverse contexts and theological perspectives of different congregations.

The concept of the Church Covenant is integral to Baptist ecclesiology, underscoring the voluntary nature of church membership and the mutual responsibilities it entails. Covenants serve not only to guide individual conduct but also to unify members in their collective mission, ensuring that all aspects of church life align with biblical teachings.

J. Newton Brown's Version

The version of the Church Covenant presented in J. Newton Brown's "A Declaration of Faith" (1853) represents a significant historical and doctrinal milestone. This version is characterized by its clarity and comprehensive approach, addressing various dimensions of church life and member responsibilities. It provides a structured outline of the commitments expected from church members, emphasizing both personal and communal aspects of faith.

Brown's version has been widely adopted due to its thoroughness and its alignment with core Baptist principles. It captures the essence of what it means to be part of a local church, offering a clear articulation of the commitments required to maintain a vibrant and cohesive community.

Comparison of Versions

While J. Newton Brown's version is noteworthy, it is essential to acknowledge that other versions of the Church Covenant exist. These variations often reflect differences in emphasis or context, tailored to meet the specific needs of different congregations. Some versions may focus more on social justice or individual piety, while others emphasize community engagement or doctrinal adherence.

Despite these variations, the underlying principles of the Church Covenant remain consistent. Each version seeks to express the same fundamental commitments: the recognition of Christ's lordship, mutual support within the church, and active participation in the church's mission. These core principles ensure that, regardless of the specific wording, the essence of the covenant remains intact.

Relevance of the Chosen Version

The version of the Church Covenant by J. Newton Brown continues to be relevant today, particularly within the context of the Baptist tradition addressed in this book. Its detailed approach provides valuable insights into the expectations of church members and their roles within the church community. The principles articulated in this version offer timeless guidance for maintaining a unified and effective church, reflecting the ongoing relevance of the covenant in contemporary church life.

As we move forward in examining each stanza of the Church Covenant, this chapter sets the stage for a deeper exploration of how these commitments are lived out in practical ways. Understanding the historical context and significance of the covenant enriches our appreciation of its role in shaping the life and mission of the church.

THE COVENANT

Having been led, as we believe, by the Spirit of God, to receive the Lord Jesus Christ as our Saviour, and on the profession of our faith, having been baptized in the name of the Father, and of the Son, and of the Holy Ghost, we do now in the presence of God, angels, and this assembly, most solemnly and joyfully enter into covenant with one another as one body in Christ.

We engage therefore, by the aid of the Holy Spirit to walk together in Christian love; to strive for the advancement of this church, in knowledge, holiness, and comfort; to promote its prosperity and spirituality; to sustain its worship, ordinances, discipline, and doctrines; to contribute cheerfully and regularly to the support of the ministry, the expenses of the church, the relief of the poor, and the spread of the gospel through all nations.

We also engage to maintain family and secret devotion; to religiously educate our children; to seek the salvation of our kindred and acquaintances; to walk circumspectly in the world; to be just in our dealings, faithful in our engagements, and exemplary in our deportment; to avoid all tattling, backbiting, and excessive anger; to abstain from the sale and use of intoxicating drink as a beverage, and to be zealous in our efforts to advance the kingdom of our Saviour.

We further engage to watch over one another in brotherly love; to remember each other in prayer; to aid each other in sickness and distress; to cultivate Christian sympathy in feeling and courtesy in speech; to be slow to take offense, but always ready for reconciliation, and mindful of the rules of our Saviour, to secure it without delay.

We moreover engage that, when we remove from this place, we will as soon as possible unite with some other church where we can carry out the spirit of this covenant and the principles of God's Word.

And now unto Him, who brought again from the dead our Lord Jesus, be Power and Glory forever. Amen.

In conclusion, the Church Covenant, as articulated in J. Newton Brown's version, serves as a vital document that encapsulates the core commitments of Baptist church membership. By understanding its historical context, we gain insight into its significance and the enduring principles it represents. The Covenant's detailed stipulations guide members in their spiritual journey, fostering a unified and supportive community dedicated to advancing the mission of the church.

As we delve into the specific stanzas in the subsequent chapters, this foundational understanding will illuminate how these commitments are practically applied in the life of the church. The Church Covenant stands as a testament to the shared faith and responsibilities of its members, reinforcing the collective dedication to living out the teachings of Christ in both personal and communal spheres.

In embracing the Covenant's call to walk together in Christian love and support, members contribute to the ongoing vitality and effectiveness of the church, ensuring that it remains a beacon of faith and a source of strength for its community. The principles outlined in this Covenant are not merely historical artifacts but active components of a living, dynamic faith that continues to shape the life of the church today.

CHAPTER SIX
A PROFOUND PRONOUNCEMENT

The first stanza of the Church Covenant marks a solemn and joyous declaration of faith and commitment. It serves as a foundational statement that establishes the basis for the covenantal relationship among church members. This initial pledge sets the stage for the subsequent commitments by emphasizing the spiritual journey that brings individuals into fellowship with one another and with Christ.

Understanding the First Stanza

The first stanza of the Church Covenant reads:

"Having been led, as we believe, by the Spirit of God to receive the Lord Jesus Christ as our Saviour; and, on the profession of our faith, having been baptized in the name of the Father, and of the Son, and of the Holy Ghost, we do now, in the presence of God, angels, and this assembly, most solemnly and joyfully enter into covenant with one another, as one body in Christ."

This opening statement encapsulates the core elements of Christian initiation and communal commitment. It highlights the role of the Holy Spirit in leading believers to faith, the significance of baptism, and the formal nature of entering into a covenant relationship within the body of Christ.

The Role of the Holy Spirit in Leading to Faith

The reference to being "led by the Spirit of God" underscores the fundamental role of the Holy Spirit in guiding individuals toward faith in Christ. John 16:13 (NKJV) states, "However, when He, the Spirit of truth, has come, He will guide you into all truth." This guidance is essential in leading individuals to recognize their need for a Savior and to respond to the call of God.

The Holy Spirit's role is not just to lead but also to transform. 2 Corinthians 5:17 (NKJV) declares, "Therefore, if anyone is in Christ, he is a new creation; old things have passed away; behold, all things have become new." This transformation is central to the believer's new identity in Christ and their entry into the covenant community.

The Significance of Baptism

Baptism, as described in the stanza, is an outward sign of an inward change. Matthew 28:19 (NKJV) commands, "Go therefore and make disciples of all nations, baptizing them in the name of the Father and of the Son and of the Holy Spirit." This ordinance symbolizes the believer's identification with Christ's death, burial, and resurrection.

Acts 2:38 (NKJV) also emphasizes the importance of baptism in the context of repentance and faith: "Then Peter said to them, 'Repent, and let every one of you be baptized in the name of Jesus Christ for the remission of sins; and you shall receive the gift of the Holy Spirit.'" This act of obedience signifies a public declaration of faith and a commitment to live according to Christ's teachings.

Entering into Covenant in the Presence of God

The act of entering into covenant "in the presence of God, angels, and this assembly" reflects the solemnity and gravity of the commitment being made. Hebrews 12:22-24 (NKJV) describes the heavenly assembly, stating, "But you have come to Mount Zion and to the city of the living God, the heavenly Jerusalem, to an innumerable company of angels, to the general assembly and church of the firstborn who are registered in heaven, to God the Judge of all, to the spirits of just men made perfect, to Jesus the Mediator of the new covenant, and to the blood of sprinkling that speaks better things than that of Abel."

This celestial witness serves as a reminder of the sacred nature of the covenant and the accountability that comes with it. The presence of the assembly underscores the communal aspect of this commitment, emphasizing that it is not just an individual pledge but a collective undertaking.

The Joy and Solemnity of the Covenant

The covenant is described as both "solemn" and "joyful," highlighting the dual nature of this commitment. It is solemn because it involves a serious and binding promise before God and the community. At the same time, it is joyful because it marks the beginning of a new chapter in the believer's spiritual journey and their integration into the body of Christ.

Psalm 100:1-2 (NKJV) captures this sense of joyful worship: "Make a joyful shout to the Lord, all you lands! Serve the Lord with gladness; come before His presence with singing." This joy reflects the new identity and belonging that come with entering into covenant and being part of the church community.

Challenges and Encouragements

The commitment to enter into covenant is a significant step that comes with its challenges. It requires a sincere and enduring dedication to living out the principles of faith and actively participating in the life of the church. Yet, it also offers profound rewards in the form of fellowship, spiritual growth, and the fulfillment of God's purpose for His people.

As members of the church embrace this covenant, they do so with the understanding that they are joining a community bound together by a shared commitment to Christ. This covenantal relationship provides a foundation for mutual support, encouragement, and accountability as they navigate their spiritual journey together.

In embracing this first stanza, church members acknowledge the transformative power of the Holy Spirit, the significance of baptism, and the solemn yet joyful nature of their covenantal commitment. This declaration sets the stage for the deeper commitments outlined in the subsequent stanzas, guiding the church community in their shared mission and purpose.

As we reflect on the profound declaration of the first stanza, we recognize the depth and significance of entering into a covenant relationship with one another as one body in Christ. This initial pledge, led by the Holy Spirit and marked by the act of baptism, is more than a mere formality; it is the bedrock of our shared faith and commitment.

By acknowledging the role of the Holy Spirit in guiding us to Christ, we affirm that our journey of faith is divinely orchestrated. Baptism, as an outward symbol of our inner transformation, not only signifies our new identity in Christ but also marks our official entry into the covenant community. This act, performed in the presence of God, angels, and the assembly, underscores the gravity and solemnity of our promise.

The dual nature of this covenant—as both solemn and joyful—reflects the seriousness with which we undertake our responsibilities and the profound joy we experience in belonging to the body of Christ. It is a reminder of the transformative power of our faith and the communal bond we share.

In embracing this covenant, we commit ourselves to walking in love, supporting one another, and contributing to the mission of the church. This foundational commitment prepares us to fully engage with the subsequent pledges, guiding us in our collective journey of faith. As we move forward, may we be ever mindful of the grace and responsibility that comes with being part of this sacred covenant, living out its principles with sincerity and joy.

CHAPTER SEVEN
A COMMITMENT TO CHURCH
ADVANCEMENT

T he second stanza of the Church Covenant provides a comprehensive framework for advancing the mission and well-being of the church. It emphasizes a collective effort to foster Christian love, promote the church's growth in various dimensions, and support its ministries and outreach. This commitment is integral to the health and vitality of the church community and aligns with the teachings of Scripture on communal living and stewardship.

Understanding the Second Stanza

The second stanza reads:

"We engage, therefore, by the aid of the Holy Spirit, to walk together in Christian love; to strive for the advancement of this church, in knowledge, holiness, and comfort; to promote its prosperity and spirituality; to sustain its worship, ordinances, discipline, and doctrines; to contribute cheerfully and regularly to the support of the ministry, the expenses of the church, the relief of the poor, and the spread of the gospel through all nations."

This stanza outlines several key areas of commitment: walking together in love, advancing the church in knowledge and holiness, promoting its prosperity, sustaining its practices, and contributing to its financial support and outreach.

Walking Together in Christian Love

The call to "walk together in Christian love" underscores the importance of unity and mutual support within the church. This principle is supported by Scripture in passages such as John 13:34-35 (NKJV), where Jesus commands, "A new commandment I give to you, that you love one another; as I have loved you, that you also love one another. By this all will know that you are My disciples, if you have love for one another." This command highlights love as the defining characteristic of the Christian community, fostering a supportive and nurturing environment.

Walking together in love involves practical actions such as encouragement, forgiveness, and compassion, creating a sense of belonging and unity among members. Ephesians 4:2-3 (NKJV) further instructs, "With all lowliness and gentleness, with long-suffering, bearing with one another in love, endeavoring to keep the unity of the Spirit in the bond of peace." This passage emphasizes the need for humility and patience in maintaining unity and peace within the church.

Striving for Advancement in Knowledge, Holiness, and Comfort

The commitment to "strive for the advancement of this church, in knowledge, holiness, and comfort" reflects a holistic approach to church growth. Advancing in knowledge involves a deepening understanding of God's Word and doctrine, as emphasized in 2 Peter 3:18 (NKJV): "But grow in the grace and knowledge of our Lord and Savior Jesus Christ." This growth is essential for a mature and thriving church.

Holiness is another key focus, as believers are called to live lives set apart for God. 1 Peter 1:15-16 (NKJV) states, "But as He who called you is holy, you also be holy in all your conduct, because it is written, 'Be holy, for I am holy.'" Striving for holiness involves pursuing personal righteousness and encouraging others to do the same.

Comfort, in this context, relates to providing spiritual and emotional support within the church community. 2 Corinthians 1:3-4 (NKJV) highlights this aspect: "Blessed be the God and Father of our Lord Jesus Christ, the Father of mercies and God of all comfort, who comforts us in all our tribulation, that we may be able to comfort those who are in any trouble, with the comfort with which we ourselves are comforted by God."

Promoting Prosperity and Spirituality

Promoting the "prosperity and spirituality" of the church involves fostering both material and spiritual well-being. Prosperity in this sense includes ensuring that the church is financially stable and able to carry out its mission effectively. Malachi 3:10 (NKJV) encourages this aspect of stewardship: "Bring all the tithes into the storehouse, that there may be food in My house, and try Me now in this," says the Lord of hosts, "if I will not open for you the windows of heaven and pour out for you such blessing that there will not be room enough to receive it."

Spirituality refers to the church's commitment to maintaining a vibrant and dynamic spiritual life, including active worship, prayer, and discipleship. Philippians 4:13 (NKJV) provides encouragement: "I can do all things through Christ who strengthens me," reflecting the empowerment found in Christ for all aspects of church life.

Sustaining Worship, Ordinances, Discipline, and Doctrines

The covenant calls for the sustaining of "worship, ordinances, discipline, and doctrines," which are central to the life of the church.

Worship includes both communal and personal expressions of reverence and adoration for God. John 4:24 (NKJV) states, "God is Spirit, and those who worship Him must worship in spirit and truth," emphasizing the importance of sincerity and truth in worship.

The ordinances, such as baptism and the Lord's Supper, are vital practices that symbolize and reinforce the faith of the church. Matthew 28:19-20 (NKJV) commands, "Go therefore and make disciples of all nations, baptizing them in the name of the Father and of the Son and of the Holy Spirit," reflecting the significance of baptism in the life of the church.

Discipline involves maintaining order and purity within the church community. Matthew 18:15-17 (NKJV) provides guidelines for resolving conflicts and addressing issues of sin, ensuring the health and integrity of the church body.

Doctrines refer to the essential teachings of the Christian faith. 2 Timothy 4:2 (NKJV) instructs, "Preach the word! Be ready in season and out of season. Convince, rebuke, exhort, with all longsuffering and teaching," highlighting the importance of upholding sound doctrine.

Contributing to Ministry, Expenses, and Outreach

The commitment to "contribute cheerfully and regularly" to the support of the ministry, church expenses, relief of the poor, and gospel outreach emphasizes the role of stewardship and generosity. 2 Corinthians 9:7 (NKJV) encourages, "So let each one give as he purposes in his heart, not grudgingly or of necessity; for God loves a cheerful giver." This verse underscores the importance of giving with a joyful and willing heart.

Supporting the ministry and expenses of the church ensures that it can function effectively and fulfill its mission. Acts 4:34-35 (NKJV) provides an example of early church generosity: "Nor was there anyone among them who lacked; for all who were possessors of lands or houses sold them, and brought the proceeds of the things that were sold, and laid them at the apostles' feet; and they distributed to each as anyone had need."

The relief of the poor and the spread of the gospel are central to the church's mission. James 1:27 (NKJV) states, "Pure and undefiled religion before God and the Father is this: to visit orphans and widows in their trouble, and to keep oneself unspotted from the world." This passage highlights the church's responsibility to care for those in need and to live a life of purity.

Challenges and Encouragements

Implementing these commitments involves both challenges and rewards. Balancing the diverse needs of the church and its members requires careful management and collaboration. However, the support and encouragement found in Scripture and the communal aspect of the church provide strength and motivation.

Encouragement can be drawn from the knowledge that these efforts contribute to the growth and vitality of the church, fulfilling its mission and reflecting the love of Christ. By embracing these commitments, we participate in the ongoing work of God's kingdom and witness His faithfulness in our lives and the lives of others.

In conclusion, the second stanza of the Church Covenant captures the essence of collective commitment to the advancement of the church and the enrichment of its ministry. By pledging to walk together in Christian love, strive for growth in knowledge and holiness, and support the church's various needs, members contribute to the vitality and effectiveness of the church's mission.

The commitment to mutual love fosters a united and supportive community, while the pursuit of knowledge, holiness, and comfort strengthens the church's spiritual foundation. Sustaining worship, ordinances, discipline, and doctrines ensures that the church remains faithful to its core principles and practices. Furthermore, cheerful and regular contributions to the church's support and outreach initiatives reflect a heart of stewardship and generosity, crucial for fulfilling the church's role in spreading the gospel and meeting the needs of its members and the broader community.

These commitments are not without challenges. Balancing personal and communal responsibilities requires dedication and perseverance. Yet, the rewards of seeing the church thrive and the gospel advance far outweigh these challenges. As members embrace these commitments, they play a vital role in nurturing a vibrant and effective church community.

Let us be encouraged by the knowledge that our efforts contribute to the fulfillment of God's purpose for His church. By living out the principles of this covenant, we not only honor our pledge but also advance the mission of Christ's kingdom. May our dedication to these commitments inspire us to continue striving for the growth and prosperity of the church, reflecting the love and grace of our Savior in all that we do.

CHAPTER EIGHT
A COMMITMENT TO PERSONAL FAITH

The third stanza of the Church Covenant presents a comprehensive vision for personal devotion and ethical conduct, emphasizing the integration of faith into every aspect of life. This commitment encompasses private and family worship, moral integrity, and active efforts to advance the kingdom of God. By exploring this stanza, we gain insight into how these principles shape the lives of believers and contribute to a faithful Christian witness.

Understanding the Third Stanza

The third stanza reads:

"We also engage to maintain family and secret devotion; to religiously educate our children; to seek the salvation of our kindred and acquaintances; to walk circumspectly in the world; to be just in our dealings, faithful in our engagements, and exemplary in our deportment; to avoid all tattling, backbiting, and excessive anger; to abstain from the sale and use of intoxicating drinks as a beverage, and to be zealous in our efforts to advance the kingdom of our Saviour."

This stanza outlines a robust commitment to personal and family faith practices, moral conduct, and a proactive approach to evangelism. It reflects the holistic nature of Christian living, where personal holiness and active engagement in God's work are intertwined.

Maintaining Family and Secret Devotion

The call to "maintain family and secret devotion" emphasizes the importance of both public and private spiritual practices. Family devotion might involve regular family prayers, Bible study, and worship, fostering a spiritual environment at home. This practice is supported by passages such as Deuteronomy 6:6-7 (NKJV), which instructs, "And these words which I command you today shall be in your heart. You shall teach them diligently to your children, and shall talk of them when you sit in your house, when you walk by the way, when you lie down, and when you rise up." This passage underscores the importance of integrating faith into daily family life.

Personal, secret devotion is equally crucial, as it involves cultivating a private relationship with God through prayer and meditation. Jesus' teaching in Matthew 6:6 (NKJV) highlights this practice: "But you, when you pray, go into your room, and when you have shut your door, pray to your Father who is in the secret place; and your Father who sees in secret will reward you openly." This verse encourages believers to seek a genuine, personal connection with God, away from public recognition.

Religious Education of Children and Evangelism

The commitment to "religiously educate our children" reflects the role of parents in nurturing the next generation of believers. Proverbs 22:6 (NKJV) states, "Train up a child in the way he should go, and when he is old he will not depart from it." This directive underscores the importance of instilling biblical values and teachings in children from a young age.

Equally important is the call to "seek the salvation of our kindred and acquaintances." This involves sharing the Gospel with family, friends, and others within our sphere of influence. Acts 1:8 (NKJV) records Jesus' instruction, "But you shall receive power when the Holy Spirit has come upon you; and you shall be witnesses to Me in Jerusalem, and in all Judea and Samaria, and to the end of the earth." This verse highlights the role of believers in evangelism, empowered by the Holy Spirit to reach others with the message of salvation.

Walking Circumspectly and Moral Integrity

Walking "circumspectly in the world" calls for careful and deliberate conduct in all areas of life. Ephesians 5:15-16 (NKJV) instructs, "See then that you walk circumspectly, not as fools but as wise, redeeming the time, because the days are evil." This passage encourages believers to live wisely and make the most of every opportunity, reflecting the light of Christ in their daily interactions.

Being "just in our dealings, faithful in our engagements, and exemplary in our deportment" underscores the call to ethical behavior and integrity. Proverbs 11:3 (NKJV) asserts, "The integrity of the upright will guide them, but the perversity of the unfaithful will destroy them." Integrity in business and personal affairs demonstrates a commitment to honesty and faithfulness.

Avoiding Tattling, Backbiting, and Excessive Anger

The covenant calls believers to "avoid all tattling, backbiting, and excessive anger." James 1:19 (NKJV) provides guidance on controlling anger: "So then, my beloved brethren, let every man be swift to hear, slow to speak, slow to wrath." This verse encourages a disciplined approach to managing emotions and avoiding harmful speech.

Tattling and backbiting are addressed in Proverbs 16:28 (NKJV), which states, "A perverse man sows strife, and a whisperer separates the best of friends." This passage highlights the destructive impact of gossip and slander on relationships and community harmony.

Abstaining from Intoxicating Drinks

The commitment to "abstain from the sale and use of intoxicating drinks as a beverage" reflects a desire to avoid behaviors that can lead to moral and spiritual compromise. Ephesians 5:18 (NKJV) advises, "And do not be drunk with wine, in which is dissipation; but be filled with the Spirit." This verse contrasts the effects of drunkenness with the fulfillment of the Holy Spirit, emphasizing the need for self-control and spiritual focus.

Being Zealous for the Advancement of God's Kingdom

Finally, the call to be "zealous in our efforts to advance the kingdom of our Saviour" reflects a proactive engagement in God's work. Matthew 6:33 (NKJV) encourages, "But seek first the kingdom of God and His righteousness, and all these things shall be added to you." This verse underscores the priority of pursuing God's kingdom and righteousness in every aspect of life.

Challenges and Encouragements

One challenge in maintaining personal faith commitments is balancing private devotion with the demands of daily life. The call to consistent family and secret devotion requires intentionality and discipline, particularly in a busy and often distracting world. However, the rewards of a vibrant spiritual life and the positive impact on family and community provide significant encouragement.

Another challenge is adhering to ethical standards and avoiding harmful behaviors in a culture that often promotes contrary values. The strength to live according to these commitments comes from relying on God's grace and the support of the Christian community.

Encouragement can be found in the promises of Scripture and the examples of faithful believers throughout history. By striving to live out these principles, we contribute to the growth of God's kingdom and witness the transformative power of the Gospel in our lives and the lives of those around us.

In closing, the third stanza of the Church Covenant serves as a profound guide for personal faith and conduct, encompassing a wide array of commitments that are essential for living out our Christian values. By engaging in family and private devotion, religiously educating our children, and actively seeking the salvation of those around us, we align our lives with the principles of God's Word and contribute to the expansion of His kingdom.

The call to walk circumspectly in the world and uphold moral integrity challenges us to embody the teachings of Scripture in all aspects of our lives. Through just dealings, faithful engagements, and exemplary behavior, we reflect the character of Christ and witness His transformative power. The covenant's injunction to avoid tattling, backbiting, and excessive anger highlights the importance of cultivating a spirit of grace and understanding, while abstaining from intoxicating beverages emphasizes self-control and focus on spiritual growth.

The zealous pursuit of advancing God's kingdom requires a proactive and passionate commitment to His work. As we strive to live according to these principles, we not only honor our covenant with the church but also contribute to a faithful and vibrant Christian witness in the world.

Embracing these commitments involves both challenges and rewards. The journey of living out our faith with sincerity and diligence requires perseverance, yet it is marked by the grace of God and the encouragement of our community. Let us remain steadfast in our efforts, drawing strength from Scripture and the support of fellow believers, as we endeavor to fulfill the spirit of the covenant in our daily lives.

By upholding these commitments, we reaffirm our dedication to God and to one another, strengthening the bonds of our church community and advancing the mission of our Savior. May our lives reflect the depth of our faith and the sincerity of our covenant, as we seek to live out the principles of God's Word with passion and integrity.

CHAPTER NINE
A COMMITMENT TO THE COMMUNITY
OF FAITH

The fourth stanza of the Church Covenant encapsulates the essence of Christian love and mutual support within the church community. It outlines how members should interact with one another in a spirit of brotherly love, prayer, and reconciliation, emphasizing the importance of fostering a supportive and harmonious environment.

Understanding the Fourth Stanza

The fourth stanza of the Church Covenant reads:

"We further engage to watch over one another in brotherly love; to remember each other in prayer; to aid each other in sickness and distress; to cultivate Christian sympathy in feeling and courtesy in speech; to be slow to take offense, but always ready for reconciliation, and mindful of the rules of our Saviour, to secure it without delay."

This stanza reflects a profound commitment to living out Christian values in our relationships with one another. It stresses not only the need for active support and empathy but also the importance of maintaining unity and peace within the church community.

Significance and Implications

The commitment to "watch over one another in brotherly love" highlights the essential role of mutual care and vigilance within the church. In John 13:34-35 (NKJV), Jesus commands, "A new commandment I give to you, that you love one another; as I have loved you, that you also love one another. By this all will know that you are My disciples, if you have love for one another." This passage underscores the centrality of love in the Christian life and the testimony it bears to the world.

Similarly, Paul's instructions in Galatians 6:2 (NKJV) to "bear one another's burdens, and so fulfill the law of Christ" reflect the call to actively support and uplift one another, particularly in times of difficulty.

Aiding in Sickness and Distress

The commitment to aid each other in sickness and distress aligns with the biblical principle of compassion and practical support. James 5:14-15 (NKJV) advises, "Is anyone among you sick? Let him call for the elders of the church, and let them pray over him, anointing him with oil in the name of the Lord. And the prayer of faith will save the sick, and the Lord will raise him up." This passage emphasizes the church's role in providing spiritual and practical assistance to those in need.

The early church exemplified this commitment through their actions. Acts 2:44-45 (NKJV) describes how "Now all who believed were together, and had all things in common, and sold their possessions and goods, and divided them among all, as anyone had need." This communal approach to meeting needs demonstrates how the early Christians prioritized mutual support and generosity.

Cultivating Christian Sympathy and Courtesy

The call to "cultivate Christian sympathy in feeling and courtesy in speech" speaks to the need for empathy and respectful communication. In Romans 12:15 (NKJV), Paul writes, "Rejoice with those who rejoice, and weep with those who weep." This directive encourages believers to share in one another's joys and sorrows, fostering a deeper sense of connection and understanding.

Colossians 4:6 (NKJV) further advises, "Let your speech always be with grace, seasoned with salt, that you may know how you ought to answer each one." This guidance highlights the importance of speaking with kindness and thoughtfulness, reflecting the character of Christ in our interactions.

Being Slow to Take Offense and Ready for Reconciliation

The commitment to being "slow to take offense, but always ready for reconciliation" addresses the importance of maintaining peace and resolving conflicts promptly. Proverbs 19:11 (NKJV) states, "The discretion of a man makes him slow to anger, And his glory is to overlook a transgression." This verse emphasizes the value of patience and forgiveness in preserving harmony within the church community.

Jesus' teaching in Matthew 18:15 (NKJV) provides a clear approach to reconciliation: "Moreover if your brother sins against you, go and tell him his fault between you and him alone; if he hears you, you have gained your brother." This process of addressing conflicts directly and seeking resolution reflects the commitment to unity and reconciliation outlined in the covenant.

Practical Application

Applying this commitment involves several practical steps. Members should actively engage in prayer for one another, offering support during times of illness, distress, and personal struggle. This can include visiting the sick, providing meals, or offering financial assistance when needed.

Cultivating Christian sympathy and courtesy requires intentional efforts to listen empathetically, communicate respectfully, and extend grace in our interactions. This might involve participating in small group discussions, engaging in one-on-one conversations, and practicing active listening.

Addressing conflicts and seeking reconciliation should be approached with humility and a willingness to forgive. Encouraging open communication, providing mediation when necessary, and adhering to the biblical guidelines for resolving disputes are essential in maintaining a healthy and unified church community.

Challenges and Encouragements

One challenge in maintaining this commitment is dealing with interpersonal conflicts and misunderstandings. It can be difficult to navigate relationships when emotions run high or when disagreements arise. However, the biblical call to reconciliation and forgiveness provides a framework for addressing these challenges with grace and patience.

Another challenge is consistently demonstrating sympathy and support, especially when it requires significant time, effort, or resources. Yet, the promise of God's support and the example of Christ's love encourage believers to persevere in their commitment to one another.

Encouragement can be found in the knowledge that fostering a loving and supportive church community reflects the heart of God and contributes to the overall health and vitality of the church. As Paul writes in Philippians 2:1-2 (NKJV), "Therefore if there is any consolation in Christ, if any comfort of love, if any fellowship of the Spirit, if any affection and mercy, fulfill my joy by being like-minded, having the same love, being of one accord, of one mind."

This passage inspires believers to strive for unity and mutual care within the church.

Examples of Commitment to the Community of Faith

Consider a church that organizes regular prayer meetings and support groups to address the needs of its members. These gatherings offer a space for individuals to share their struggles, receive prayer, and find practical assistance from the community. This active engagement in mutual support reflects the commitment outlined in the covenant.

Another example is a church that implements a conflict resolution process, encouraging members to address grievances directly and seek reconciliation in a timely manner. By providing training and resources for effective communication and mediation, the church fosters a culture of forgiveness and unity.

In conclusion, the fourth stanza of the Church Covenant calls us to a profound commitment to one another, emphasizing the values of brotherly love, mutual support, and reconciliation. This commitment is foundational to the life of the church and essential for nurturing a vibrant and cohesive community of faith.

Our dedication to "watch over one another in brotherly love" involves not only providing practical support and aid in times of need but also cultivating a spirit of empathy and courtesy in our interactions. By remembering each other in prayer, assisting during illness and distress, and fostering a culture of understanding and forgiveness, we embody the heart of the covenant and reflect the love of Christ to one another.

The challenge of maintaining this commitment lies in our ability to navigate the complexities of human relationships and respond with grace and patience. Yet, the encouragement found in Scripture and the example of Christ guide us in fulfilling this covenant with sincerity and dedication. As we strive to live out these principles, we contribute to a church community that is marked by unity, compassion, and mutual respect.

Let us embrace the call to support and uplift one another, remaining vigilant in our efforts to resolve conflicts and practice forgiveness. In doing so, we honor the spirit of the covenant and strengthen the bonds that unite us as the body of Christ. May our commitment to one another reflect the love and grace of our Savior, and may our church community flourish as a testament to His enduring faithfulness.

CHAPTER TEN
A COMMITMENT TO CONTINUAL
FELLOWSHIP

The fifth stanza of the Church Covenant captures a vital aspect of Christian commitment: the promise to seek continued fellowship with a church community, even in the event of relocation. This pledge reflects the enduring nature of the believer's commitment to living out the principles of the covenant and the teachings of Scripture, regardless of changes in geographical location.

Understanding the Fifth Stanza

The fifth stanza of the Church Covenant reads:

"We moreover engage, that when we remove from this place, we will as soon as possible unite with some other church, where we can carry out the spirit of this covenant, and the principles of God's Word."

This statement underscores the importance of continuity in the believer's spiritual journey. It affirms that even when individuals or families move away from their current church, their commitment to the covenant and to living out the teachings of Scripture should persist. The pledge to unite with another church is a testament to the enduring nature of one's commitment to the Christian community and its principles.

Significance and Implications

The significance of this commitment lies in its affirmation of the necessity for believers to remain connected to a church body. Hebrews 10:24-25 instructs us: "And let us consider one another to provoke unto love and to good works: Not forsaking the assembling of ourselves together, as the manner of some is; but exhorting one another: and so much the more, as ye see the day approaching." This passage highlights the essential role of regular fellowship and mutual encouragement within the Christian life.

The early church also modeled this commitment to fellowship and community. In Acts 9:26-27, we see how the apostle Paul, after his conversion, sought to join the fellowship of the disciples in Jerusalem, despite initial hesitations about his past. His desire to be integrated into the church community reflects the natural inclination of believers to seek out fellowship with other Christians as a means of growth and accountability.

This commitment is not merely a practical consideration but a spiritual imperative. The church serves as the primary context for spiritual nourishment, accountability, and service. As Paul writes in Ephesians 4:16, "From whom the whole body fitly joined together and compacted by that which every joint supplieth, according to the effectual working in the measure of every part, maketh increase of the body unto the edifying of itself in love." This verse emphasizes the vital role each member plays in contributing to the health and growth of the church.

Practical Application

Applying this commitment involves several practical steps. First, it requires planning for continuity in one's church involvement when a move is anticipated. This includes researching potential new churches in the area of relocation and making connections with those congregations prior to the move. By proactively seeking out a new church home, individuals can ensure that their spiritual needs are met and that they can continue to contribute to a new community of believers.

Another aspect is the integration process once a new church is found. This involves actively participating in the life of the new church, joining in its activities, and aligning oneself with its mission and values. The transition to a new church should be seen as an opportunity to renew and deepen one's commitment to the principles of the covenant and the teachings of Scripture.

Churches can also facilitate this process by offering resources and support for members who are relocating. Providing information about potential churches in different areas, offering guidance on how to find a church that aligns with one's values, and encouraging members to maintain their covenantal commitments are ways in which churches can support members in their transitions.

Challenges and Encouragements

One challenge in maintaining this commitment is finding a church that aligns with the principles of the covenant and one's personal beliefs in a new location. This may require diligence and patience, as it can be difficult to identify a church that closely mirrors one's previous congregation in terms of doctrine, fellowship, and community involvement.

Additionally, adapting to a new church community can be a complex and sometimes uncomfortable process. It may involve navigating new social dynamics, understanding different church cultures, and establishing new relationships. Despite these challenges, the process of integrating into a new church community is an opportunity for personal and spiritual growth.

The encouragement for those facing such transitions is found in the assurance that God's provision and guidance are present throughout the process. As Psalm 32:8 assures us, "I will instruct thee and teach thee in the way which thou shalt go: I will guide thee with mine eye." This promise provides comfort and confidence that God will lead and support believers as they seek to unite with a new church family.

Examples of Commitment to Continual Fellowship

To illustrate this commitment in action, consider a family that relocates to a new city and, before moving, reaches out to local churches in their new area. They visit several congregations, seek guidance from their current pastor, and ultimately find a new church home that aligns with their values and beliefs. This proactive approach allows them to transition smoothly into their new church community, continuing their commitment to the covenant and contributing to the life of their new congregation.

In another example, a church provides support for members who are moving by maintaining a network of contacts with other churches across different regions. This network helps relocating members find new church homes that fit their needs and ensures that their commitment to the covenant is carried forward.

As we conclude our exploration of the fifth stanza of the Church Covenant, we are reminded of the enduring significance of maintaining our commitment to Christian fellowship, even in the midst of change. This pledge to unite with a new church when relocating is more than a logistical consideration; it is a testament to the unwavering dedication of believers to live out the principles of God's Word and to continue their journey of faith within a supportive community.

The biblical mandate to remain connected to a church body, as emphasized in Hebrews 10:24-25 and illustrated by the early church's example, underscores the importance of this commitment.

It is a call to actively seek out and integrate into new communities of faith, ensuring that our spiritual growth and communal support continue uninterrupted.

Navigating the transition to a new church can present challenges, including finding a congregation that aligns with one's beliefs and adapting to a new community. However, these challenges are met with the assurance of God's guidance and provision, as promised in Psalm 32:8. The process of seeking and joining a new church offers opportunities for personal growth and renewal in one's commitment to the covenant.

Real-life examples of individuals and families successfully integrating into new church communities highlight the practical outworking of this commitment. By taking proactive steps and seeking support from existing congregations, believers can maintain their covenantal promises and contribute to the life of their new church home.

In embracing the call to continual fellowship, we honor the spirit of the Church Covenant and affirm our dedication to living out the principles of God's Word. May we approach each transition with a spirit of faithfulness and openness, trusting that God will guide us to new communities where we can continue to grow, serve, and build meaningful relationships. As we move forward, let us carry with us the commitment to remain engaged with the body of Christ, fostering unity and support wherever we go.

CHAPTER ELEVEN
THE COVENANT IN WORSHIP AND LIFE

The Church Covenant stands as more than a declaration of beliefs; it is a living document that shapes the worship and daily life of Baptist congregations. Rooted in the rich soil of scriptural principles, the covenant functions as both a guide and a commitment for believers, influencing their worship practices and their walk with God.

Historical Practices of the Church Covenant in Worship

From the earliest days of Baptist congregations, the Church Covenant has been central to worship and church life. In the 17th and 18th centuries, it was common for Baptist churches to recite the covenant during significant moments such as the Lord's Supper, new member inductions, and church anniversaries. These recitations were not mere formalities but profound communal affirmations of shared faith and mutual responsibility.

One historical account from a Baptist church in New England describes how, during covenant services, the congregation would rise as one to recite the covenant. The act of standing together symbolized the unity of the body of Christ, as each member publicly reaffirmed their commitment to the church and to God. This practice served to bind the congregation together, fostering a sense of belonging and mutual accountability.

The covenant was also used during times of church discipline. When a member was found to be living contrary to the covenant's principles, the church would refer back to the covenant during disciplinary proceedings. This was not done in a spirit of legalism but out of a desire to restore the erring member to fellowship, as Galatians 6:1 (KJV) admonishes: "Brethren, if a man be overtaken in a fault, ye which are spiritual, restore such an one in the spirit of meekness."

Exploring the Historical Context of Covenant Renewal Practices

Covenant renewal services have deep historical roots in the Baptist tradition, often reflecting periods of revival and spiritual renewal within the church. These services provided congregations with a formal opportunity to reaffirm their commitments to God and to one another.

The practice of covenant renewal gained particular prominence during the Great Awakenings of the 18th and 19th centuries. As revival spread across the American colonies and later the United States, many Baptist churches incorporated covenant renewal services as a way to solidify the spiritual gains of the revival. These services often took place during special seasons of prayer and fasting, and were accompanied by fervent preaching and heartfelt worship.

An example of such a service can be found in the history of a Baptist church in Virginia in the early 1800s. After a season of revival, the church held a covenant renewal service in which members, both young and old, stood together to recite the covenant. The service was marked by a deep sense of repentance and renewal, as members recommitted themselves to living out the covenant's principles in their daily lives.

Covenant renewal also served as a means of spiritual protection for the church. In a time when churches faced both internal and external challenges, renewing the covenant was a way to ensure that the congregation remained united in purpose and firm in their commitments. As Hebrews 10:23 (KJV) encourages, "Let us hold fast the profession of our faith without wavering; (for he is faithful that promised;)"

Challenges and Adaptations in Modern Contexts

In today's rapidly changing world, Baptist churches face unique challenges in maintaining the relevance and significance of the Church Covenant. Modern congregations often struggle with issues of individualism, cultural shifts, and differing interpretations of biblical principles, all of which can impact how the covenant is understood and practiced.

One significant challenge is the rise of individualism in contemporary society. In a culture that often prioritizes personal autonomy and self-expression, the communal commitments of the Church Covenant can seem restrictive or outdated. Churches must navigate this tension by emphasizing the biblical foundation of the covenant and its role in fostering a healthy, interconnected church community.

Another challenge is the diversity of modern congregations. As Baptist churches grow to include members from various cultural, ethnic, and socioeconomic backgrounds, the application of the covenant's principles may require adaptation. Churches must find ways to honor the covenant's core values while also respecting the diverse experiences and perspectives of their members.

In some cases, churches have adapted the language of the covenant to make it more accessible to contemporary audiences. While the traditional wording of the covenant is cherished for its historical significance, some congregations have opted to use modernized versions that retain the covenant's essence while making it easier to understand. This approach allows the covenant to remain a living document, relevant to the needs and challenges of the present day.

Examples of Modern Applications of the Covenant

Despite these challenges, many Baptist churches today continue to find meaningful ways to integrate the Church Covenant into their worship and daily life. These modern applications demonstrate the covenant's enduring power to shape the spiritual lives of believers.

One example can be seen in the practice of small group covenant recitations. In some churches, members gather in small groups to discuss and recite the covenant together. These intimate settings allow for deeper reflection and discussion of the covenant's principles, as members share personal experiences and challenges related to living out the covenant. This practice not only strengthens individual faith but also builds a sense of community within the church.

Another modern application is the use of the covenant in church membership classes. Many Baptist churches require new members to study the Church Covenant as part of their membership process. This study often includes a discussion of the covenant's biblical foundations and practical implications, helping new members understand what it means to be part of the church community. By integrating the covenant into the membership process, churches ensure that new members are fully aware of the commitments they are making and the expectations of the church.

Additionally, some churches have incorporated the covenant into their digital platforms. In today's digital age, many churches have created online resources that explain the Church Covenant, including video teachings, downloadable study guides, and interactive discussion forums. These resources make the covenant more accessible to members who may not be able to attend in-person services or classes, ensuring that the covenant's principles continue to be taught and upheld in a variety of contexts.

Deeper Theological Exploration of the Covenant

At its core, the Church Covenant is deeply rooted in the theological concept of covenant-making with God, a theme that runs throughout the Bible. From the Old Testament covenants with Abraham, Moses, and David, to the New Covenant established through Jesus Christ, the idea of a covenant is central to understanding the relationship between God and His people.

The Church Covenant reflects this biblical concept by outlining the commitments that believers make to God and to each other. Just as the Old Testament covenants were formal agreements that defined the relationship between God and His people, the Church Covenant serves as a formal declaration of the commitments that bind a church community together.

Theologically, the covenant emphasizes the corporate nature of the Christian faith. While personal faith in Christ is essential, the covenant reminds believers that they are also part of a larger community of faith. This communal aspect of the covenant is reflected in the repeated use of the plural pronouns "we" and "our," emphasizing that the commitments made in the covenant are not just individual but collective.

The covenant also reflects the New Testament's emphasis on living out one's faith in practical ways. The Apostle Paul frequently exhorted the early church to live in a manner worthy of their calling, to bear one another's burdens, and to strive for unity in the body of Christ (Ephesians 4:1-3). The Church Covenant echoes these themes, calling believers to a life of holiness, service, and mutual care within the church community.

The Covenant's Connection to Ecclesiology

The Church Covenant is not just a theological statement; it is also a reflection of Baptist ecclesiology, or the doctrine of the church. In Baptist tradition, the church is understood as a local congregation of baptized believers who have covenanted together for worship, fellowship, and ministry. The Church Covenant is a key document that outlines the commitments that members of a Baptist church make to one another and to the church as a whole.

Baptist ecclesiology places a strong emphasis on the autonomy of the local church, meaning that each congregation is self-governing and free to determine its own practices and beliefs within the bounds of biblical teaching. The Church Covenant is a vital part of this autonomy, as it represents the collective agreement of the church members to live according to certain biblical principles.

The covenant also reflects the Baptist emphasis on the priesthood of all believers, the idea that every Christian has direct access to God and is called to minister to others. This concept is embedded in the covenant's call to mutual care and accountability within the church. By committing to "watch over one another in brotherly love," members of a Baptist church are embracing their role as ministers to one another, fulfilling the New Testament's vision of the church as a community of priests (1 Peter 2:9).

Profiles of Three Churches and Their Use of the Covenant

To illustrate how the Church Covenant is lived out in different contexts, here are profiles of three Baptist churches that have successfully integrated the covenant into their worship and daily life:

First Baptist Church in Atlanta, GA, a historic congregation with deep roots in the Southern Baptist tradition, has made the Church Covenant a central part of its identity. The church recites the covenant during the Lord's Supper and at the conclusion of significant church meetings, such as business meetings or pastoral installations. In recent years, the church has adapted the language of the covenant to be more inclusive and accessible, particularly to younger members and new believers. The covenant is also used as a teaching tool in its discipleship programs, helping members understand the biblical basis for each of the covenant's commitments. This practice has fostered a significant sense of unity and purpose within the congregation. Members report feeling a stronger sense of belonging and accountability, knowing that they are part of a community that takes its commitments seriously.

Mount Zion Baptist Church in Nashville, TN, a large and diverse congregation, has incorporated the Church Covenant into its digital ministry. The church's website features a detailed explanation of the covenant, along with video teachings from the pastor that explore its biblical foundations. In addition to these innovations, the church uses the covenant as a framework for its community outreach programs. Members are encouraged to view their service to the community as an extension of their covenant commitments, particularly in following the call to "walk circumspectly in the world" and "to do good unto all men" (Galatians 6:10, KJV). This approach has helped Mount Zion maintain a strong sense of purpose and mission, even as the congregation has grown in size and diversity. Members note that the covenant has helped them stay focused on the church's core values, despite the challenges of ministering in a rapidly changing urban environment.

Ebenezer Baptist Church in Richmond, VA, a historic African American congregation, has preserved the traditional practice of reciting the Church Covenant during the Lord's Supper, a practice passed down through generations and deeply cherished by the congregation. In addition to this tradition, the church holds an annual covenant renewal service, during which members publicly reaffirm their commitments. This service is often accompanied by testimonies and prayers of recommitment, creating a powerful sense of unity and spiritual renewal within the church. The covenant has also helped Ebenezer navigate the challenges of maintaining its identity and mission in a changing cultural landscape. By grounding the church in its historical commitments, the covenant provides a stable foundation for the church's ministry and outreach efforts.

Conclusion

In reflecting on the Church Covenant's role in worship and life, it becomes clear that this ancient declaration remains a living, vital part of the Baptist tradition. From its historical roots in early Baptist practice to its modern adaptations, the covenant continues to shape and inspire the worship and daily lives of believers.

The historical practices of covenant recitations and renewal services remind us of the profound communal and spiritual significance that these rituals have held over time. They anchor our faith in a shared commitment to God and to each other, reinforcing the unity and purpose of the church community. As we have seen, the covenant's adaptability in the face of modern challenges demonstrates its enduring relevance. Churches today are finding innovative ways to integrate the covenant into their practices, ensuring that its principles continue to guide and enrich their faith journey.

Moreover, the deeper theological exploration of the covenant underscores its foundational place in Baptist ecclesiology. By reflecting on the covenant's scriptural underpinnings and its role in defining the church's identity, we gain a clearer understanding of its significance in fostering a committed and vibrant church community. The profiles of diverse churches illustrate how the covenant can be lived out in various contexts, each uniquely reflecting the covenant's principles while addressing contemporary needs.

As we conclude this chapter, let us be reminded that the Church Covenant is more than a historical document; it is a dynamic and practical guide for living out our faith. It calls us to a deeper commitment to God and to one another, challenging us to uphold our shared values and to continually renew our dedication to the community of faith. May we approach the covenant not merely as a tradition to be observed but as a living testament to our collective journey of faith, guiding our worship and our daily lives as we seek to honor God and serve one another in love.

PART III. THE GUIDING PRINCIPLES

CHAPTER TWELVE
THE DECLARATION OF FAITH

Introduction

The Declaration of Faith is a central document in the life of Baptist churches, encapsulating the core beliefs and doctrinal positions that define Baptist identity. This chapter explores the history, origins, and significance of the Declaration of Faith within the Baptist tradition, tracing its development from early creeds and confessions to its role in shaping the faith and practice of Baptist congregations today.

Historical Origins

The origins of the Declaration of Faith can be traced back to the early 17th century, during a time of religious upheaval and reform in England. The Protestant Reformation had already begun to challenge the doctrines and practices of the Roman Catholic Church, leading to the formation of various Protestant denominations. Among these were the early Baptist groups, who sought to return to a more biblical form of Christianity, free from the traditions and hierarchical structures of the established Church of England.

One of the earliest and most influential Baptist confessions of faith was the **London Baptist Confession of 1644**. This document, drafted by a group of Particular Baptists in London, outlined the essential beliefs of these early Baptists, including the importance of believers' baptism, the autonomy of the local church, and the authority of Scripture. The London Confession served as a model for later Baptist confessions, including the more widely recognized **Second London Baptist Confession of 1689**, which was adopted by many Baptist churches in England and the American colonies.

In America, as the Baptist movement grew, there was a need for a more unified and concise statement of faith that could be embraced by the diverse and independent Baptist congregations. This led to the development of the **Philadelphia Baptist Confession of Faith** in 1742, which was based on the Second London Confession but included additional articles reflecting the unique experiences and challenges of Baptists in the New World.

The Declaration of Faith: Development and Adoption

The Declaration of Faith as we know it today has its roots in these early confessions but has been shaped by the unique theological and cultural contexts of Baptist life in America. By the 19th century, the rapid expansion of Baptist churches across the United States, coupled with the emergence of various Baptist conventions and associations, necessitated a more standardized declaration of beliefs.

The **New Hampshire Baptist Confession of 1833** was one of the key documents in this process. Drafted by the New Hampshire Baptist Convention, this confession sought to provide a clear and concise statement of Baptist beliefs that could be used for teaching and unifying Baptist churches. The New Hampshire Confession became widely accepted among Baptists, particularly in the northern and western states, and influenced subsequent declarations of faith.

In 1925, the **Southern Baptist Convention** adopted a revised version of the New Hampshire Confession, known as the **Baptist Faith and Message**. This document has been revised several times (most notably in 1963 and 2000) and serves as the official statement of faith for Southern Baptists, outlining their beliefs on topics such as the nature of God, the authority of Scripture, salvation, and the church.

Meaning and Significance

For Baptists, the Declaration of Faith is more than just a doctrinal statement; it is a living document that reflects the core convictions of the Baptist tradition. It serves several important functions:

1. Confession of Belief

The Declaration of Faith serves as a formal and public expression of what Baptists believe, offering a clear and authoritative summary of key doctrinal positions. This confession of belief is essential for several reasons:

Teaching Tool: The Declaration of Faith is a valuable resource for instructing both new and mature believers. It provides a structured framework for understanding the essential tenets of the Christian faith from a Baptist perspective. Churches often use it in catechism classes, Sunday School, and Bible studies to ensure that members have a sound grasp of core doctrines.

Preaching Resource: Pastors and preachers often draw upon the Declaration of Faith as a guide for sermon preparation. It ensures that the teaching from the pulpit remains consistent with Baptist doctrine and helps to prevent the spread of erroneous or heretical views within the congregation.

Evangelistic Tool: The Declaration of Faith can also serve as an evangelistic tool, providing a concise summary of the Gospel message and the key beliefs that Baptists hold. When sharing the faith with non-believers, Baptists can refer to the Declaration as a way to explain what they believe and why, making it easier for others to understand the distinctives of Baptist theology.

2. Unifying Document

The Declaration of Faith plays a crucial role in fostering unity among Baptist churches, which are known for their emphasis on the autonomy of the local congregation. Despite the independence of individual churches, the Declaration of Faith helps to maintain doctrinal continuity and a sense of shared identity across the wider Baptist community.

Doctrinal Integrity: By adhering to a common Declaration of Faith, Baptist churches are able to maintain a consistent doctrinal stance, even as they exercise their autonomy in matters of church governance and practice. This helps to prevent division and ensures that Baptist churches remain aligned in their core beliefs.

Denominational Cohesion: The Declaration of Faith serves as a foundational document for Baptist conventions, associations, and fellowships. It provides a basis for cooperation among churches, enabling them to work together in missions, education, and other collective endeavors. This shared doctrinal foundation is essential for the functioning of denominational structures, allowing for collaboration while respecting the independence of each congregation.

Global Connection: The Declaration of Faith also connects Baptists globally, serving as a point of reference for Baptist churches around the world. While there may be cultural and contextual differences, the shared Declaration of Faith unites Baptists across national and cultural boundaries, fostering a sense of global fellowship.

3. Guidance for Practice

The Declaration of Faith not only articulates what Baptists believe but also provides practical guidance for how these beliefs should be lived out in the life of the church and the individual believer.

Church Governance: The Declaration of Faith outlines principles of church governance, emphasizing the autonomy of the local congregation, the priesthood of all believers, and the importance of congregational polity. These principles guide Baptist churches in making decisions, selecting leaders, and organizing their ministries in a way that aligns with their theological convictions.

Ordinances: The Declaration of Faith provides instruction on the observance of the two key Baptist ordinances: believers' baptism and the Lord's Supper. It explains the significance of these practices, emphasizing that baptism is an outward sign of an inward faith and that the Lord's Supper is a commemoration of Christ's sacrifice. This guidance ensures that these ordinances are observed in a manner that is consistent with Baptist beliefs.

Ethical Living: The Declaration of Faith often includes teachings on Christian ethics, guiding believers in how they should conduct themselves in accordance with biblical principles. This includes instructions on issues such as marriage and family, social justice, stewardship, and personal holiness. By providing a moral and ethical framework, the Declaration helps believers to navigate the complexities of modern life while remaining faithful to their convictions.

Worship and Mission: The Declaration of Faith also informs the worship practices and missional activities of Baptist churches. It emphasizes the centrality of Scripture in worship, the importance of congregational singing, and the responsibility of the church to engage in evangelism and social ministry. This guidance helps churches to align their worship and mission with their doctrinal beliefs, ensuring that their practices are both biblically grounded and theologically sound.

4. Response to Contemporary Issues

The Declaration of Faith is not a static document; it evolves in response to new theological, cultural, and social challenges. This adaptability allows Baptists to remain rooted in their core beliefs while engaging thoughtfully with the changing world around them.

Theological Clarification: As new theological questions arise, the Declaration of Faith can be revised or expanded to provide clarity on these issues. This helps to protect the church from doctrinal errors and ensures that Baptist beliefs remain relevant and robust in the face of new challenges. For example, revisions might address contemporary issues such as bioethics, religious liberty, or the role of women in ministry.

Cultural Engagement: The Declaration of Faith also enables Baptists to engage with cultural issues from a position of faith. By articulating a biblical response to societal challenges, the Declaration equips Baptists to address matters such as racial justice, poverty, and human rights in a way that is consistent with their theological convictions. This engagement is crucial for maintaining the church's witness in the world and for promoting justice and righteousness in society.

Missional Adaptation: As the church's mission field changes, the Declaration of Faith provides a foundation for adapting missional strategies and practices. Whether addressing the needs of a post-Christian society, engaging with digital technology, or responding to global crises, the Declaration ensures that Baptist mission remains faithful to its doctrinal roots while being innovative and responsive to new opportunities for ministry.

Conclusion

The Declaration of Faith is a vital part of the Baptist heritage, representing the core beliefs and convictions that have defined Baptist life for centuries. Its history and development reflect the dynamic and evolving nature of Baptist theology, while its ongoing significance underscores the importance of a shared confession of faith in uniting and guiding Baptist churches in their mission to proclaim the Gospel and live out their faith in the world.

CHAPTER THIRTEEN
THE SCRIPTURES

We Believe that the Holy Bible was written by men divinely inspired, and is a perfect treasure of heavenly instruction; that it has God for its Author, salvation for its end, and truth without any mixture of error, for its matter; that it reveals the principles by which God will judge us; and therefore is, and shall remain to the end of the world, the true center of Christian union, and the supreme standard by which all human conduct, creeds, and opinions should be tried.

Historical Context

The belief in the divine inspiration and authority of Scripture has been foundational to Christian faith since the early church. The Old Testament scriptures were recognized by the Jewish community and affirmed by Jesus and the apostles. The New Testament writings, though initially emerging from early Christian communities, quickly gained recognition as authoritative. The process of canonization, which involved discerning which texts were truly inspired and authoritative, was a careful and prayerful task that resulted in the New Testament canon we have today.

Early church fathers like Augustine and Origen emphasized the divine inspiration of the Scriptures, arguing that all truth found in the Bible originates from God. The Reformation further solidified the centrality of Scripture in Christian doctrine, challenging prevailing ecclesiastical traditions that contradicted biblical teachings and affirming Scripture alone (sola scriptura) as the ultimate authority.

Exposition and Analysis

The doctrine of Scripture as divinely inspired and authoritative rests on several key affirmations. First, the Bible is regarded as written by men divinely inspired, meaning that while human authors penned the texts, they did so under the guidance of the Holy Spirit (2 Peter 1:21; 2 Timothy 3:16). This inspiration ensures that the Bible is a perfect treasure of heavenly instruction, containing no errors in its original manuscripts (Psalm 119:160; Proverbs 30:5-6).

Second, the Bible's primary end is salvation. It reveals God's plan for humanity, the means of redemption through Jesus Christ, and the way to eternal life (John 20:31; Romans 3:21-22). As such, it provides the principles by which God will judge humanity (John 12:47-48; Revelation 20:12).

Third, the Bible serves as the supreme standard for Christian union and the evaluation of all human conduct, creeds, and opinions. It remains the ultimate authority by which all beliefs and practices should be tested (Matthew 5:18; 2 Timothy 3:16-17). This means that while human understanding and interpretation may vary, the Bible itself is unchanging and remains central to Christian faith and practice.

Theological Significance

The belief in the Bible's divine inspiration and authority is pivotal to Christian theology. It underscores the notion that Scripture is not merely a historical or literary document but the very word of God. This belief shapes the way Christians understand divine revelation, moral authority, and the nature of truth. By affirming that the Bible is the supreme standard, Christians acknowledge that it is the final arbiter on matters of faith and practice.

This doctrine also emphasizes the Bible's role in guiding Christian life. Since it is inspired by God and free from error, it provides a trustworthy basis for understanding God's will and living a life that is pleasing to Him. It assures believers that the teachings and principles found in Scripture are valid and applicable throughout all generations.

Practical Application

The practical application of this belief involves several key practices. First, Christians are called to engage deeply with the Scriptures through regular reading, study, and meditation. This engagement helps believers understand God's will and align their lives with biblical teachings (2 Timothy 2:15; Psalm 119:105).

Second, the authority of Scripture implies that it should be the final measure against which all teachings, doctrines, and practices are evaluated. Christians are encouraged to test teachings and beliefs by the Bible, ensuring that their faith and practice remain true to its teachings (1 John 4:1; Acts 17:11).

Third, recognizing the Bible as the center of Christian union means that believers should seek unity based on shared adherence to its teachings. This perspective encourages mutual respect and dialogue within the Christian community while maintaining commitment to the truth revealed in Scripture (Ephesians 4:3; Philippians 2:2).

Common Misunderstandings

One common misunderstanding is the notion that the Bible's divine inspiration implies that it is free from human cultural and historical context. While the Bible is considered inerrant in its teachings, understanding its messages requires recognizing the historical and cultural background of its texts. This helps in accurately interpreting and applying its teachings.

Another misunderstanding is the idea that differing interpretations of Scripture indicate a failure of its authority. Diverse interpretations can arise from varying contexts and perspectives, but they should always be tested against the Bible's core teachings. The doctrine of Scripture's authority maintains that while interpretations may vary, the Bible's message remains consistent and true.

Additionally, some may misunderstand the relationship between Scripture and tradition. While tradition can offer valuable insights, the Bible remains the ultimate authority. Traditions and practices should be evaluated against Scripture to ensure they align with biblical teachings.

Conclusion

The doctrine of Scripture as divinely inspired and authoritative is foundational to the Christian faith. It affirms that the Bible is God's perfect revelation, intended to guide believers in faith and practice. By adhering to the Bible as the supreme standard, Christians ensure that their beliefs and actions align with divine truth. This belief underscores the importance of engaging with Scripture diligently and applying its teachings faithfully in all aspects of life.

CHAPTER FOURTEEN
THE TRUE GOD

We Believe that there is one and only one living and true God, an intelligent, spiritual and personal Being, the Creator, Preserver and Ruler of the universe, infinite in holiness and all other perfections to Whom we owe the highest love, reverence and obedience. He is revealed to us as Father, Son and Holy Spirit, each with distinct personal attributes, but without division of nature, essence or being.

Historical Context

The doctrine of the one true God is a cornerstone of Christian theology and has roots deeply embedded in the Judeo-Christian tradition. The affirmation of monotheism, the belief in a single, all-powerful God, distinguishes Christianity from polytheistic religions that worship multiple gods. This belief is firmly grounded in the Old Testament, where God's oneness is repeatedly affirmed (Deuteronomy 6:4).

Early Christian doctrine further developed this understanding by affirming the triune nature of God—Father, Son, and Holy Spirit—while maintaining the unity of God's essence. This concept, though complex, was articulated in early creeds and councils, such as the Nicene Creed, which sought to articulate and defend the doctrine against various heresies that threatened to distort the understanding of God's nature.

Exposition and Analysis

The Bible describes God as the only living and true God, distinguishing Him from the lifeless idols of other religions (Jeremiah 10:10; Psalm 83:18). God is presented as an intelligent, spiritual, and personal Being—qualities that underscore His active and relational nature in the universe. His role as Creator, Preserver, and Ruler illustrates His comprehensive sovereignty and involvement in all aspects of creation (Hebrews 3:4; Revelation 4:11).

The doctrine of the Trinity is central to understanding God's nature as revealed in the New Testament. God is revealed as Father, Son, and Holy Spirit—each person of the Trinity has distinct personal attributes, yet they share the same divine essence and are fully God. This is reflected in passages such as Matthew 28:19, where Jesus commands baptism in the name of the Father, Son, and Holy Spirit, and in John 14:26, where the Holy Spirit is sent by the Father in Jesus' name.

The unity of God's essence is emphasized throughout Scripture, affirming that while God is revealed in three persons, these persons are not divided in nature or being. The relationship between the Father, Son, and Holy Spirit is characterized by harmony and unity, as illustrated in John 10:30, where Jesus declares, "I and the Father are one," and in 2 Corinthians 13:14, which blesses believers with the grace of the Lord Jesus Christ, the love of God, and the fellowship of the Holy Spirit.

Theological Significance

The belief in one true God is fundamental to Christian theology. It establishes the framework for understanding God's attributes and actions. God's oneness underscores His ultimate authority and supreme power, rejecting any notion of polytheism or division within the divine essence. This belief reinforces the importance of worshiping God alone, as commanded in the Scriptures (Exodus 20:3; Deuteronomy 6:4).

The doctrine of the Trinity is significant as it provides a fuller understanding of God's nature and His relational aspects. It explains how God can be both transcendent and immanent, existing beyond creation while also actively engaging with it. This understanding shapes Christian worship and prayer, which are directed to the triune God, acknowledging the distinct roles and unity of the Father, Son, and Holy Spirit.

Practical Application

In practical terms, the belief in the one true God and the Trinity impacts Christian life and worship. It encourages believers to honor God's singular authority and to engage in worship that reflects the fullness of His nature. This means recognizing and honoring the distinct roles of the Father, Son, and Holy Spirit in one's spiritual life, from creation to salvation and ongoing sanctification.

Believers are called to live in a way that reflects their understanding of God's holiness and perfection. This involves striving to align one's life with God's commandments, showing reverence in worship, and seeking to emulate His attributes of love, justice, and mercy in their interactions with others (1 Peter 1:15-16).

Common Misunderstandings

One common misunderstanding is the notion that the Trinity implies three separate gods. In reality, Christian doctrine affirms that while God is revealed in three persons, He remains one in essence. The concept of the Trinity can be challenging to grasp, but it is crucial to understand that this doctrine does not suggest division within the Godhead but rather a complex unity.

Another misconception is that the Old Testament's emphasis on the oneness of God conflicts with the New Testament's revelation of the Trinity. However, Christian doctrine maintains that the one true God revealed in the Old Testament is the same God revealed in the New Testament in three persons. The Trinity does not introduce a new god but rather clarifies the nature of the one true God.

Conclusion

The belief in one living and true God, revealed as Father, Son, and Holy Spirit, is central to Christian faith. This doctrine affirms God's unique position as the Creator, Preserver, and Ruler of the universe while recognizing His complex nature as a triune Being. Understanding and embracing this belief shapes Christian worship, ethics, and spiritual life, ensuring that all aspects of faith align with the true nature of God as revealed in Scripture.

CHAPTER FIFTEEN
THE FALL OF MAN

We Believe that man was created by the special act of God, as recorded in Genesis. "So God created man in His own image, in the image of God created He him; male and female created He them" (Genesis 1:27). "And the Lord God formed man of the dust of the ground, and breathed into his nostrils the breath of life; and man became a living soul" (Genesis 2:7). He was created in a state of holiness under the law of his Maker, but through the temptation of Satan, he transgressed the command of God and fell from his original holiness and righteousness; whereby his posterity inherit a nature corrupt and in bondage to sin, are under condemnation, and as soon as they are capable of moral action, become actual transgressors.

Historical Context

The doctrine of the Fall of Man is rooted in the Genesis account of creation and the subsequent fall of Adam and Eve. According to the Scriptures, man was initially created in a state of righteousness and holiness, reflecting God's own image (Genesis 1:27). This creation narrative establishes humanity's unique relationship with God and its intended purpose.

The Fall, as described in Genesis 3, marks a pivotal moment in biblical history. The serpent's temptation and the subsequent disobedience of Adam and Eve introduced sin into the human experience. This event is foundational for understanding the nature of human sinfulness and the need for redemption. The implications of the Fall are addressed throughout Scripture, influencing theological and doctrinal discussions on human nature, sin, and salvation.

Exposition and Analysis

The biblical account in Genesis reveals that man was created by God with intentionality and purpose. Genesis 1:27 emphasizes that humanity was made in the image of God, which signifies inherent dignity and value. Genesis 2:7 further details the special act of creation, where God formed man from the dust and breathed life into him, illustrating the intimate relationship between God and humanity.

Despite this original state of holiness, the narrative of the Fall demonstrates how Adam and Eve succumbed to the serpent's temptation (Genesis 3:6). This act of disobedience led to their expulsion from Eden and introduced a corrupt nature into the human lineage. Romans 5:12 and Romans 5:19 articulate how Adam's sin resulted in death and condemnation spreading to all people, emphasizing the universality of sin's impact.

The Fall of Man has significant theological implications. It underscores the concept of original sin, which asserts that humanity's fall into sin affects all subsequent generations. As Psalm 51:5 suggests, all people inherit a sinful nature from birth. This corruption is not merely an external condition but a fundamental alteration of humanity's moral state, leading to a propensity towards sin (Romans 8:7).

Theological Significance

The doctrine of the Fall is crucial for understanding the need for salvation. It explains why all humans are born with a corrupt nature and are under condemnation. This understanding of human depravity lays the groundwork for the necessity of Christ's redemptive work. The Fall highlights the gravity of sin and its pervasive influence on human nature, which the Gospel addresses through the redemptive work of Jesus Christ.

The Fall also provides context for the concept of human responsibility and the necessity of divine grace. The recognition of one's fallen state leads to a deeper appreciation of the grace offered through Christ. This doctrine shapes Christian views on human nature, the moral struggle, and the transformative power of salvation.

Practical Application

Understanding the Fall of Man has practical implications for how Christians view human behavior and moral responsibility. It fosters humility, acknowledging that all people are susceptible to sin and in need of redemption. This awareness encourages believers to rely on God's grace and strive for moral integrity while recognizing the ongoing struggle against sin in their lives.

In pastoral care and counseling, this doctrine helps address issues related to human suffering, temptation, and moral failure. It provides a framework for understanding why individuals and societies experience brokenness and conflict, pointing to the need for Christ's healing and transformative power.

Common Misunderstandings

One common misunderstanding is the notion that the Fall of Man implies a deterministic view of human nature, where individuals are seen as unable to choose good over evil. However, Christian doctrine maintains that while human nature is corrupt, individuals still possess the ability to make moral choices and are called to exercise their free will in alignment with God's commands.

Another misconception is that the doctrine of original sin suggests that individuals are personally responsible for Adam and Eve's sin. In reality, original sin explains the inherited condition of human nature, not personal guilt. Each person is accountable for their own actions and sins, as outlined in Ezekiel 18:19-20.

Conclusion

The Fall of Man is a foundational doctrine that explains the entrance of sin into the human experience and its consequences for all humanity. By understanding this doctrine, believers gain insight into the nature of human sinfulness and the profound need for redemption. This understanding shapes Christian theology, ethics, and the appreciation of God's grace through Jesus Christ.

CHAPTER SIXTEEN
THE WAY OF SALVATION

We believe that the salvation of sinners is wholly of grace, through the mediatorial office of the Son of God, Who by the Holy Spirit was born of the Virgin Mary and took upon Him our nature, yet without sin; honored the divine law by His personal obedience and made atonement for our sins by His death. Being risen from the dead, He is now enthroned in Heaven, and, uniting in His person the tenderest sympathies with divine perfections, He is in every way qualified to be a compassionate and all-sufficient Saviour.

Introduction

The doctrine of salvation is the cornerstone of the Christian faith, and for Baptists, it stands as a powerful testament to God's unmerited favor toward humanity. We believe that salvation is entirely by grace, a gift extended to sinners through the mediatorial work of Jesus Christ. This chapter explores the profound theological implications of the way of salvation, focusing on the work of Christ, His incarnation, His sinless life, and His atoning death. Salvation is not something humanity can earn; it is freely given by God through Christ, who now reigns as a compassionate and all-sufficient Savior.

Historical Context

Origins

The understanding of salvation by grace alone has deep biblical roots. From the time of the apostles, the church has affirmed that salvation is not something humans can attain by their own effort but is entirely a work of God. This teaching finds its origin in Scripture, particularly in the New Testament writings of Paul, who proclaimed that "by grace are ye saved through faith; and that not of yourselves: it is the gift of God" (Ephesians 2:8). Early Christians believed that Jesus Christ's life, death, and resurrection were the fulfillment of God's plan for redemption, grounded in grace.

Development

During the Reformation, this doctrine became a focal point as the Reformers, such as Martin Luther and John Calvin, opposed the idea that human works or merit could contribute to salvation. The emphasis on *sola gratia* (grace alone) as the basis for salvation was reinforced in contrast to the prevailing view that salvation involved a combination of grace and works. Baptist theology, rooted in this Reformation heritage, continues to uphold that salvation is a divine gift, achieved solely through Christ's mediating role and offered to humanity without regard to their own righteousness.

Exposition and Analysis

The article lays out several important aspects of Christ's role in salvation:

The Mediator: Christ, as the divine Mediator, bridges the gap between a holy God and sinful humanity. Born of the Virgin Mary, He took on human flesh, yet remained without sin (Hebrews 4:14-15). His role as Mediator is essential to understanding salvation as

He alone could fulfill the divine law, offering Himself as the perfect sacrifice for sin.

The Incarnation: By taking on human nature, Christ demonstrated God's love and commitment to redeem humanity. His incarnation means that He fully identifies with us in our weaknesses, yet without compromising His divinity (John 1:14). He lived a life of perfect obedience to the divine law, which we, as sinners, could never achieve.

Atonement and Resurrection: Through His death on the cross, Christ made full atonement for sin. He bore the punishment that humanity deserved, fulfilling Isaiah's prophecy: "He was wounded for our transgressions, he was bruised for our iniquities" (Isaiah 53:5, KJV). Christ's resurrection further affirms the completeness of His work, as He conquered death and secured eternal life for all who believe (1 Corinthians 15:1-4).

Enthroned in Heaven: Following His resurrection, Christ ascended to Heaven, where He now reigns with compassion and power (Hebrews 1:3). As both divine and human, He is uniquely qualified to sympathize with our weaknesses and intercede on our behalf (Hebrews 7:25).

Theological Significance

The doctrine of salvation by grace alone emphasizes that salvation is wholly a work of God. Ephesians 2:8-9 reminds us, "For by grace are ye saved through faith; and that not of yourselves: it is the gift of God: not of works, lest any man should boast." This truth underscores the nature of God's grace—it is unearned and undeserved. Salvation is initiated by God's love and accomplished through Christ's obedience and atonement.

The mediatorial office of Christ, highlighted in passages such as 1 Timothy 2:5 which states, "For there is one God, and one mediator between God and men, the man Christ Jesus," reinforces the central role of Jesus in bridging the gap between sinful humanity and a holy God. His dual nature—both fully divine and fully human—allows Him to effectively represent us before God, making salvation accessible to all.

Places in the Bible Where Taught

- **Ephesians 2:8** – "For by grace are ye saved through faith..."
- **Matthew 18:11** – "For the Son of man is come to save that which was lost."
- **1 John 4:10** – "Herein is love, not that we loved God, but that he loved us, and sent his Son to be the propitiation for our sins."
- **John 3:16** – "For God so loved the world, that he gave his only begotten Son..."
- **Hebrews 4:14-15** – "We have a great high priest... Jesus the Son of God."

Practical Application

Understanding that salvation is a work of grace has profound implications for the Christian life. First, it cultivates humility, as believers recognize that they are saved not by their own merit but by God's unmerited favor. This leads to a life of gratitude and worship, as Paul writes in Romans 12:1, "present your bodies a living sacrifice, holy, acceptable unto God, which is your reasonable service."

Additionally, this doctrine challenges believers to live lives marked by grace toward others. Just as God extended His grace to us through Christ, we are called to reflect that grace in our relationships, forgiving as we have been forgiven (Colossians 3:13). The knowledge that salvation is a gift should inspire believers to share the gospel freely, offering others the hope of salvation through Christ.

For the church, this doctrine shapes both its mission and message. The church exists to proclaim the gospel of grace, ensuring that every ministry, sermon, and outreach effort emphasizes the centrality of Christ's atoning work. Furthermore, understanding salvation as grace-based underscores the importance of depending on God's power rather than human efforts in all spiritual endeavors.

Common Misunderstandings

One common misunderstanding is the belief that good works are necessary to earn salvation. While good works are a natural result of salvation, they are not a means to obtain it. Paul clarifies this in Titus 3:5, stating that it is "not by works of righteousness which we have done, but according to his mercy he saved us."

Another misconception is that salvation is temporary or can be lost. While salvation demands perseverance in faith, Scripture assures us of the eternal nature of Christ's saving work (John 10:28), where Jesus promises, "I give unto them eternal life; and they shall never perish, neither shall any man pluck them out of my hand."

Conclusion

The way of salvation is the heart of the Christian message. It is the good news that God, in His infinite grace, has provided a way for sinners to be reconciled to Him through the mediatorial work of Jesus Christ. This salvation, rooted in Christ's perfect obedience and sacrificial death, is a gift offered to all who will believe. As we embrace this truth, it transforms our lives, fills us with gratitude, and compels us to share the hope of salvation with the world.

CHAPTER SEVENTEEN
JUSTIFICATION

We believe that justification is God's gracious and full acquittal upon principles of righteousness of all sinners who believe in Christ. This blessing is bestowed, not in consideration of any works of righteousness, which we have done, but through the redemption that is in and through Jesus the Christ. It brings us into a state of most blessed peace and favor with God, and secures every other needed blessing.

Introduction

Justification is one of the most pivotal doctrines in Christian theology. It speaks to the heart of the gospel, affirming that believers are declared righteous before God, not because of any merit or good works, but solely through faith in Jesus Christ. This chapter will explore the meaning of justification, its biblical basis, and its implications for believers today. The fact that we can be fully acquitted of sin and clothed in the righteousness of Christ is a profound truth that transforms the believer's relationship with God, bringing peace and security in His presence.

Historical Context

Origins

The doctrine of justification is rooted in the Bible, particularly in the teachings of the Apostle Paul. In the early church, Paul confronted those who sought to combine faith in Christ with adherence to the Jewish law as a basis for righteousness. Paul's epistles, especially to the Romans and Galatians, emphasize that justification is a gracious act of God, received through faith, not works (Romans 3:28, KJV). The early church fathers, including Augustine, expanded on this teaching, highlighting that justification was a gift of grace, made possible by Christ's sacrifice.

Development

During the Reformation, the doctrine of justification became a central issue. Reformers like Martin Luther and John Calvin emphasized *sola fide* (faith alone), arguing that justification comes through faith in Christ apart from human efforts. This doctrine stood in contrast to the Roman Catholic view of justification, which involved both faith and works. For Baptists, this Reformation understanding of justification continues to be a core belief. We affirm that righteousness is imputed to believers by God through faith in Jesus Christ, a divine exchange where our sins are placed on Christ and His righteousness is given to us.

Exposition and Analysis

The article outlines several key aspects of justification:

Full Acquittal: Justification means being fully acquitted of all charges of sin. In a legal sense, God declares the believer righteous, not on the basis of their works, but on the righteousness of Christ. Romans 5:1 affirms, "Therefore being justified by faith, we have peace with God through our Lord Jesus Christ."

By Faith in Christ: Justification is not something that can be earned or achieved through personal merit or good works. Ephesians 2:8-9 states, "For by grace are ye saved through faith; and that not of yourselves: it is the gift of God: not of works, lest any man should boast." Our faith in Christ brings us into right standing with God because Christ's righteousness is imputed to us (Romans 4:4-5).

Through the Redemption in Christ: The basis of our justification is the redemption achieved through Christ's sacrificial death. Jesus bore the penalty for our sins, and His death on the cross satisfied the demands of God's justice (Romans 3:24-26). Through His resurrection, we are justified and assured of eternal life (Romans 4:23-25).

Peace and Favor with God: Justification brings believers into a state of peace with God. No longer under the wrath of God for sin, believers experience His favor and are reconciled to Him. Romans 5:9 speaks of this, stating, "Much more then, being now justified by his blood, we shall be saved from wrath through him."

Secures Every Needed Blessing: The blessings of justification extend beyond acquittal from sin. As children of God, believers are granted access to every spiritual blessing, including sanctification, adoption, and ultimately glorification (Romans 8:1). Justification opens the door to a lifelong process of being transformed into the image of Christ, securing for us eternal blessings.

Theological Significance

Justification by faith alone stands as a central tenet of Christian faith because it underscores the sufficiency of Christ's atonement and the grace of God. Romans 3:23-24 makes it clear that "all have sinned, and come short of the glory of God; being justified freely by his grace through the redemption that is in Christ Jesus." This means that no one can boast of their own righteousness but must trust solely in Christ for their salvation.

Paul's words in Philippians 3:9 summarize this beautifully: "And be found in him, not having mine own righteousness, which is of the law, but that which is through the faith of Christ, the righteousness which is of God by faith." It is Christ's righteousness, imputed to us by faith, that brings us into a right relationship with God.

Places in the Bible Where Taught

- **John 1:16** – "And of his fulness have all we received, and grace for grace."
- **Ephesians 3:8** – "Unto me...is this grace given, that I should preach among the Gentiles the unsearchable riches of Christ."
- **Acts 13:39** – "By him all that believe are justified from all things, from which ye could not be justified by the law of Moses."
- **Isaiah 53:11-12** – "By his knowledge shall my righteous servant justify many; for he shall bear their iniquities."
- **Romans 5:1** – "Therefore being justified by faith, we have peace with God through our Lord Jesus Christ."
- **Titus 3:5-7** – "Not by works of righteousness which we have done, but according to his mercy he saved us..."

Practical Application

The doctrine of justification by faith alone should produce several important responses in the believer's life. First, it humbles us. Knowing that our standing before God is not based on anything we have done should keep us from pride. Instead, we live in gratitude for the unmerited favor we have received.

Second, justification gives us peace and assurance. We do not have to live in fear of losing our salvation because it is based on Christ's finished work, not our ongoing efforts. Romans 8:1 reminds us, "There is therefore now no condemnation to them which are in Christ Jesus." This knowledge frees us to live joyfully and confidently in the grace of God.

Lastly, justification compels us to live righteously. Though our works do not justify us, they are the evidence of our justification. As James 2:18 states, "I will shew thee my faith by my works." Our justified standing with God leads us to pursue holiness, not to earn salvation, but as a response to the salvation already secured for us.

Common Misunderstandings

One common misunderstanding of justification is the belief that it can be lost through sin. While believers may struggle with sin, the Bible teaches that justification is a once-for-all declaration that secures the believer's eternal standing with God (Romans 8:33-34).

Another misconception is the idea that justification is incomplete without works. While good works are a necessary fruit of faith, they are not the basis of justification. Justification is solely through faith in Christ, as Paul writes in Romans 4:5, "But to him that worketh not, but believeth on him that justifieth the ungodly, his faith is counted for righteousness."

Conclusion

Justification by faith is a glorious doctrine that reveals the fullness of God's grace. Through the finished work of Christ, we are declared righteous, acquitted of sin, and granted peace with God. This truth transforms our lives, bringing us into a secure relationship with our Creator and empowering us to live lives that reflect His righteousness. As believers, we rejoice in the knowledge that our salvation is not based on our own merit but on the perfect righteousness of Christ.

CHAPTER EIGHTEEN
THE FREENESS OF SALVATION

We believe that the blessings of salvation are made free to all by the gospel. It is the duty of all to accept them by penitent and obedient faith. Nothing prevents the salvation of the greatest sinner except his own voluntary refusal to accept Jesus the Christ as Teacher, Saviour, and Lord.

Introduction

The doctrine of the freeness of salvation emphasizes the inclusive and universal nature of God's grace. The blessings of salvation, offered through the gospel, are freely available to all who are willing to receive them in faith. This chapter will explore the biblical foundation for this doctrine, the responsibility of individuals to respond, and the consequences of rejecting God's free offer of salvation. The good news is that no one is beyond the reach of God's saving power, and it is through faith in Jesus Christ that salvation is received.

Historical Context

Origins

The freeness of salvation has always been at the heart of the Christian message. From the prophets in the Old Testament to the apostles in the New Testament, the consistent call has been for all people to repent and turn to God. Isaiah 55:1 (KJV) echoes this call: "Ho, every one that thirsteth, come ye to the waters, and he that hath no money; come ye, buy, and eat; yea, come, buy wine and milk without money and without price."

In the early church, the message of salvation was proclaimed to both Jews and Gentiles, breaking down cultural and ethnic barriers. The Apostle Paul declared in Romans 1:16 (KJV), "For I am not ashamed of the gospel of Christ: for it is the power of God unto salvation to every one that believeth; to the Jew first, and also to the Greek." This universal offer of salvation was a radical departure from the idea that God's favor was limited to a specific group of people.

Development

Throughout church history, the doctrine of the freeness of salvation has been a point of emphasis in various movements. During the Protestant Reformation, reformers like Martin Luther and John Calvin reasserted the importance of salvation by grace through faith, emphasizing that salvation was not something earned by human effort or merit. Baptists have consistently upheld this belief, teaching that the gospel is offered freely to all, and that individuals have the responsibility to respond in faith and repentance.

Exposition and Analysis

The article on the freeness of salvation highlights three important truths:

Salvation Is Free to All: The gospel offers salvation to everyone, without discrimination. Isaiah 55:1 (KJV) beautifully captures this: "Come, buy wine and milk without money and without price." This imagery speaks to the unmerited nature of salvation—there is no cost to the individual because Christ has already paid the full price. The invitation is extended to all, regardless of social status, ethnicity, or past sins. Revelation 22:17 (KJV) also affirms this: "And whosoever will, let him take the water of life freely."

It Is the Duty of All to Accept: While salvation is freely offered, individuals are not passive recipients. They must respond to God's offer by exercising penitent and obedient faith. Mark 1:15 (KJV) records the words of Jesus: "The time is fulfilled, and the kingdom of God is at hand: repent ye, and believe the gospel." Faith and repentance are essential responses to the gospel message. Romans 16:25-26 (KJV) also speaks of "the obedience of faith" as the proper response to God's gracious offer of salvation.

Rejection of Salvation Is Voluntary: The only thing that prevents a person from receiving salvation is their own refusal to believe in and accept Jesus Christ. John 5:40 (KJV) records Jesus lamenting over the unwillingness of people to come to Him for life: "And ye will not come to me, that ye might have life." The Bible is clear that God desires all to be saved (1 Timothy 2:4, KJV), but He does not force salvation on anyone. Those who reject the gospel do so by their own willful choice, as illustrated in Matthew 23:37 (KJV): "O Jerusalem, Jerusalem...how often would I have gathered thy children together...and ye would not!"

Theological Significance

The freeness of salvation underscores the boundless grace of God. It declares that no person, regardless of their past, is beyond the reach of God's saving power. Romans 10:13 (KJV) states, "For whosoever shall call upon the name of the Lord shall be saved." This promise is universal in its scope and highlights God's desire for all people to be reconciled to Him.

At the same time, the doctrine reminds us that salvation requires a response. Faith and repentance are necessary conditions for receiving the blessings of salvation. Jesus Himself preached, "Repent ye, and believe the gospel" (Mark 1:15, KJV), signaling the need for a personal decision to trust in Him. The freeness of salvation is not a license to live however we please but a call to submit to the lordship of Christ.

This doctrine also confronts the reality of human responsibility. While salvation is available to all, not everyone will be saved. Those who reject Christ do so of their own volition, and the consequences of that rejection are eternal. John 3:19 (KJV) declares, "And this is the condemnation, that light is come into the world, and men loved darkness rather than light, because their deeds were evil."

Places in the Bible Where Taught

- **Isaiah 55:1** – "Ho, every one that thirsteth, come ye to the waters, and he that hath no money; come ye, buy, and eat; yea, come, buy wine and milk without money and without price."
- **Revelation 22:17** – "And the Spirit and the bride say, Come. And let him that heareth say, Come. And let him that is athirst come. And whosoever will, let him take the water of life freely."
- **Luke 14:17** – "And sent his servant at supper time to say to them that were bidden, Come; for all things are now ready."
- **Romans 1:16-17** – "For I am not ashamed of the gospel of Christ: for it is the power of God unto salvation to every one that believeth; to the Jew first, and also to the Greek."
- **John 5:40** – "And ye will not come to me, that ye might have life."
- **Matthew 23:37** – "O Jerusalem, Jerusalem...how often would I have gathered thy children together, even as a hen gathereth her chickens under her wings, and ye would not!"
- **Mark 1:15** – "The time is fulfilled, and the kingdom of God is at hand: repent ye, and believe the gospel."

Practical Application

The doctrine of the freeness of salvation should deeply shape the way believers live and interact with others. First and foremost, it reminds us of the importance of evangelism. Since salvation is freely available to all, it is the responsibility of every Christian to share the gospel without discrimination, trusting that God's grace is sufficient to save the most hardened of sinners. This conviction should propel believers to reach out to people from all walks of life, recognizing that no one is beyond the scope of God's redemptive power. The inclusiveness of the gospel calls believers to have compassion on those who have yet to experience the transformative grace of Jesus Christ.

Moreover, the freeness of salvation underscores the personal responsibility each individual has in responding to God. It is not enough to hear the message of salvation; one must actively receive it through faith and repentance. This understanding brings clarity to the Christian's call to not only share the gospel but to encourage others to make a conscious and obedient decision to follow Christ. It is a constant reminder that salvation requires more than a mental acknowledgment of Jesus' sacrifice—it demands a life lived in obedience to His lordship. As believers, this truth should inspire a life of faithful discipleship, demonstrating what it means to live under the grace that has been freely offered.

The freeness of salvation also teaches believers to live in a posture of humility and gratitude. Since salvation is a gift given by God and not earned by human merit, there is no room for boasting or self-righteousness. Understanding that our salvation is purely the result of God's grace should fill our hearts with deep thankfulness, leading us to treat others with grace, knowing that we, too, were undeserving of such love. This awareness should create a humility that permeates every aspect of our lives, recognizing that we are recipients of a gift that cannot be repaid.

Finally, this doctrine places an urgency on the believer's mission. Salvation is available to all, but it can also be rejected. The reality that people can turn away from the free offer of salvation means that Christians must take their witness seriously. There is an eternal significance to the decisions people make about Christ, and believers should feel a pressing responsibility to present the gospel clearly and compellingly. This urgency compels us to see every opportunity as a moment where someone might make the most important decision of their life, accepting or rejecting Christ.

The freeness of salvation, therefore, not only comforts believers in the boundless reach of God's grace but also challenges them to live with purpose, humility, and a sense of mission in their walk with Christ.

Common Misunderstandings

One misunderstanding is the belief that because salvation is free, it is automatic. Some may think that since salvation is offered to all, everyone will be saved regardless of their response. This view, known as universalism, is unbiblical. Jesus clearly taught that some would reject Him and face eternal separation from God (Luke 19:27, KJV).

Another misconception is that the freeness of salvation allows for a passive or superficial faith. While salvation is free, it requires genuine repentance and obedient faith. Saving faith is not mere intellectual assent but involves a heartfelt commitment to follow Christ as both Savior and Lord.

Conclusion

The freeness of salvation is a profound and glorious truth that reflects the depth of God's love and grace. The gospel extends an open invitation to all, offering eternal life through faith in Jesus Christ. Yet, it also calls for a personal response—faith and repentance are necessary to receive the blessings of salvation. As we reflect on this doctrine, may it inspire us to share the good news with others and to live lives that reflect the grace we have freely received.

CHAPTER 19
GRACE IN REGENERATION

We Believe that regeneration or the new birth is a change of heart wrought by the Holy Spirit, whereby we become partakers of the divine nature and a holy disposition is given, leading to the love and practice of righteousness. It is a work of God's free grace conditioned upon faith in Christ and made manifest by the fruit which we bring forth to the glory of God.

Historical Context

Origins

The doctrine of regeneration, or the new birth, has its roots in early Christian theology and can be traced back to the teachings of Jesus Christ. In John 3:3, Jesus tells Nicodemus, "Except a man be born again, he cannot see the kingdom of God." This new birth was understood as a spiritual transformation brought about by the Holy Spirit. Regeneration is one of the key doctrines that distinguishes Christianity from other worldviews, as it emphasizes an internal, divinely initiated transformation of the heart, rather than external compliance to religious rules.

Development

Throughout church history, the concept of regeneration has been explored and expanded by various theologians, including Augustine, Martin Luther, and John Calvin. During the Protestant Reformation, the doctrine was articulated in opposition to the Catholic emphasis on sacramental grace. Reformers emphasized that regeneration was an act of God's grace alone, not dependent on any human effort. Baptists have historically upheld regeneration as a work of the Holy Spirit, contingent on personal faith in Christ, and have rejected the notion that it can be achieved through infant baptism or other rituals.

Exposition and Analysis

Regeneration, often referred to as the new birth, marks the beginning of a believer's spiritual life. It is a divine work of grace, initiated by God and carried out by the Holy Spirit. Regeneration is not merely a reform of character, but a radical transformation of the heart, where the individual receives a new nature inclined toward righteousness and love for God. This transformation enables the believer to love, obey, and serve God in ways that were impossible before.

The Scriptures teach that regeneration is a supernatural event. In John 3:6, Jesus explains that "That which is born of the flesh is flesh, and that which is born of the Spirit is spirit." The new birth is not achieved by human effort but is entirely the work of God. It brings the believer into spiritual life, enabling them to comprehend spiritual truths and live in a way that reflects their new nature in Christ. This work of regeneration is often accompanied by an observable change in behavior and desires, as the believer now seeks to honor God with their life.

Theological Significance

Regeneration is essential to salvation because it is the means by which sinners are made spiritually alive. Without it, no one can enter the kingdom of God (John 3:3). It is an act of God's free grace, grounded in the redemptive work of Christ, and is conditioned upon faith. This transformation results in the believer becoming a "new creation" (2 Corinthians 5:17, KJV), where old sinful desires are replaced by new godly affections.

The indwelling of the Holy Spirit is the hallmark of regeneration. Ezekiel 36:26 promises, "A new heart also will I give you, and a new spirit will I put within you." This new heart enables believers to walk in obedience to God's commandments and produce spiritual fruit, such as love, joy, and peace (Galatians 5:22-23, KJV). Regeneration is not an isolated event but a continual process of growth in holiness, as the believer becomes more like Christ over time.

Places in the Bible Where Taught:

- John 3:3, 6-7
- 1 Corinthians 2:14
- 2 Corinthians 5:17
- Ezekiel 36:26
- Romans 2:28-29
- 1 John 4:7
- Philippians 2:13
- 1 Peter 1:22-25
- Colossians 3:9-11

Key Figures and Influences

The doctrine of regeneration has been championed by key figures in Christian history. Augustine's understanding of original sin and grace laid the groundwork for the need for spiritual rebirth. Martin

Luther emphasized regeneration in his teachings on justification, linking the new birth to faith in Christ. John Calvin expanded on the regenerative work of the Holy Spirit in his doctrine of election, explaining that regeneration is an integral part of God's plan for salvation. In the modern era, theologians such as Charles Spurgeon and Jonathan Edwards have preached extensively on the necessity of the new birth for true conversion.

Practical Application

The doctrine of regeneration calls believers to reflect on the radical change that has occurred in their lives as a result of the new birth. Understanding that regeneration is solely the work of God's grace should evoke deep gratitude and humility in the believer's heart. It is a reminder that salvation is not something we can earn, but a gift of God that transforms us from the inside out.

Moreover, regeneration challenges believers to live lives that reflect the reality of their new birth. If we have been made new by the Holy Spirit, we should exhibit the fruit of that transformation in our daily conduct. This involves a commitment to growing in holiness, loving others, and practicing righteousness. The believer's new nature should compel them to live in obedience to God's commands and reject sinful desires. Furthermore, the assurance that we have been made partakers of the divine nature encourages believers to rely on the Holy Spirit for strength in their spiritual walk.

Understanding regeneration also compels the church to emphasize the necessity of true conversion. Pastors and church leaders must ensure that their congregations understand that merely attending church or participating in religious activities is not sufficient for salvation. True regeneration is evidenced by a changed life, one that is marked by love for God, obedience to His Word, and the pursuit of holiness. As a result, evangelistic efforts should focus not only on calling people to make a decision for Christ but on the transformative power of the Holy Spirit in bringing about the new birth.

Common Misunderstandings

One common misunderstanding of regeneration is the belief that it is simply a moral reform or self-improvement. Some think that becoming a Christian is about changing external behavior or adopting religious practices. However, regeneration is much deeper than that—it is a complete transformation of the heart by the Holy Spirit. As Jesus explained to Nicodemus, regeneration is not something that can be achieved by human effort, but only by the Spirit of God (John 3:5).

Another misunderstanding is that regeneration happens gradually over time, rather than as a specific moment of spiritual rebirth. While spiritual growth and sanctification are lifelong processes, regeneration itself is an instantaneous act of God's grace. It occurs at the moment of salvation when the Holy Spirit indwells the believer, giving them new life in Christ (2 Corinthians 5:17).

A third misunderstanding is the belief that baptism or other sacraments are necessary for regeneration. While baptism is an important act of obedience and a public declaration of faith, it is not the means by which a person is regenerated. Regeneration is solely the work of the Holy Spirit and is conditioned on faith in Christ, not any external ritual (Titus 3:5).

Conclusion

The doctrine of regeneration is a fundamental aspect of the Christian faith, highlighting the necessity of a new birth for entry into the kingdom of God. It is a work of God's grace that transforms sinners into new creations, enabling them to live lives of obedience and righteousness. As believers, we are called to reflect on the significance of this transformation and live in accordance with the new nature we have received. This understanding of regeneration not only deepens our appreciation for God's grace but also challenges us to live lives that bear witness to the reality of the new birth.

CHAPTER 20
REPENTANCE AND FAITH

We believe that repentance and faith are sacred duties and inseparable graces, wrought in our souls by the regenerating Spirit of God; whereby, being deeply convinced of our guilt, danger, and helplessness, and of the way of salvation by Christ, we turn to God with unfeigned contrition, confession, and supplication for mercy; at the same time, heartily receiving the Lord Jesus Christ as our Prophet, Priest, and King, and relying on Him alone as the only and all-sufficient Savior.

Historical Context

Origins

The doctrine of repentance and faith has been central to the Christian message since the early church. These two concepts are often presented together in Scripture as necessary responses to the gospel. Repentance and faith are not merely intellectual acknowledgments but deep spiritual transformations. The call to "repent and believe" echoes through the teachings of John the Baptist, Jesus Christ, and the apostles (Mark

1:15), emphasizing the turning away from sin and a sincere trust in Christ for salvation.

Development

Over the centuries, theologians like Augustine, John Calvin, and Martin Luther have emphasized the importance of repentance and faith as gifts of God, made possible through the work of the Holy Spirit. Luther, in particular, spoke of repentance as a daily act for the believer, a continual turning away from sin and reliance on the grace of Christ. The Baptist tradition, rooted in the Protestant Reformation, has maintained the essential connection between repentance, faith, and the experience of salvation, teaching that both are responses to the grace of God made possible through regeneration.

Exposition and Analysis

Repentance and faith are the two sides of the same coin in the Christian experience of salvation. Repentance involves a heartfelt turning away from sin, a recognition of our guilt, and an acknowledgment of our inability to save ourselves. Faith, on the other hand, is a turning toward Christ in complete trust, receiving Him as Savior and Lord. Together, they mark the beginning of the Christian life and form the foundation for a continuing relationship with God.

Repentance, as taught in Scripture, is not merely feeling sorry for sin but involves a deep sense of contrition and a determination to change. It is a recognition of our rebellion against God, our need for His mercy, and the desire to turn away from sinful behavior. True repentance always leads to action, as the repentant person seeks to live in a way that pleases God (Acts 2:37-38).

Faith is the response to God's grace, a complete trust in Christ as the only means of salvation. It is not merely intellectual assent but involves the whole person—mind, heart, and will—accepting Jesus as Prophet, Priest, and King. As our Prophet, Christ reveals the truth of God; as our Priest, He intercedes on our behalf, offering Himself as the perfect sacrifice; as our King, He rules over our lives with love and authority.

Theological Significance

Repentance and faith are inseparable graces. They occur simultaneously in the soul of a believer at the moment of salvation and continue throughout the Christian life. Both are initiated by the Holy Spirit, who convicts us of sin and leads us to trust in Christ (John 16:8). Ephesians 2:8 teaches that "by grace are ye saved through faith; and that not of yourselves: it is the gift of God" (KJV). This reminds us that neither repentance nor faith are human achievements, but are graciously given by God.

Repentance brings about a change in the believer's relationship with sin. Prior to salvation, we are slaves to sin, living in rebellion against God. In repentance, we turn away from this rebellion, acknowledging the righteousness of God's law and our failure to keep it. In doing so, we seek God's mercy and forgiveness, knowing that only through Christ can we be reconciled to God.

Faith, on the other hand, is the means by which we receive the gift of salvation. It is by faith that we are justified, made right with God, and brought into a new relationship with Him. Faith is not a one-time act but a continual reliance on Christ for all that we need. As we grow in faith, we come to understand more deeply the sufficiency of Christ's sacrifice and His ongoing work in our lives.

Places in the Bible Where Taught:

- Mark 1:15
- Acts 11:18
- Ephesians 2:8
- John 16:8
- Acts 2:37-38

- Luke 15:18-21
- James 4:7-10
- Romans 10:9-11
- Hebrews 4:14

Key Figures and Influences

The doctrine of repentance and faith has been emphasized by key figures throughout Christian history. John the Baptist preached a message of repentance in preparation for the coming of Christ, calling people to turn from their sins and believe in the One who was to come. Jesus Himself preached repentance and faith, commanding His followers to repent and believe the gospel (Mark 1:15).

During the Reformation, Martin Luther and John Calvin articulated a clear understanding of repentance as a daily, ongoing process for the believer. Luther famously wrote in his Ninety-Five Theses that the entire Christian life should be one of repentance. Calvin emphasized the role of the Holy Spirit in producing repentance and faith in the heart of the believer, teaching that both are gifts of grace rather than human accomplishments.

In the Baptist tradition, Charles Spurgeon, known as the "Prince of Preachers," frequently emphasized the necessity of repentance and faith for salvation. He declared, "Repentance and faith are distaff and spindle in the hands of the Spirit to bring forth the soul's garments of salvation." These two graces are woven together in the experience of every believer, brought about by the regenerating work of the Holy Spirit.

Practical Application

The doctrine of repentance and faith calls believers to a life of continual transformation and trust in Christ. Understanding that repentance is not a one-time event but an ongoing response to God's grace, we are challenged to examine our hearts regularly, turning away from sinful thoughts and behaviors that dishonor God. This requires humility, as we acknowledge our failures and seek God's mercy.

In the same way, faith is not merely the means by which we are saved, but the foundation for our entire Christian walk. Living by faith means trusting in Christ for every aspect of our lives, relying on His wisdom, provision, and strength. As we grow in faith, we learn to trust God more deeply, even in the midst of trials, knowing that He is faithful to His promises.

This doctrine also shapes the way we share the gospel with others. Evangelism must include both a call to repentance and an invitation to faith in Christ. People need to understand their sin and need for a Savior, and they need to be directed to Christ as the only solution. True conversion is marked by both a turning away from sin and a turning toward Christ.

Common Misunderstandings

One common misunderstanding is the idea that repentance is merely feeling sorry for one's sins. While sorrow for sin is an important part of repentance, true repentance involves more than just emotion. It is a complete change of mind and heart that leads to a change in behavior. True repentance results in a turning away from sin and a desire to live in obedience to God.

Another misconception is that faith is simply intellectual agreement with certain facts about Jesus. While understanding the truth about Christ is essential, biblical faith involves a deep trust and reliance on Him as Savior and Lord. It is not enough to acknowledge Jesus with our minds; we must also surrender our lives to Him and follow Him as our King.

A third misunderstanding is that repentance and faith are separate events in the Christian life. In reality, they are inseparable. Repentance without faith leads to despair, while faith without repentance is superficial and ineffective. Both must be present in the heart of the believer for true salvation.

Conclusion

The doctrines of repentance and faith are foundational to the Christian life. They represent the twofold response to the gospel: turning away from sin and trusting in Christ for salvation. As believers, we are called to live lives marked by ongoing repentance and growing faith, relying on the grace of God to transform us and sustain us. These sacred duties are also gifts of God's grace, given to us through the regenerating work of the Holy Spirit, and they mark the beginning of a life lived in fellowship with God.

CHAPTER TWENTY-ONE
GOD'S PURPOSE OF GRACE

We believe that election is the gracious purpose of God, according to which He regenerates, sanctifies, and saves sinners. It is perfectly consistent with the free agency of man and in no way interferes with the salvation of any individual. It is a most glorious display of God's sovereign goodness and is infinitely wise, holy, and unchangeable. It excludes boasting and promotes humility. It encourages the use of means in the highest degree.

Historical Context

Origins

The doctrine of election, or predestination, has been a subject of theological debate for centuries, especially following the Protestant Reformation. Rooted in Scripture, it highlights God's sovereign choice in salvation, where He elects or chooses individuals to be saved. Early Christian theologians like Augustine championed the idea of God's grace as the ultimate source of salvation, which was further developed by Reformers like John Calvin. Calvin's view, often referred to as "unconditional election," argued that God chooses to save certain individuals based on His sovereign will, not on any foreseen merit or action of the individual.

Development

In Baptist theology, the belief in God's election as gracious and sovereign is upheld, while maintaining that it does not negate human responsibility or free will. This tension between God's sovereignty and human responsibility is essential in understanding the biblical teaching on salvation. The Baptist tradition affirms that while God's election is unchangeable and eternal, it also operates in harmony with human free agency, making the offer of salvation accessible to all.

Exposition and Analysis

The doctrine of election emphasizes God's sovereign grace as the source of salvation. According to this doctrine, God, in His wisdom and love, chooses certain individuals to be recipients of His grace, ensuring their regeneration, sanctification, and ultimate salvation. Ephesians 1:3-14 beautifully describes this purpose of grace, noting that God chose us in Christ before the foundation of the world. This choosing is not arbitrary but reflects God's unchanging wisdom, goodness, and love.

Election and Human Responsibility

One of the key concerns with election is whether it contradicts the free will of man. However, Baptist teaching maintains that election is fully compatible with human free agency. Though God elects individuals for salvation, this does not prevent anyone from responding to the gospel. Instead, it guarantees that those whom God has chosen will indeed come to faith through the regenerating work of the Holy Spirit (John 6:37-40). This balance preserves the biblical tension between God's sovereignty and human responsibility, where

God's purpose of grace does not negate the need for individual faith and repentance.

Theological Significance

The doctrine of election is often misunderstood as promoting fatalism or making human effort unnecessary. However, properly understood, it fosters deep humility and reliance on God's grace. Since salvation is entirely God's work, there is no room for boasting (Romans 3:27; Ephesians 2:8-9). Election also inspires gratitude and assurance, as believers understand that their salvation is rooted in God's eternal purpose, not in their own merit or efforts.

Furthermore, the doctrine of election encourages the use of means. Rather than promoting passivity, it energizes the church to preach the gospel, pray, and engage in evangelism, knowing that God uses these means to bring His elect to salvation (Acts 13:48). The certainty of God's purpose provides confidence in the effectiveness of gospel proclamation.

Places in the Bible Where Taught:

- 2 Timothy 1:8-9
- Ephesians 1:3-14
- Romans 11:5-6
- John 15:16
- Romans 8:28-31

Key Figures and Influences

The understanding of election has been shaped by notable theologians and pastors throughout Christian history. Augustine first formulated the doctrine of grace in a way that heavily influenced both Catholic and Protestant traditions. During the Reformation, John Calvin became one of the most prominent defenders of election, teaching that God's grace alone determines who is saved. His doctrine, often called "Calvinism," included the belief in unconditional election, meaning that God's choice is not based on human merit.

The Baptist tradition, while influenced by Calvinist thought, has also emphasized human responsibility. Notable Baptist theologians like Charles Haddon Spurgeon and Andrew Fuller preached on God's sovereign election while simultaneously urging sinners to repent and believe the gospel. Spurgeon, in particular, preached that God's election does not hinder evangelism but compels it, since the elect must be brought to faith through the hearing of the gospel.

Practical Application

The doctrine of election offers profound comfort and encouragement for believers. Knowing that our salvation is rooted in God's eternal purpose rather than our own efforts gives us assurance of our security in Christ. This understanding should lead to greater humility, as we recognize that our standing before God is entirely by His grace and not our own merit.

Additionally, this doctrine inspires urgency in evangelism. Since we do not know who the elect are, we must share the gospel freely with all people, trusting that God will use our efforts to bring His elect to faith. Acts 13:48 demonstrates that as many as were appointed to eternal life believed, showing that God uses the preaching of the gospel to accomplish His purposes.

Common Misunderstandings

One common misunderstanding of election is that it leads to a belief that human actions or decisions are irrelevant. This fatalistic view is not supported by Scripture or Baptist teaching. While God's election is certain, it works in harmony with human responsibility. God's purpose does not override the need for individuals to repent, believe, and persevere in faith.

Another misconception is that election promotes pride or elitism. In fact, the doctrine teaches the opposite: it emphasizes that salvation is entirely of grace and excludes boasting (Romans 3:27). The more we understand the depth of our sin and the greatness of God's grace, the more humility and gratitude should characterize our lives.

Finally, some believe that election negates the need for evangelism. However, Scripture teaches that the gospel must be preached to all people, and it is through the preaching of the Word that the elect are brought to faith (Romans 10:14-17). The doctrine of election should motivate believers to engage in evangelism with confidence, knowing that God's purpose will be accomplished.

Conclusion

The doctrine of God's purpose of grace, or election, is a profound mystery that demonstrates His sovereign love and wisdom in saving sinners. It brings assurance, promotes humility, and encourages the diligent use of means such as prayer, evangelism, and gospel proclamation. As we trust in God's gracious purposes, we are reminded that salvation belongs to the Lord and that His sovereign plan will be fulfilled.

CHAPTER TWENTY-TWO
SANCTIFICATION

We Believe that sanctification is the process by which, according to the will of God, we are made partakers of His holiness; that it is a progressive work; that it is begun in regeneration; and that it is carried on in the hearts of believers by the presence and power of the Holy Spirit, the Sealer and Comforter, in the continual use of the appointed means, especially the Word of God, self-examination, self-denial, watchfulness, and prayer.

Historical Context

Origins

Sanctification, as a theological concept, has its roots deeply embedded in the Old Testament, where the idea of being set apart for God's purposes is a recurring theme. In the Old Testament, the concept of holiness is central to the understanding of sanctification. For instance, in Leviticus 20:7, God commands the Israelites to consecrate themselves and be holy, for He is holy. This sets a precedent for the understanding of sanctification as being set apart from sin and dedicated to God's service.

Development

In the New Testament, the understanding of sanctification evolves as it becomes more explicitly linked to the work of Christ and the Holy Spirit. The New Testament emphasizes that sanctification is not just about external adherence to the law but about an internal transformation that occurs through the Holy Spirit. This transformation is linked to the believer's union with Christ and is seen as a process that continues throughout the believer's life.

Exposition and Analysis

Sanctification, according to the New Testament, is a process initiated and sustained by God. It begins at the moment of regeneration, when a person is born again through faith in Jesus Christ. This new birth marks the beginning of a transformative journey where believers are progressively made more like Christ. The Apostle Paul underscores this process in 2 Corinthians 3:18 (NKJV), where he writes, "But we all, with unveiled face, beholding as in a mirror the glory of the Lord, are being transformed into the same image from glory to glory, just as by the Spirit of the Lord."

The role of the Holy Spirit in sanctification is crucial. The Holy Spirit works within believers to cultivate spiritual growth and holiness. Ephesians 1:4 (NKJV) notes that God chose believers to be holy and blameless before Him, highlighting the divine intent for sanctification. Additionally, Philippians 2:12-13 (NIV) encourages believers to "continue to work out your salvation with fear and trembling, for it is God who works in you to will and to act in order to fulfill his good purpose." This passage emphasizes both the human responsibility and divine assistance in the sanctification process.

Sanctification is not a passive process but involves active participation from believers. This includes engaging in spiritual disciplines such as reading Scripture, self-examination, prayer, and self-denial. The process is described as progressive, meaning that it continues throughout a believer's life, with the ultimate goal of becoming more like Christ. The practical outworking of sanctification is reflected in the believer's growing ability to live in accordance with God's commands and to exhibit the fruits of the Spirit, as detailed in Galatians 5:22-23 (NKJV).

Theological Significance

Sanctification holds significant theological importance as it embodies the transformative work of God in the believer's life. It reflects the nature of salvation as a holistic process that encompasses not only justification but also a continuous, dynamic work of renewal and growth. Theologically, sanctification underscores the believer's participation in the divine nature (2 Peter 1:4) and the manifestation of God's holiness in everyday life.

Firstly, sanctification highlights the distinction between positional and progressive sanctification. Positional sanctification refers to the believer's standing before God as being set apart and holy due to their union with Christ. This is a completed work achieved through Christ's sacrifice. Progressive sanctification, on the other hand, is the ongoing process where believers grow in holiness and spiritual maturity. This dynamic process illustrates the ongoing nature of salvation and the believer's active role in their spiritual growth.

Secondly, sanctification is the means by which believers reflect God's character and advance His purposes on earth. It aligns with God's will for His people to be holy as He is holy (1 Thessalonians 4:3). The process of sanctification is a response to God's call to live a life that reflects His moral and ethical standards. Through sanctification, believers participate in God's redemptive mission, demonstrating the transformative power of the gospel in their lives and influencing the world around them.

Lastly, the doctrine of sanctification reinforces the importance of the Holy Spirit's role in the believer's life. The Spirit not only empowers believers to live according to God's commands but also ensures that their efforts in sanctification are rooted in divine strength and guidance. This theological perspective emphasizes the interplay between divine sovereignty and human responsibility in the sanctification process.

Practical Application

Understanding sanctification has profound implications for the believer's daily life. Sanctification is a call to live out one's faith in practical ways, demonstrating the transformative power of the Holy Spirit. This involves ongoing efforts to align one's life with God's will, pursuing holiness in thought, word, and deed.

Believers are encouraged to cultivate spiritual disciplines that facilitate growth in sanctification. Regular reading of Scripture helps in understanding God's will and provides guidance for living a holy life. Prayer is essential for maintaining a close relationship with God and seeking His strength to overcome sin. Self-examination allows believers to assess their spiritual progress and make necessary adjustments. Self-denial and watchfulness help in resisting temptations and living a life that reflects Christ's character.

Moreover, sanctification involves community support. Being part of a church community provides encouragement, accountability, and opportunities for growth. Engaging in fellowship and service allows believers to practice love and humility, further reflecting the sanctifying work of the Holy Spirit in their lives.

Common Misunderstandings

One common misunderstanding about sanctification is that it is a one-time event rather than a progressive process. Some may believe that sanctification occurs instantaneously at conversion, but Scripture presents it as an ongoing work. The notion of sanctification as a lifelong journey is supported by passages like 1 Thessalonians 5:23 (NKJV), which refers to the "God of peace" sanctifying believers "completely," and Philippians 1:6 (NIV), which assures that God "who began a good work in you will carry it on to completion."

Another misunderstanding is the belief that sanctification is solely the result of human effort. While believers are called to actively pursue holiness, it is essential to recognize that sanctification is ultimately a work of the Holy Spirit. Philippians 2:13 (NIV) clarifies that it is God who works in believers "to will and to act in order to fulfill his good purpose," highlighting the divine partnership in the process of sanctification.

Conclusion

Sanctification is a central aspect of the Christian faith, reflecting the transformative power of God's grace in the life of a believer. It begins with regeneration and continues as a progressive work of the Holy Spirit, who enables believers to grow in holiness and Christlikeness. Understanding sanctification helps believers appreciate the ongoing work of God in their lives and motivates them to engage actively in spiritual disciplines.

CHAPTER TWENTY-THREE
THE PERSEVERANCE OF SAINTS

We Believe that such only are real believers as endure unto the end: that their persevering attachment to Christ is the grand mark which distinguishes them from superficial professors; that a special Providence watches over their welfare; and that they are kept by the power of God through faith unto salvation.

Historical Context

Origins

The doctrine of the perseverance of the saints has its roots in the early church and was further developed during the Reformation. Early church fathers like Augustine emphasized the notion that true believers are sustained by God's grace throughout their lives. This idea was further refined by Reformers such as John Calvin, who articulated the concept of "eternal security" or "perseverance of the saints" as a central tenet of Reformed theology.

Development

During the Reformation, the doctrine of perseverance was articulated as part of the broader Reformed emphasis on the sovereignty of God and the security of the believer. Calvin's teachings on the perseverance of the saints were grounded in his understanding of the covenant of grace and the eternal nature of God's promises. This doctrine was affirmed in various confessions and catechisms, such as the Westminster Confession of Faith, which asserts that "they who are included in the covenant of grace shall never totally or finally fall away from the state of grace, but shall certainly persevere therein to the end."

Exposition and Analysis

The perseverance of the saints is based on the belief that those who are truly regenerated and justified by God will continue in faith until the end of their lives. This doctrine asserts that genuine believers are kept by God's power and will not ultimately fall away from their state of grace.

John 6:39 (NKJV) states, "This is the will of the Father who sent Me, that of all He has given Me I should lose nothing, but should raise it up at the last day." This verse highlights the assurance that Christ will preserve those whom the Father has given Him. Similarly, John 8:31 (NKJV) underscores the idea that true disciples of Christ will remain steadfast in His word: "If you abide in My word, you are My disciples indeed."

The distinction between genuine believers and superficial professors is a crucial aspect of this doctrine. Matthew 13:20-21 (NKJV) describes how some receive the word with joy but fall away when trouble arises, illustrating the difference between those who endure in their faith and those who do not. In contrast, genuine believers are characterized by their enduring faith and attachment to Christ, as shown in 1 John 2:27-28 (NKJV), which says, "But the anointing which you have received from Him abides in you... And now, little children, abide in Him, that when He appears, we may have confidence and not be ashamed before Him at His coming."

The concept of divine preservation is also emphasized. Philippians 1:6 (NKJV) assures believers, "Being confident of this very thing, that He who has begun a good work in you will complete it until the day of Jesus Christ." This assurance is based on the belief that God's providential care ensures that true believers are preserved in faith until the end.

Theological Significance

Theologically, the perseverance of the saints underscores several key aspects of Christian doctrine:

Divine Sovereignty and Faithfulness: The doctrine affirms God's sovereignty and faithfulness in the process of salvation. It emphasizes that salvation is not dependent on human effort but on God's unchanging purpose and power. Romans 8:28 (NKJV) reinforces this, stating, "And we know that all things work together for good to those who love God, to those who are the called according to His purpose."

Eternal Security: The perseverance of the saints provides assurance of eternal security for believers. This assurance is rooted in the belief that God's promises are reliable and His power is sufficient to sustain believers through all trials and temptations. Jude 24-25 (NKJV) reflects this confidence: "Now to Him who is able to keep you from stumbling, and to present you faultless before the presence of His glory with exceeding joy."

Genuine Faith vs. Temporary Belief: The doctrine distinguishes between genuine faith that endures and temporary belief that does not. It underscores the importance of a persevering faith as evidence of true salvation. 1 John 2:19 (NKJV) highlights this by stating, "They went out from us, but they were not of us; for if they had been of us, they would have continued with us."

Encouragement for Believers: Understanding the perseverance of the saints provides encouragement for believers facing difficulties.

It assures them that their efforts to live faithfully are not in vain, and that they are supported by God's providential care. Hebrews 13:5 (NKJV) promises, "For He Himself has said, 'I will never leave you nor forsake you.'"

Practical Application

The doctrine of perseverance calls believers to remain steadfast in their faith and to live in a manner consistent with their identity in Christ. It encourages believers to cultivate a strong relationship with God through prayer, Scripture reading, and community fellowship. Recognizing that God's power sustains them, believers are motivated to live with confidence and resilience in the face of trials.

Practically, this doctrine also calls believers to avoid complacency and to actively engage in their spiritual growth. This includes participating in church life, pursuing personal holiness, and supporting one another in the faith. The assurance of perseverance should inspire believers to live out their faith with diligence and commitment.

Common Misunderstandings

One common misunderstanding is that the doctrine of perseverance implies that believers can live however they want, assuming they are secure regardless of their actions. However, the doctrine asserts that genuine faith will produce a life marked by holiness and perseverance. It is not a license for sin but a call to a life that reflects true faith.

Another misunderstanding is the conflation of perseverance with eternal security without recognizing the ongoing responsibility of the believer. While the doctrine assures that God will preserve believers, it also emphasizes the believer's role in remaining faithful and diligent in their spiritual walk.

Conclusion

The perseverance of the saints is a doctrine that provides profound assurance of God's faithfulness and the enduring nature of true salvation. It highlights the distinction between genuine believers who are sustained by God's power and those who only superficially embrace the faith. This doctrine encourages believers to remain steadfast, knowing that God's providential care ensures their ultimate security.

CHAPTER TWENTY-FOUR
THE HARMONY OF THE LAW AND THE GOSPEL

We Believe that the law of God is the eternal and unchangeable rule of His moral government; that it is holy, just, and good; and that the inability which the Scriptures ascribe to fallen men to fulfill its precepts arises entirely from their love of sin; to deliver them from which, and to restore them through a Mediator to unfeigned obedience to the holy law, is one great end of the gospel, and of the means of grace connected with the establishment of the visible Church.

Historical Context

Origins

The relationship between the law and the gospel has been a central topic in Christian theology since the early church. Early Christian leaders sought to understand how the Mosaic law related to the new covenant established by Jesus Christ. The law's role in revealing sin and the gospel's role in offering redemption became a focal point of theological reflection and debate.

Development

During the Reformation, key figures such as Martin Luther and John Calvin made significant contributions to the understanding of the law and the gospel. Luther argued that the law exposes human sinfulness and the gospel provides the remedy through faith in Christ. The Reformation reinforced the idea that the law and the gospel are complementary rather than contradictory, with the law highlighting the need for grace and the gospel fulfilling that need.

Exposition and Analysis

The law of God, as presented in Scripture, is described as eternal, unchangeable, holy, just, and good. Romans 7:12 (NKJV) states, "Therefore the law is holy, and the commandment holy and just and good." The law serves as a reflection of God's moral character and a guide for human conduct. However, due to the fall and humanity's inherent sinfulness, there is an inability to fully comply with the law's demands.

Romans 3:20 (NKJV) explains, "Therefore by the deeds of the law no flesh will be justified in His sight, for by the law is the knowledge of sin." The law's purpose is to reveal sin rather than to provide a means of salvation. This is further emphasized in Galatians 3:21 (NKJV), which asserts, "Is the law then against the promises of God? Certainly not! For if there had been a law given which could have given life, truly righteousness would have been by the law."

The gospel, on the other hand, addresses the inability of fallen humanity to fulfill the law. It presents Jesus Christ as the Mediator who fulfills the law's requirements and provides redemption. Romans 10:4 (NKJV) declares, "For Christ is the end of the law for righteousness to everyone who believes." The gospel restores humanity's relationship with God and empowers believers to live in accordance with God's will.

The relationship between the law and the gospel is one of complementarity rather than opposition. The law points to humanity's need for redemption, and the gospel provides the means of that redemption. Hebrews 8:10 (NKJV) states, "For this is the covenant that I will make with the house of Israel after those days, says the Lord: I will put My laws in their mind and write them on their hearts; and I will be their God, and they shall be My people."

Theological Significance

Theologically, the harmony between the law and the gospel underscores several key aspects of Christian doctrine:

Purpose of the Law: The law serves to reveal sin and guide believers in righteousness. It is an expression of God's holy character and His expectations for human conduct. It highlights humanity's need for grace and sets the standard for living in accordance with God's will.

Fulfillment in Christ: The gospel demonstrates that Jesus Christ is the fulfillment of the law. He perfectly obeyed the law and, through His death and resurrection, provided a means for believers to be reconciled to God. This fulfillment underscores the unity of the Old and New Testaments and the continuity of God's redemptive plan.

Role of Grace: The gospel introduces the concept of grace as the means by which believers are empowered to live according to God's standards. Grace does not abolish the law but enables believers to fulfill its requirements through the power of the Holy Spirit. This relationship is captured in Romans 8:2-4 (NKJV): "For the law of the Spirit of life in Christ Jesus has made me free from the law of sin and death. For what the law could not do in that it was weak through the flesh, God did by sending His own Son in the likeness of sinful flesh, on account of sin: He condemned sin in the flesh, that the righteous requirement of the law might be fulfilled in us who do not walk according to the flesh but according to the Spirit."

Unity of Scripture: The harmony of the law and the gospel affirms the unity of Scripture. Both the Old and New Testaments reveal different aspects of God's redemptive work. The law prepares the way for the gospel, and the gospel fulfills and completes the law's promises.

Practical Application

Understanding the relationship between the law and the gospel deeply influences how Christians live out their faith. The law continues to serve as a moral guide, highlighting the standards of righteousness that God expects. However, it is through the gospel that believers find the strength and motivation to meet these standards. The recognition that salvation comes through grace alone encourages believers to rely on the Holy Spirit's power rather than their own efforts to achieve righteousness. This realization fosters a deeper appreciation for Christ's sacrifice and a more profound sense of gratitude.

Furthermore, integrating both the law and the gospel in teaching and preaching ensures a balanced approach to spiritual growth. Presenting the law helps believers understand their need for redemption, while the gospel offers the solution and empowerment for living out God's commands. This approach not only upholds the moral teachings of Scripture but also reinforces the grace that makes obedient living possible.

Common Misunderstandings

A common misunderstanding is the belief that the gospel nullifies the law. Some might think that emphasizing grace means dismissing the law's moral teachings. In reality, the gospel fulfills the law rather than abolishes it, maintaining the relevance of the law's ethical principles while providing a means to live according to them. Another misconception is that adherence to the law is unnecessary for believers. While the gospel provides salvation through grace, it does not negate the law's role in guiding righteous living. Believers are called to uphold the law's moral teachings, empowered by grace rather than bound by legalism.

Conclusion

The harmony of the law and the gospel reveals the coherence and unity of God's redemptive plan. The law, while exposing human sinfulness, sets the stage for the gospel's promise of salvation. The gospel fulfills and completes the law's requirements through Christ, highlighting the continuity of Scripture and the comprehensive nature of God's plan for humanity. This understanding enriches the believer's faith and guides them in living a life that reflects God's righteousness and grace.

CHAPTER TWENTY-FIVE
A GOSPEL CHURCH

We Believe that a visible Church of Christ is a congregation of baptized believers, associated by covenant in the faith and fellowship of the gospel; observing the ordinances of Christ; governed by His laws; and exercising the gifts, rights, and privileges invested in them by His word; that its only Scripture officers are bishops or pastors, and deacons, whose qualifications, claims, and duties are defined in the Epistles to Timothy and Titus.

Historical Context

Origins

The concept of the church as a visible and organized body of believers is rooted in the New Testament. Jesus Christ established the Church during His earthly ministry, and the early Christians, guided by His teachings, began to form local congregations. The early church's structure and practices were shaped by the directives of Christ and the Apostles, emphasizing the importance of community, fellowship, and governance according to divine principles.

Development

As the early church grew, it faced various challenges that led to the development of more formal structures and practices. The Apostles, particularly Paul, wrote letters to the churches providing guidance on church governance, membership, and the role of church officers. These Epistles to Timothy and Titus outline the qualifications for church leaders and the essential functions of a gospel-centered church. The church's structure evolved to include bishops or pastors and deacons, reflecting the need for effective leadership and service within the congregation.

Exposition and Analysis

A visible church of Christ is defined as a congregation of baptized believers who are united by a covenant in the faith and fellowship of the gospel. This definition emphasizes the importance of both individual commitment and collective association in the life of the church. According to 1 Corinthians 1:1-13, the church is a community of believers who share a common faith and are called to live out the gospel together.

The observance of Christ's ordinances, including baptism and the Lord's Supper, is central to the church's identity and practice. Acts 2:41-42 illustrates the early church's commitment to these ordinances, as well as their dedication to teaching, fellowship, and prayer. The church is governed by Christ's laws, as outlined in Scripture, and exercises the gifts, rights, and privileges given by Him.

The church's leadership structure includes bishops or pastors and deacons, as defined in the Epistles to Timothy and Titus. Bishops or pastors are responsible for teaching, shepherding, and guiding the congregation (1 Timothy 3; Titus 1), while deacons serve in roles of practical ministry and support (Acts 6:1-6; 1 Timothy 3:8-13). These officers are appointed based on specific qualifications and are entrusted with responsibilities that contribute to the church's health and mission.

Theological Significance

The concept of the gospel church highlights several theological principles. First, it underscores the importance of the church as the visible manifestation of the body of Christ on earth. The church is not merely a gathering of individuals but a cohesive community united by faith and governed by divine principles. This understanding emphasizes the church's role in advancing God's kingdom and living out the gospel.

The structure and governance of the church reflect the order and authority established by Christ. The roles of bishops or pastors and deacons are essential for maintaining the church's mission and ensuring effective ministry. These offices are not only practical but also symbolic of the church's commitment to uphold the teachings and example of Christ.

Additionally, the church's observance of ordinances and adherence to Christ's laws reflect its dedication to living according to God's will. This commitment to obedience and fellowship is central to the church's witness and effectiveness in carrying out its mission.

Practical Application

In practical terms, understanding the nature of a gospel church influences how believers engage with their local congregations. Being part of a visible church means committing to a community of faith that observes Christ's ordinances and follows His teachings. This commitment involves participating in baptism, celebrating the Lord's Supper, and contributing to the church's mission through service and fellowship.

Church members are called to respect and support their leaders, recognizing the roles of bishops or pastors and deacons in guiding and serving the congregation. This includes honoring their qualifications and responsibilities as outlined in Scripture and working collaboratively to fulfill the church's mission.

Moreover, the structure of the church provides a framework for accountability and growth. Believers are encouraged to engage in regular fellowship, adhere to the church's teachings, and exercise their spiritual gifts in service to others. This holistic approach ensures that the church remains faithful to its calling and effectively advances the gospel.

Common Misunderstandings

One common misunderstanding is the notion that the church's organizational structure is secondary to its mission. In reality, a well-ordered structure is crucial for fulfilling the church's mission and maintaining its health. The roles of bishops or pastors and deacons are essential for effective leadership and service, and their qualifications are important for ensuring that the church operates according to biblical principles.

Another misconception is the belief that church membership is a mere formality. Membership in a gospel church involves a genuine commitment to the faith and fellowship of the gospel. It is not just about attending services but actively participating in the life of the church, observing its ordinances, and supporting its mission.

Conclusion

The concept of a gospel church as a congregation of baptized believers united by faith and governed by divine principles highlights the importance of both individual commitment and collective fellowship. The church's structure, including the roles of bishops or pastors and deacons, reflects the order and authority established by Christ. Understanding and engaging with these principles ensures that the church remains true to its mission and effectively lives out the gospel.

CHAPTER TWENTY-SIX
BAPTISM AND THE LORD'S SUPPER

We Believe that Christian baptism is the immersion in water of a believer, in the name of the Father, and the Son, and the Holy Spirit; to show forth, in a solemn and beautiful emblem, our faith in the crucified, buried, and risen Savior with its effect in our death to sin and resurrection to a new life; that it is prerequisite to the privileges of a Church relation; and to the Lord's Supper, in which the members of the Church, by the sacred use of bread and wine, are to commemorate together the dying love of Christ – preceded always by solemn self-examination.

Historical Context

Origins of Baptism

Baptism in the early church was rooted in the Jewish practice of ritual purification, which symbolized cleansing and renewal. However, Christian baptism, as instituted by Jesus and practiced by His followers, introduced new significance. It became a public declaration of faith, symbolizing identification with

Christ's death, burial, and resurrection. Jesus Himself was baptized by John (Matthew 3:13-17), setting an example for His disciples. The Great Commission (Matthew 28:19) commanded His followers to baptize new believers, making baptism a central rite of initiation into the Christian faith.

Origins of the Lord's Supper

The Lord's Supper, or Eucharist, was instituted by Jesus during the Passover meal with His disciples (Matthew 26:26-29; Mark 14:22-25; Luke 22:14-20). It commemorates Christ's sacrifice and serves as a tangible reminder of the new covenant established through His blood. Early Christians observed the Lord's Supper as part of their communal worship and fellowship, recognizing it as a sacred act of remembrance and proclamation of Christ's death until He comes again (1 Corinthians 11:26).

Exposition and Analysis

Baptism symbolizes the believer's identification with Christ's death, burial, and resurrection. Romans 6:4 and Colossians 2:12 emphasize that baptism represents the believer's transition from death to sin to new life in Christ. It is performed by immersion, which reflects the fullness of the symbolism—being buried with Christ and rising to walk in newness of life. Baptism is not only a personal act of faith but also a prerequisite for church membership and participation in the Lord's Supper.

The Lord's Supper, observed with bread and wine, commemorates Christ's sacrificial death. The bread represents His body, and the wine represents His blood, shed for the forgiveness of sins (1 Corinthians 11:23-26). The practice of solemn self-examination before partaking (1 Corinthians 11:28) underscores the importance of approaching the table with a pure heart and understanding of its significance. The Lord's Supper serves as a means of grace, reinforcing believers' faith and unity within the church.

Theological Significance

The theological significance of baptism and the Lord's Supper lies in their role as means of grace and signs of covenant relationship. Baptism represents the believer's entry into the new covenant with God, symbolizing purification, transformation, and incorporation into the body of Christ. It affirms the believer's faith and commitment to live according to the teachings of Jesus.

The Lord's Supper is a continual reminder of Christ's atoning work and the believer's participation in the new covenant. It reinforces the unity of believers as they collectively remember and proclaim the death of Christ. The Supper is both a memorial and a means of spiritual nourishment, reminding believers of their ongoing dependence on Christ's sacrifice and the promise of His return.

Practical Application

In practice, the observance of baptism and the Lord's Supper should be approached with reverence and understanding. Baptism should be seen as an essential step in the believer's spiritual journey, signifying a public declaration of faith and commitment to Christ. It is an opportunity for believers to express their faith openly and to be welcomed into the fellowship of the church.

The Lord's Supper should be observed with thoughtful preparation and reflection. Believers are encouraged to engage in self-examination and repentance before partaking of the elements, ensuring that they approach the table with sincerity and gratitude. The Supper is an occasion for communal worship and renewal of faith, as believers collectively remember Christ's sacrifice and reaffirm their commitment to His teachings.

Churches should maintain the integrity of these ordinances by ensuring that baptism and the Lord's Supper are conducted according to biblical guidelines. This includes administering baptism by immersion and observing the Lord's Supper in a manner that respects its significance and fosters unity within the church.

Common Misunderstandings

A common misunderstanding about baptism is that it is merely a symbolic act without significant spiritual implications. In reality, baptism is a profound expression of faith and obedience, signifying a believer's identification with Christ and His work. It is an essential step in the believer's spiritual journey and a prerequisite for church membership.

Regarding the Lord's Supper, some may view it as a mere ritual rather than a meaningful act of worship. It is crucial to recognize the Supper's deep significance as a commemoration of Christ's sacrifice and a means of grace. The practice of self-examination before partaking ensures that believers approach the Supper with the right attitude and understanding.

Conclusion

Baptism and the Lord's Supper are integral to the life of the church, serving as means of grace and signs of the believer's covenant relationship with God. Baptism symbolizes the believer's new life in Christ and entry into the church, while the Lord's Supper commemorates Christ's sacrificial death and fosters unity within the church. Approaching these ordinances with reverence and understanding is essential for their proper observance and the spiritual growth of believers.

CHAPTER TWENTY-SEVEN
THE CHRISTIAN SABBATH

We Believe that the first day of the week is the Lord's Day, or Christian Sabbath; and is to be kept sacred to religious purposes, by abstaining from all secular labor and sinful recreations; by the devout observance of all the means of grace, both private and public; and by preparation for that rest that remaineth for the people of God.

Historical Context

Origins of the Sabbath

The concept of a Sabbath originates in the Old Testament with the seventh day of creation, when God rested from His work (Genesis 2:3). The Sabbath was instituted as a day of rest and worship for the Israelites (Exodus 20:8-11) and was a sign of the covenant between God and His people. The observance of the Sabbath was integral to Jewish religious life, marked by rest from work and dedication to spiritual activities.

Transition to the Christian Sabbath

With the resurrection of Jesus Christ on the first day of the week, Christians began to observe Sunday, the first day of the week, as a

161

day of worship and rest (John 20:19; Acts 20:7). This transition reflects the significance of the resurrection and the new creation inaugurated through Christ's victory over death. The early church gathered on the first day to break bread, teach, and fellowship (Acts 2:42; 1 Corinthians 16:1-2), establishing Sunday as a day distinct from the traditional Jewish Sabbath.

Exposition and Analysis

The Christian Sabbath, or Lord's Day, is rooted in the resurrection of Jesus and the early Christian practice of gathering for worship on the first day of the week. Colossians 2:16-17 and Mark 2:27 highlight that while the Sabbath was a part of the Old Covenant, the principles of rest and worship continue in the New Covenant through the observance of Sunday. The day is set apart for spiritual growth and reflection, contrasting with secular work and activities.

Observing the Lord's Day involves abstaining from secular labor and activities that detract from its spiritual significance. This is not about legalistic adherence but about dedicating the day to God, engaging in private and public worship, and preparing for the ultimate rest that awaits the people of God (Hebrews 4:3-11). The day should be marked by devotion, reflection, and preparation for the eternal rest promised in Christ.

Theological Significance

The theological significance of the Christian Sabbath lies in its role as a weekly reminder of Christ's resurrection and the new creation He has brought about. The observance of Sunday underscores the believer's identity in Christ and the transformation that has occurred through His work. It serves as a weekly celebration of the victory over sin and death, and a foretaste of the eternal rest promised to believers.

The day also functions as a practical expression of the believer's relationship with God, providing an opportunity to focus on spiritual matters and engage in communal worship. The principle of setting aside a day for rest and worship reflects the broader biblical theme of Sabbath rest, which is ultimately fulfilled in Christ.

Practical Application

In practice, observing the Christian Sabbath involves prioritizing spiritual activities and refraining from secular labor and distractions that may interfere with worship and rest. This includes participating in corporate worship, engaging in personal devotions, and spending time in reflection and prayer. It is a day for believers to recharge spiritually, connect with fellow believers, and grow in their faith.

Churches should encourage practices that honor the Sabbath, such as offering regular worship services and providing opportunities for fellowship and spiritual growth. Believers should prepare for the Sabbath by planning ahead to minimize secular activities and create a space for worship and reflection.

Observing the Sabbath also means recognizing it as a day of rest and renewal. It should be approached with joy and anticipation, rather than as a burdensome obligation. The focus should be on celebrating the new creation and the hope of eternal rest that is ours in Christ.

Common Misunderstandings

A common misunderstanding about the Christian Sabbath is that it imposes a legalistic burden, akin to Old Testament Sabbath laws. In reality, the observance of the Lord's Day is a voluntary act of devotion and celebration, reflecting the freedom and joy of the New Covenant. It is about honoring God and engaging in practices that nurture spiritual growth, rather than adhering to a set of rigid rules.

Another misunderstanding is equating the Sabbath with mere inactivity or a day of boredom. Proper observance involves active engagement in worship, community, and spiritual reflection, making it a meaningful and enriching experience. It is not just a day off from work but an opportunity to deepen one's relationship with God and with the church community.

Conclusion

The Christian Sabbath is a significant aspect of the believer's spiritual life, serving as a weekly reminder of Christ's resurrection and the promise of eternal rest. Observing the Lord's Day involves dedicating time to worship, reflection, and renewal, and refraining from activities that detract from its spiritual significance. By honoring the Sabbath, believers celebrate the new creation in Christ and anticipate the ultimate rest that awaits them.

CHAPTER TWENTY-EIGHT
CIVIL GOVERNMENT

We Believe that civil government is of divine appointment for the interests and good order of human society; and that magistrates are to be prayed for, conscientiously honored, and obeyed; except only in things opposed to the will of our Lord Jesus the Christ, Who is the only Lord of the conscience, and the Prince of the kings of the earth.

Historical Context

Origins and Purpose of Civil Government

Civil government, as an institution, is rooted in the divine order established by God for maintaining societal order and justice. The concept of governance is reflected in the Old Testament where God's laws and instructions provided the framework for Israel's societal structure. The role of civil authorities was to uphold justice, ensure order, and serve the people. This notion of governance as a divine appointment is underscored in the scriptures and has been a fundamental part of the Judeo-Christian worldview.

New Testament Perspective

In the New Testament, civil government continues to be affirmed as part of God's plan for human society. Jesus acknowledged the legitimacy of civil authority when He instructed His followers to "render to Caesar the things that are Caesar's" (Matthew 22:21). The Apostle Paul also emphasized the role of government in maintaining order and justice, urging believers to respect and obey governing authorities as they are instituted by God (Romans 13:1-7). However, the New Testament also recognizes the limits of civil authority, particularly when it conflicts with divine commandments.

Exposition and Analysis

The Biblical view of civil government as described in Romans 13:1-7 and 1 Peter 2:13 highlights its role in maintaining societal order and justice. Government is seen as a divine institution that functions under God's sovereignty. Magistrates, or rulers, are to be respected and obeyed in all matters that do not conflict with the will of God. This respect and obedience are part of the Christian's duty to live peaceably within society.

However, the Bible also acknowledges the limits of civil authority. When civil laws or decrees contradict the commands of Christ, believers are instructed to follow divine authority over human authority (Acts 5:29). This principle is evident in instances such as Daniel's refusal to worship the king's statue (Daniel 3:15-18) and the Apostles' defiance of the Sanhedrin's orders (Acts 4:18-20).

The balance between honoring civil authorities and adhering to God's commands requires wisdom and discernment. Believers are called to be conscientious in their civic responsibilities, while also recognizing that Christ is the ultimate authority over their consciences.

Theological Significance

The theological significance of civil government is that it represents God's concern for human order and justice. It serves as an extension of God's authority in the earthly realm, reflecting His commitment to upholding righteousness and order. By respecting and obeying civil authorities, Christians honor God's sovereign rule over all aspects of life.

The limits of civil authority also underscore the sovereignty of Christ as the ultimate ruler. Christians are reminded that while they are to honor and respect government, their highest allegiance is to Christ. This duality highlights the need for believers to navigate their responsibilities in society while remaining faithful to their ultimate allegiance to God.

Practical Application

In practical terms, believers should actively engage in their civic duties, including voting, obeying laws, and contributing to societal well-being. This involvement demonstrates respect for the institutions established by God for maintaining order and justice. It is important to approach these responsibilities with integrity, ensuring that actions are in alignment with Biblical principles.

When faced with situations where civil laws or policies conflict with Christian values, believers should seek guidance through prayer, scripture, and counsel from mature Christian leaders. Standing firm in faith while engaging respectfully with governing authorities is essential for navigating such conflicts.

Churches can play a role in educating and equipping members on their civic responsibilities and how to engage with government from a Christian perspective. Encouraging active participation in societal matters while maintaining a focus on spiritual priorities helps believers live out their faith in all areas of life.

Common Misunderstandings

A common misunderstanding is the idea that Christians should never oppose government authority. While the Bible calls for respect and obedience to civil rulers, it also acknowledges the right of believers to resist unjust laws that conflict with God's commands. This resistance should be conducted in a manner that is respectful and nonviolent, reflecting the teachings of Christ.

Another misunderstanding is the belief that all government actions are inherently just or divinely sanctioned. The Bible recognizes that human governments can be flawed and fallible. Believers are encouraged to engage critically and thoughtfully with governmental policies, seeking to uphold justice and righteousness.

Conclusion

Civil government is a divinely appointed institution designed to promote order and justice within human society. Christians are called to respect and obey governing authorities as part of their duty to God. However, when civil laws conflict with divine commands, believers are to uphold their allegiance to Christ above all. By balancing civic responsibilities with spiritual priorities, Christians can contribute positively to society while remaining faithful to their ultimate calling.

CHAPTER TWENTY-NINE
THE RIGHTEOUS AND WICKED

We Believe that there is a radical and essential difference between the righteous and the wicked. Those only who are justified through the name of the Lord Jesus the Christ and sanctified by the Holy Spirit are truly righteous in His sight. Those who continue in impenitence and unbelief are in His sight wicked and are under condemnation. This distinction between the righteous and the wicked holds in and after death, and will be made manifest at the judgment when final and everlasting awards are made to all men.

Historical Context

Old Testament Foundations

The distinction between the righteous and the wicked is deeply rooted in the Old Testament. This division is often portrayed through contrasting examples of individuals and their outcomes based on their righteousness or wickedness. The righteous are depicted as those who follow God's commandments and live in accordance with His will, while the wicked are characterized by their rebellion against God and their disregard for His laws. The Old Testament provides numerous examples of this dichotomy, including the fate of Sodom and Gomorrah (Genesis 18:23) and the contrasting lives of the righteous and the wicked as seen in Proverbs and Psalms.

New Testament Revelation

In the New Testament, this distinction is further clarified through the teachings of Jesus and the Apostles. Jesus, in His parables and teachings, often highlighted the differences between the righteous and the wicked, emphasizing that righteousness is found through faith in Him (Matthew 25:31-46). The Apostle Paul and other New Testament writers also emphasize that righteousness comes through justification by faith and sanctification by the Holy Spirit, while those who persist in sin and unbelief are considered wicked and are under condemnation (Romans 6:16; 1 John 3:7).

Exposition and Analysis

Definition of Righteousness and Wickedness

Righteousness, according to Scripture, is not merely an external adherence to laws but a state of being justified and sanctified by faith in Christ. This righteousness is granted through the grace of God and involves a transformative work of the Holy Spirit. On the other hand, wickedness is defined as a state of rebellion against God, characterized by impenitence and unbelief. The Bible clearly delineates these two states, showing that true righteousness is a result of divine intervention and grace, while wickedness leads to condemnation.

Implications for the Afterlife

The distinction between the righteous and the wicked extends beyond this life into the afterlife. The righteous are promised eternal life and rewards, while the wicked face judgment and condemnation. This is supported by numerous passages that describe the final judgment where the separation between the righteous and the wicked will be fully realized (Matthew 25:31-46;

Revelation 20:11-15). The eternal consequences of these distinctions underscore the importance of living a life of faith and obedience.

Theological Significance

Theologically, the distinction between the righteous and the wicked highlights the concept of divine justice and grace. It emphasizes that righteousness is not achieved through human effort alone but through the grace of God and the work of Christ. This distinction also reinforces the importance of repentance and faith as prerequisites for righteousness and the dire consequences of remaining in wickedness. The final judgment serves as a culmination of God's justice, where the eternal destinies of all individuals are determined based on their response to God's offer of grace.

Practical Application

Believers are called to live out their righteousness through a life of faith, obedience, and sanctification. This involves not only believing in Christ but also demonstrating that belief through righteous living. The distinction between the righteous and the wicked should motivate Christians to remain steadfast in their faith, pursue holiness, and actively seek to share the gospel with those who remain in unbelief. Additionally, understanding this distinction helps Christians approach others with compassion, recognizing the urgency of repentance and the reality of eternal consequences.

Churches can support this by teaching and modeling righteous living, encouraging repentance, and fostering an environment where individuals are equipped to live out their faith. Preaching, teaching, and personal discipleship should consistently reinforce the biblical understanding of righteousness and wickedness and their implications for both this life and the next.

Common Misunderstandings

A common misunderstanding is the belief that righteousness can be achieved through human effort or good deeds alone. The Bible makes it clear that righteousness comes through faith in Christ and the work of the Holy Spirit, not by human merit (Romans 3:22-24). Another misunderstanding is the notion that God's judgment is arbitrary or unjust. Scripture consistently teaches that God's judgments are righteous and based on His perfect justice and grace (Revelation 19:2).

Conclusion

The distinction between the righteous and the wicked is a central theme in Scripture, emphasizing the profound difference between those who are justified by faith and those who remain in sin. This distinction has eternal significance, influencing the believer's conduct in this life and their eternal destiny. Understanding this difference calls believers to live righteously, engage in repentance, and uphold the truth of God's justice and grace.

CHAPTER THIRTY
CHRISTIAN EDUCATION

We Believe that Christianity is the religion of enlightenment and intelligence. In Jesus the Christ are hidden all the treasures of wisdom and knowledge. All sound learning is therefore a part of our Christian heritage. The new birth opens all human faculties and creates a thirst for knowledge. An adequate system of schools is necessary to a complete spiritual program for Christ's people. The cause of education in the Kingdom of Christ is co-ordinate with the causes of missions and general benevolence, and should receive along with these the liberal support of the Churches.

Historical Context

Early Christian Education

From the early days of the Christian church, education has played a critical role in the development and expansion of the faith. The New Testament reveals that early Christians were encouraged to pursue knowledge and wisdom as part of their spiritual growth. The Apostles, including Paul, emphasized the importance of learning and teaching. For instance, the Apostle Paul commended the Bereans for their eagerness to examine the

Scriptures daily (Acts 17:11), reflecting an early commitment to understanding and applying Biblical truth.

Medieval and Reformation Contributions

During the medieval period, monastic schools and cathedral schools became centers of Christian learning, preserving and expanding theological and philosophical knowledge. The Reformation further emphasized the importance of education in the church, with figures like Martin Luther advocating for the education of clergy and laity alike to ensure a well-informed and spiritually grounded church.

Modern Perspectives

In modern times, the role of Christian education has evolved but remains crucial. The establishment of Christian schools and seminaries continues to reflect the belief that education is integral to spiritual development. The emphasis on integrating faith with learning underscores the belief that all knowledge is ultimately derived from and directed towards God.

Exposition and Analysis

The Role of Education in Christianity

Christian education is rooted in the belief that all knowledge and wisdom find their source in God. The pursuit of knowledge is seen as a way to honor God and understand His creation better. Jesus Christ, as the embodiment of divine wisdom, serves as the ultimate model for learning and intellectual pursuit. The Bible encourages believers to seek wisdom and understanding, as seen in Proverbs 2:6 and John 8:32, which highlight the value of knowledge in living a Christian life.

Integration of Faith and Learning

Christian education seeks to integrate faith with learning, ensuring that all subjects are taught in a manner consistent with Biblical principles. This approach emphasizes that education is not just about acquiring information but about shaping a worldview that reflects Christian values and beliefs. The new birth, as described in John 3:3, transforms the believer's mind, fostering a deeper desire for knowledge that aligns with God's truth.

Theological Significance

Theologically, Christian education affirms the belief that all truth is God's truth and that education is a means of understanding and living out that truth. It supports the idea that intellectual development and spiritual growth are interconnected, with the pursuit of knowledge being an expression of one's faith. This perspective reinforces the notion that education should be supported and prioritized within the Christian community as part of its broader mission.

Practical Application

Churches and Christian communities are encouraged to support and develop educational programs that promote both academic excellence and spiritual growth. This includes establishing and maintaining Christian schools, supporting educational initiatives, and integrating Biblical principles into all areas of learning. Educators in Christian settings are called to model and teach according to a Christian worldview, helping students to apply their learning in ways that reflect their faith. Additionally, parents are encouraged to engage in their children's education, ensuring that it aligns with their Christian values.

Common Misunderstandings

A common misunderstanding is that Christian education is solely about Bible knowledge and not about academic excellence. In reality, Christian education encompasses both aspects, aiming to provide a well-rounded education that integrates faith and learning. Another misunderstanding is the belief that Christian education is only for the church community and not for broader society. In fact, Christian education contributes positively to society by promoting values such as integrity, compassion, and responsibility.

Conclusion

Christian education plays a vital role in the life of the church and the broader community. It reflects the belief that all knowledge is ultimately from God and should be pursued with a view toward glorifying Him. By integrating faith with learning, Christian education supports spiritual growth and intellectual development, contributing to the overall mission of the church.

CHAPTER THIRTY-ONE
SOCIAL SERVICE

We Believe that every Christian is under obligation to seek to make the will of Christ regnant in his own life and in human society; to oppose in the Spirit of Christ every form of greed, selfishness, and vice; to provide for the orphaned, the aged, the helpless, and the sick; to seek to bring industry, government, and society as a whole under the sway of the principles of righteousness, truth, and brotherly love; to promote these ends Christians should be ready to work with all men of good will in any good cause, always being careful to act in the spirit of love without compromising their loyalty to Christ and his truth. All means and methods used in social service for the amelioration of society and the establishment of righteousness among men must finally depend on the regeneration of the individual by the saving grace of God in Christ Jesus.

Historical Context

Early Christian Social Service

In the early church, Christians were recognized for their care for the poor and marginalized, reflecting the teachings and example of Jesus Christ. The New Testament shows the early believers' commitment to social service as an extension of their faith. Acts 11:29 and Acts 5:11 highlight the early church's efforts to provide for those in need, including the collection for the poor in Judea and the support of widows and orphans.

Medieval and Reformation Contributions

Throughout the medieval period and the Reformation, the church continued to engage in social service, establishing hospitals, orphanages, and educational institutions. Reformers like Martin Luther and John Calvin emphasized social responsibility as a reflection of one's faith. Calvin's Geneva, for instance, became known for its social welfare programs and efforts to address poverty and inequality.

Modern Perspectives

In contemporary times, the church's role in social service has expanded to address a wide range of social issues, including poverty, injustice, and human rights. Christian organizations and churches actively participate in various forms of social service, advocating for justice and providing practical support to those in need. The integration of faith with social action remains a significant aspect of Christian witness today.

Exposition and Analysis

The Christian Obligation to Social Service

Christian social service is deeply rooted in the teachings and example of Jesus Christ. Throughout His ministry, Jesus demonstrated a profound concern for the poor, the oppressed, and the marginalized. In Matthew 25:35-36, Jesus identifies Himself with the needy, stating that acts of kindness toward the hungry, the thirsty, the stranger, the naked, the sick, and the imprisoned are considered acts done unto Him. This passage emphasizes that

Christian social service is not just a charitable act but a sacred duty that reflects one's devotion to Christ.

Early Christian communities took this mandate seriously, as evidenced by the Acts of the Apostles, which recounts how the early church organized collections for the needy and cared for widows and orphans (Acts 11:29; Acts 6:1). This historical context highlights that social service was integral to the church's mission from its inception.

In addition, the New Testament letters encourage believers to support those in need and live out their faith through deeds of love and mercy (James 1:27; 1 John 3:17-18). This reflects a broader biblical principle that true faith is evidenced by actions that align with God's commands to love one's neighbor as oneself.

Integration of Faith and Social Action

Christian social service is fundamentally about integrating faith with action. Ephesians 5:5 and James 1:27 provide a framework for understanding this integration. Ephesians 5:5 calls believers to live lives of holiness and righteousness, while James 1:27 defines pure religion as caring for orphans and widows in their distress and keeping oneself unstained from the world. This indicates that social service is an expression of one's faith, not separate from it.

The call to integrate faith with social action means that Christians should approach social issues with a worldview shaped by biblical principles. This involves advocating for justice, providing tangible help to those in need, and working towards systemic change while upholding Christian values. For example, Christians are encouraged to work towards alleviating poverty, fighting injustice, and supporting humanitarian causes through a lens of faith, ensuring that their efforts reflect Christ's love and righteousness.

Theological Significance

Theologically, social service is a manifestation of the Kingdom of God on earth. It reflects the values of the Kingdom as taught by Jesus, including justice, mercy, and compassion. Romans 15:26 underscores the importance of supporting those in need as part of the Christian mission, while Ephesians 5:5 emphasizes living a life that embodies these values.

Social service also demonstrates the practical outworking of the regenerate life. The belief is that the regeneration brought about by Christ transforms individuals' hearts, creating a desire to act justly and compassionately. This transformation is central to the Christian understanding of social service, as it is not merely about performing good deeds but about living out the implications of one's new identity in Christ.

The ultimate goal of social service is to reflect the character of Christ and advance His Kingdom. By addressing societal issues and promoting justice, Christians are participating in God's redemptive work in the world. This perspective aligns with the view that the ultimate solution to societal problems is the transformation of individuals through the gospel. As believers engage in social service, they are also bearing witness to the power of Christ's love and grace in addressing both immediate needs and broader social injustices.

Practical Application

Christians are called to actively engage in social service as a manifestation of their faith. This involves participating in and supporting programs that address the needs of the poor, the sick, and the vulnerable. Churches and Christian organizations are encouraged to develop and support initiatives that promote justice, provide aid, and advocate for the rights of the marginalized. Additionally, Christians are to collaborate with others who share similar values while maintaining their commitment to Christ and His teachings.

Common Misunderstandings

A common misunderstanding is that social service is a substitute for personal salvation and spiritual growth. In reality, social service is an extension of one's faith and a response to the regeneration brought about by Christ. Another misconception is that social service should be performed solely within church settings. Effective social service often involves working with broader community organizations and partnerships to achieve meaningful change.

Conclusion

Social service is a vital aspect of the Christian life, reflecting the love and compassion of Christ through practical actions. By addressing societal needs and promoting justice, Christians fulfill their obligation to make Christ's will manifest in the world. The integration of faith and social action remains central to the mission of the church and the witness of individual believers.

CHAPTER THIRTY-TWO
STEWARDSHIP

We Believe that God is the source of all blessings, temporal and spiritual; all that we have and are we owe to Him. We have a spiritual debtorship to the whole world, a holy trusteeship in the gospel, and a binding stewardship in our possessions. We are therefore under obligation to serve Him with our time, talents, and material possessions; and should recognize all these as entrusted to use for the glory of God and helping others. Christians should cheerfully, regularly, systematically, proportionately, and liberally contribute of their means to advancing the redeemer's cause on earth.

Historical Context

The concept of stewardship has its roots deeply embedded in the biblical narrative, beginning with the Genesis account where humanity is placed in the Garden of Eden with the responsibility to tend and keep it (Genesis 2:15). This early example sets the stage for understanding stewardship as a fundamental aspect of human existence and responsibility. Throughout the Old Testament, the idea of stewardship is reflected in various laws and teachings about managing resources and caring for the vulnerable, such as the instructions for leaving the edges of fields for the poor (Leviticus 19:9-10).

In the New Testament, Jesus uses parables like the Parable of the Talents (Matthew 25:14-30) to illustrate the expectations of faithful stewardship. The early church also exemplified this principle through their communal sharing of resources and support for those in need (Acts 2:44-45). The apostle Paul further elaborates on stewardship in his epistles, emphasizing the importance of managing resources wisely and supporting the work of the ministry (1 Corinthians 16:1-2; 2 Corinthians 9:6-7).

Exposition and Analysis

The biblical understanding of stewardship involves recognizing that everything we possess—our time, talents, and material resources—ultimately belongs to God. This recognition comes from the understanding that God is the creator and owner of all things. Consequently, stewardship is not merely about managing resources but about honoring God through their use. Financial stewardship involves more than just giving; it encompasses how we manage our entire financial life, including budgeting, saving, and investing in ways that align with biblical principles. Believers are encouraged to give generously and systematically, reflecting their trust in God's provision and their commitment to His kingdom work.

Time management is another critical aspect of stewardship. Scripture encourages believers to use their time wisely, making the most of every opportunity (Ephesians 5:15-16). This involves prioritizing spiritual growth, engaging in acts of service, and participating in the life of the church. The use of talents and spiritual gifts also falls under stewardship. Christians are called to use their abilities for the benefit of others and the advancement of God's work, whether through ministry, service, or everyday interactions. Effective stewardship means integrating these elements into a cohesive approach to living out one's faith.

Theological Significance

Theologically, stewardship is a reflection of God's sovereignty and human responsibility. The doctrine of creation establishes that God is the ultimate owner of all things, and humanity is entrusted with the care and management of His creation. This stewardship is a sacred trust, and how we handle our resources speaks to our understanding of God's ownership and our role as caretakers.

Stewardship is not merely about managing material possessions; it encompasses every aspect of life under God's lordship. The concept highlights the inherent relationship between divine ownership and human responsibility, emphasizing that all our actions should align with God's purposes. By fulfilling our stewardship responsibilities, we participate in God's redemptive plan and contribute to the flourishing of His creation.

Practical Application

Applying the principle of stewardship involves a holistic approach to managing one's resources in alignment with biblical teachings. For financial stewardship, this means creating a budget that reflects priorities consistent with Christian values, such as supporting the church, aiding the needy, and avoiding excessive debt. It also involves regular and proportionate giving, which demonstrates trust in God's provision and commitment to advancing His work.

Time management should focus on making intentional decisions that reflect spiritual priorities, such as dedicating time for prayer, worship, and service, while also balancing work and personal responsibilities in a way that honors God. Using talents and gifts effectively means actively engaging in areas where one can contribute to the church and community, whether through teaching, leadership, or service. Overall, effective stewardship requires intentionality and a willingness to align all aspects of life with God's purposes.

Common Misunderstandings

A prevalent misunderstanding of stewardship is the narrow view that it only pertains to financial giving. While financial stewardship is a significant aspect, it is only one part of a broader responsibility that includes managing time and talents. Another misconception is that stewardship is a burdensome obligation rather than a joyful and purposeful expression of faith. Some may see stewardship as merely an administrative task rather than a spiritual practice that reflects one's relationship with God.

Additionally, there can be confusion about the balance between personal needs and sacrificial giving, with some believing that stewardship requires neglecting personal well-being in favor of giving. It is crucial to understand that stewardship involves a balanced approach, recognizing both the importance of supporting God's work and the need to manage personal resources wisely.

Conclusion

Stewardship is an essential component of the Christian life, reflecting our understanding of God's sovereignty and our role as caretakers of His creation. By managing our resources—time, talents, and material possessions—in ways that honor God and advance His kingdom, we align our lives with His purposes and contribute to His redemptive work. Effective stewardship is both a responsibility and a privilege, requiring a heart of gratitude and a commitment to living in accordance with biblical principles.

CHAPTER THIRTY-THREE
EVANGELISM AND MISSIONS

We Believe that it is the duty of every Christian man and woman, and the duty of every Church of Christ to seek to extend the gospel to the ends of the earth. The new birth of man's spirit by God's Holy Spirit means the birth of love for others. Missionary effort on the part of all rests thus upon a spiritual necessity of the regenerate life. It is also expressly and repeatedly commanded in the teachings of Christ. It is the duty of every child of God to seek constantly to win the lost to Christ by personal effort and by all other methods sanctioned by the gospel of Christ.

Historical Context

The call to evangelism and missions is deeply rooted in the teachings and actions of Jesus Christ and the early church. Jesus' Great Commission, as recorded in Matthew 28:19-20 and Mark 16:15, explicitly commands His followers to make disciples of all nations and to preach the gospel to every creature. This mandate reflects the central purpose of the church's mission on earth. The early church, as seen in the Acts of the Apostles, demonstrated a vibrant commitment to spreading the gospel despite facing significant opposition and persecution (Acts 8:30-35; 1 Corinthians 9:19-27).

The New Testament letters also emphasize the importance of evangelism and missions, portraying them as integral to the life of the believer and the church. Paul's letters often address the necessity of proclaiming the gospel and engaging in missionary work as central to Christian living and ministry.

Exposition and Analysis

The theological significance of evangelism and missions is grounded in the understanding that salvation through Jesus Christ is available to all people, regardless of their background or location. The gospel's transformative power is not limited to a specific group but is meant to reach every corner of the world. This universal scope of the gospel highlights the inclusivity of God's redemptive plan and the church's role in it.

Evangelism involves actively sharing the message of Christ with others, while missions extends this effort by seeking to establish and support churches and ministries in areas where the gospel has not yet reached or is not well-established. Both aspects are driven by the conviction that eternal destinies are at stake and that the love of Christ compels believers to act. The imperative to evangelize and engage in missions is not an optional part of Christian life but a fundamental expression of the regenerated life.

Theological Significance

Theologically, evangelism and missions underscore the essential nature of the church's mission as dictated by Christ Himself. The command to go and make disciples is a direct reflection of God's desire for all people to come to the knowledge of the truth (1 Timothy 2:4). This mission is rooted in the Great Commission, which frames evangelism as a central aspect of the church's existence and purpose. Evangelism demonstrates the church's commitment to fulfilling God's redemptive plan, while missions represent the church's role in advancing that plan globally. Theological reflection on these practices reveals a commitment to the Great Commission and the understanding that the church is an active participant in God's mission to redeem and restore humanity.

Practical Application

In practical terms, evangelism and missions require both personal and corporate engagement. On an individual level, Christians are called to live out their faith openly, share their testimony, and engage in conversations about the gospel with friends, family, and acquaintances. This involves being prepared to give a reason for the hope that is within them (1 Peter 3:15) and demonstrating Christ's love through actions as well as words.

Churches, on the other hand, are called to support and participate in mission efforts both locally and globally. This can include organizing outreach programs, supporting missionaries financially and prayerfully, and participating in mission trips. Additionally, churches should foster an environment where evangelism is encouraged and equipped through teaching, training, and providing resources. By actively engaging in evangelism and missions, both individuals and congregations contribute to the fulfillment of the Great Commission and the expansion of God's kingdom on earth.

Common Misunderstandings

One common misunderstanding is that evangelism and missions are solely the responsibility of a few individuals or specialized groups within the church, such as missionaries or evangelists. In reality, the call to share the gospel and participate in missions is a universal mandate for all believers. Another misconception is that evangelism is merely about making converts rather than nurturing new believers and integrating them into the life of the church.

Additionally, some may view missions as an activity for those with a particular calling, rather than a core aspect of Christian life that involves every believer. It is also important to address the idea that missions only involve international or cross-cultural work, whereas local outreach and community engagement are equally vital aspects of fulfilling the Great Commission.

Conclusion

Evangelism and missions are central to the life of the church and the individual believer. They reflect the core purpose of spreading the message of Christ and engaging in God's redemptive work. By embracing the call to evangelize and participate in missions, Christians fulfill their role in God's global plan and contribute to the advancement of His kingdom. Understanding and addressing common misunderstandings about these practices can lead to a more effective and inclusive approach to fulfilling the Great Commission.

CHAPTER THIRTY-FOUR
THE RESURRECTION

We Believe that the Scriptures clearly teach that Jesus rose from the dead. His grave was emptied of its contents. He appeared to the disciples after His resurrection in many convincing manifestations. He now exists in His glorified body at God's right hand. There will be a resurrection of the righteous and the wicked. The bodies of the righteous will conform to the glorious spiritual body of Jesus.

Historical Context

The resurrection of Jesus is a cornerstone of Christian faith and doctrine, rooted deeply in the New Testament narratives and teachings. The accounts of Jesus' resurrection are found in the Gospels of Matthew, Mark, Luke, and John, each offering unique details but converging on the central fact of His rising from the dead (Matthew 28:1-6; Mark 16:1-7; Luke 24:1-7; John 20:1-10). These accounts emphasize not only the empty tomb but also the numerous post-resurrection appearances of Jesus to His disciples and followers.

Paul's writings, particularly in 1 Corinthians 15, provide an extensive theological reflection on the significance of the resurrection. The resurrection is presented as a guarantee of believers' future resurrection and a demonstration of Christ's victory over death.

Exposition and Analysis

Theologically, the resurrection of Jesus is foundational to Christian hope and doctrine. It confirms His divine nature and validates His teachings and promises. The resurrection signifies the ultimate victory over sin and death, establishing Jesus as the Lord of life and the source of eternal hope. It is the cornerstone of the Christian gospel, as Paul asserts that if Christ has not been raised, then the faith is futile (1 Corinthians 15:14).

The resurrection also assures believers of their future resurrection. Just as Jesus was raised in a glorified body, so too will those who are in Christ be resurrected to eternal life. This future resurrection involves a transformation of the body into a form that is imperishable and glorious, in alignment with the glorified body of Christ.

Theological Significance

The resurrection of Jesus is significant because it is the triumph of divine power over the ultimate human adversary, death. It validates Jesus' claim to be the Son of God and affirms the truth of His promises regarding eternal life. The resurrection is not merely a past event but a present reality that impacts the believer's life and future. It assures Christians that death has been defeated and that there is a future hope of resurrection and eternal life with God.

The resurrection also has profound implications for Christian living. It provides a basis for hope and assurance in the face of suffering and death. It calls believers to live in the light of Christ's victory, embracing a life of faith and obedience.

Practical Application

Believers are called to live in the light of the resurrection, embracing the hope and assurance it provides. This involves living a life that reflects the newness and vitality of the resurrection, characterized by a transformed nature and a focus on eternal values. The resurrection should inspire Christians to live boldly in their faith, knowing that their labor in the Lord is not in vain (1 Corinthians 15:58).

Practically, the resurrection encourages believers to view their struggles and sufferings through the lens of eternal hope. It offers comfort in times of grief, knowing that death is not the end but a transition to eternal life. The resurrection also motivates believers to share the message of hope with others, emphasizing the transformative power of the resurrection in their lives and in the world.

Common Misunderstandings

A common misunderstanding regarding the resurrection is to view it as merely a metaphorical or symbolic event rather than a literal historical fact. Some may interpret the resurrection as a spiritual or allegorical concept, missing its foundational role in the Christian faith. Another misconception is that the resurrection applies only to Jesus, without recognizing its implications for all believers. Additionally, some may downplay the physical aspect of the resurrection, focusing solely on the spiritual dimensions.

It is also important to address the confusion between the resurrection of Jesus and the general resurrection of the dead. While Jesus' resurrection is the firstfruits of the future resurrection, there is a distinction between His unique resurrection and the future resurrection that awaits all who are in Christ.

Conclusion

The resurrection of Jesus Christ is a pivotal doctrine in Christianity, affirming His divinity, victory over death, and the promise of eternal life for believers. It has profound theological implications, offering hope and assurance to Christians and calling them to live in light of this victorious reality. Understanding and embracing the true nature of the resurrection helps believers to live with hope, purpose, and confidence in their faith.

CHAPTER THIRTY-FIVE
THE RETURN OF THE LORD

We Believe that the New Testament teaches in many places the visible and personal return of Jesus to this earth. "This same Jesus which is taken up from you into heaven, shall so come in like manner as ye have seen Him go into heaven." The time of His coming is not revealed. "Of that day and hour knoweth no man, no, not the angels of heaven, but My Father only (Matthew 24:36). It is the duty of all believers to live in readiness for His coming and by diligence in good works to make manifest to all men the reality and power of their hope in Christ.

Historical Context

The doctrine of Christ's return is a central theme in New Testament eschatology. It is rooted in the promises made by Jesus Himself and the prophetic visions given to the apostles. Jesus' ascension into heaven, as recorded in Acts 1:11, is coupled with the promise of His return in the same manner. This promise is echoed in various New Testament passages, emphasizing that His return will be visible and personal, not a mere metaphor or symbolic event.

In Matthew 24, Jesus speaks extensively about His return and the signs preceding it, though He emphasizes that the exact time is unknown. The book of Revelation, particularly chapters 19:11-16, portrays the return of Christ as a dramatic and triumphant event, where He comes as a victorious King to judge and reign.

Exposition and Analysis

Theologically, the return of Christ is significant as it concludes the current age and ushers in the final phase of God's redemptive plan. It affirms the promise of Christ's ultimate victory over evil and His establishment of God's kingdom on earth. This event will bring about the final judgment, where righteousness will be vindicated and sin will be judged.

The return of Christ is not only a future hope but also a present motivation for Christian living. It underlines the reality of God's promises and the certainty of His ultimate plan for the world. The anticipation of Christ's return should influence how believers live, guiding them to live righteously and with a sense of urgency.

Theological Significance

The return of Christ holds profound theological implications. It affirms the ultimate triumph of Christ and the establishment of His kingdom, which will fulfill the promises made throughout Scripture. This event signifies the culmination of human history and the realization of God's redemptive purposes. It confirms the truth of the Christian hope and the promises of Scripture.

The anticipation of Christ's return also reinforces the concept of accountability. Believers are reminded that their lives should reflect the hope and reality of Christ's imminent return. This hope influences their actions, encouraging them to live in accordance with God's will and to witness to the transformative power of Christ in their lives.

Practical Application

Living in light of Christ's return involves maintaining a posture of readiness and diligence. Believers are called to live with an awareness of the nearness of Christ's return, which should inspire them to engage in good works and to reflect the reality of their hope in Christ. This means living a life of integrity, compassion, and righteousness, actively seeking to make a positive impact in the world.

Practical readiness includes engaging in evangelism and discipleship, as the anticipation of Christ's return should drive believers to share the gospel and help others grow in their faith. It also involves personal holiness, where believers strive to align their lives with God's standards, demonstrating the transformative power of their hope in Christ.

Common Misunderstandings

One common misunderstanding about the return of Christ is to speculate on the exact time or date of His coming. Despite numerous predictions and theories throughout history, Jesus Himself stated that no one knows the day or hour of His return (Matthew 24:36). Such speculation can lead to confusion and distraction from the core message of readiness and faithfulness.

Another misconception is the tendency to view Christ's return as a distant or abstract concept rather than a tangible and imminent reality. This can lead to complacency and a lack of urgency in living out one's faith. It is important to recognize that while the exact timing is unknown, the call to live in readiness and to embody the hope of Christ's return is ever-present.

Additionally, some might misunderstand the nature of Christ's return, expecting it to be symbolic rather than literal. The New Testament portrays His return as a literal, visible event that will have real-world implications, rather than a purely spiritual or metaphorical occurrence.

Conclusion

The return of the Lord is a foundational belief in Christian eschatology, signifying the culmination of God's redemptive plan and the establishment of Christ's kingdom. It carries significant theological implications, offering hope and motivation for Christian living. By living in readiness and reflecting the hope of Christ's return in their actions, believers are called to embody the reality of this promise and to faithfully await the fulfillment of God's promises.

CHAPTER THIRTY-SIX
THE WORLD TO COME

We Believe that the end of the world is approaching; that at the last day Christ will descend from heaven, and raise the dead from the grave to final retribution; that a solemn separation will then take place; that the wicked will be adjudged to endless punishment, and the righteous to endless joy; and that this judgment will fix forever the final state of men in heaven or hell, on principles of righteousness.

Historical Context

The doctrine of the world to come is deeply embedded in the biblical narrative and prophetic literature. The Old Testament offers early glimpses into the eschatological visions of God's final justice and the establishment of His kingdom. For instance, Isaiah describes a future time when God's rule will bring peace and righteousness to the world (Isaiah 2:2-4), and Daniel speaks of an everlasting kingdom that will succeed all earthly kingdoms (Daniel 7:13-14).

In the New Testament, the teachings of Jesus and the apostles elaborate on these themes. Jesus foretold His return and the end of the world in passages like Matthew 24 and Mark 13, where He describes signs and events leading up to His second coming. The Apostle Paul also emphasizes the resurrection and final judgment in 1 Thessalonians 4:13-18 and 1 Corinthians 15:52-54, affirming the belief in the resurrection of the dead and the transformation of believers into glorified bodies.

The Book of Revelation provides a comprehensive vision of the end times, detailing the final judgment and the eternal destinies of the righteous and the wicked. Revelation 20:11-15 portrays the great white throne judgment where all are judged according to their deeds, while Revelation 21:1-4 describes the new heaven and new earth where God dwells with His people, wiping away every tear.

Exposition and Analysis

The doctrine of the world to come includes several crucial aspects. The New Testament affirms the certainty of Christ's return, an event that will be both visible and personal. Acts 1:11 and Revelation 1:7 highlight that Christ's second coming will be a dramatic and unmistakable event. This return will usher in the resurrection of the dead, as described in John 5:28-29 and 1 Corinthians 15:52-54, where all the dead will be raised to face final judgment.

The final judgment will result in a definitive separation between the righteous and the wicked. The righteous, those who have lived according to God's will and accepted His grace, will be rewarded with eternal life in the presence of God. This is affirmed in Matthew 25:31-46 and Revelation 21:8, which describe the eternal joy of the righteous and the endless punishment of the wicked. The righteous will experience eternal joy and fellowship with God, while the wicked will face eternal separation and suffering.

The doctrine underscores that God's justice will ultimately prevail, and every individual's final state will be determined by divine righteousness. This final separation reflects the outcome of each person's response to God's grace and their earthly conduct.

Theological Significance

The belief in the world to come holds profound theological significance. It reinforces the certainty of divine justice and the ultimate fulfillment of God's promises. This doctrine provides a framework for understanding the end of human history and assures believers that their faith and actions have eternal consequences. The concept of final judgment highlights the importance of living a life that aligns with God's will, knowing that earthly actions have eternal implications.

Furthermore, this doctrine emphasizes the transformative nature of Christian hope. The anticipation of Christ's return and the final establishment of God's kingdom should inspire believers to live righteously and faithfully. It serves as a reminder that the current world is not the end but a stage in the unfolding of God's redemptive plan, which culminates in eternal justice and joy.

Practical Application

The doctrine of the world to come has significant implications for Christian living. Believers are called to live in a state of readiness and vigilance, reflecting the teachings of Matthew 24:42-44. This means adopting a lifestyle of faithfulness and preparedness, always anticipating Christ's return.

Additionally, the belief in final judgment underscores the importance of righteous living. Christians are encouraged to embody God's principles of justice, mercy, and love in their daily lives. This includes seeking to reflect Christ's character and pursuing holiness, as emphasized in 2 Corinthians 5:10.

Finally, the awareness of eternal consequences motivates believers to be diligent stewards of their resources and opportunities. Living in light of the coming world should inspire Christians to use their time, talents, and possessions for the advancement of God's kingdom and the well-being of others.

Common Misunderstandings

There are several common misunderstandings regarding the doctrine of the world to come. One such misunderstanding is the preoccupation with predicting specific dates or events related to the end times. This focus can divert attention from the primary call to live faithfully and righteously. The emphasis should be on readiness and faithfulness rather than speculative predictions.

Another misunderstanding involves misconceptions about the nature of eternal punishment. Some may perceive eternal punishment as unjust or disproportionate. It is important to understand that final judgment reflects God's perfect justice, which transcends human comprehension and operates on principles of righteousness.

Additionally, there can be a tendency to neglect present responsibilities while focusing on future expectations. The belief in the world to come should not lead to disengagement from current duties but rather should motivate believers to live actively and faithfully in the present.

Conclusion

The doctrine of the world to come is a central element of Christian eschatology, providing insight into the ultimate end of human history and the final state of every individual. It affirms the certainty of Christ's return, the reality of final judgment, and the ultimate fulfillment of God's justice. This belief encourages believers to live in readiness, uphold righteousness, and remain steadfast in their faith, knowing that their actions have eternal significance.

PART IV. GOVERNANCE

CHAPTER THIRTY-SEVEN
INTRODUCTION TO CHURCH
GOVERNANCE

Introduction

Effective governance is fundamental to the health and vitality of any church. For Baptist churches, governance involves a blend of biblical principles and practical strategies that ensure the church operates smoothly, remains accountable, and fulfills its mission. This introductory chapter lays the groundwork for understanding the governance structures that support Baptist churches, providing an overview of key concepts, roles, and practices.

The Biblical Foundation of Church Governance

Church governance is deeply rooted in Scripture. 1 Corinthians 12:4-7 emphasizes the diversity of gifts within the body of Christ, highlighting the need for organized leadership that harnesses these gifts effectively. Acts 15:1-35 illustrates early church decision-making and conflict resolution, offering a model for structured and collaborative governance. The Bible provides clear guidance on leadership, accountability, and community involvement, setting a foundation for Baptist church governance.

Key Concepts in Church Governance

1. Church Composition: Understanding the makeup of the church body is essential for effective governance. This includes recognizing the roles and responsibilities of different members and leaders within the congregation.

2. Church Officers: Church officers, such as pastors, deacons, and trustees, play critical roles in church management. Each officer has specific duties that contribute to the church's mission and operations.

3. Relation to Other Bodies: Baptist churches often interact with larger denominational bodies, local associations, and other churches. These relationships influence church operations and decision-making processes.

4. Church Discipline: Maintaining discipline within the church is crucial for preserving its integrity and promoting spiritual growth. Discipline should be conducted with love and respect, aiming for restoration and reconciliation.

Importance of Governance

Effective governance ensures that the church is well-organized, operates efficiently, and remains true to its mission. It provides a framework for decision-making, resource management, and conflict resolution. Governance structures help maintain transparency, accountability, and consistency in church operations.

1. Strategic Leadership: Governance provides strategic direction, guiding the church in fulfilling its mission and adapting to changes in its environment.

2. Financial Oversight: Proper governance ensures that financial resources are managed responsibly, with transparency and accountability.

3. Policy Development: Governance involves creating and implementing policies that support the church's mission and operational needs.

4. Conflict Resolution: Governance structures help address conflicts and challenges within the church, ensuring that issues are resolved in a manner that upholds biblical principles.

Overview of Governance Structures

This part of the book will explore various aspects of church governance, including:

- **Church Composition:** Examining the structure and membership of the church body.
- **Church Officers:** Defining the roles and responsibilities of key officers.
- **Relation to Other Bodies:** Understanding the church's interaction with denominational and local bodies.
- **Church Discipline:** Implementing and maintaining discipline according to biblical guidelines.
- **Church Boards:** Outlining the key responsibilities and functions of church boards.
- **Policies for Auxiliaries:** Developing and implementing effective policies for church auxiliaries.

Setting the Stage for Effective Governance

Effective governance in Baptist churches requires a clear understanding of roles, responsibilities, and processes. By setting a strong foundation, this part of the book aims to equip church leaders and members with the knowledge and tools needed for successful governance. Each chapter will build upon this introduction, providing detailed insights into the various elements of church governance.

Conclusion

The introduction to church governance sets the stage for a deeper exploration of how Baptist churches are organized and managed. By understanding the biblical principles and practical aspects of governance, church leaders can foster a healthy and effective church environment. This chapter provides a roadmap for navigating the complexities of church governance, ensuring that the church remains true to its mission and responsive to its members' needs.

CHAPTER THIRTY-EIGHT
CHURCH COMPOSITION

Introduction

C hurch composition refers to the structure and organization of the church body, including its membership, leadership, and organizational framework. Understanding church composition is essential for effective governance and for ensuring that the church functions smoothly and fulfills its mission. This chapter explores the various aspects of church composition, including membership categories, roles, and the importance of each member's contribution to the life of the church.

Biblical Foundation of Church Composition

The concept of church composition is rooted in Scripture, where the church is described as the body of Christ with diverse members who each have unique roles and functions. 1 Corinthians 12:12-27 highlights the idea that the church is one body with many parts, each essential and interdependent. This biblical perspective emphasizes the importance of every member's role in the church and the need for a well-organized structure to support the church's mission.

Membership Categories

Church membership is typically categorized into several types, each with specific roles and responsibilities. Regular members are those who have formally joined the church through baptism and a membership process. They are active participants in church life, attending services regularly, engaging in church activities, and contributing to the church's financial needs and volunteer efforts.

Associate members, on the other hand, are individuals who may be affiliated with the church but have not completed the full membership process. They might be regular attendees or individuals who participate in church activities while maintaining membership with another congregation. Their involvement in church life is generally more limited compared to regular members.

Inactive members are those who were once active but are no longer regularly involved in the church. They may have moved away, joined another church, or become disengaged from church activities. It is important for the church to maintain contact with these individuals and make efforts to re-engage them through outreach and supportive initiatives.

Roles and Responsibilities within the Church

In any church, the congregation plays a vital role in both governance and the daily life of the church. Members are essential for participating in church activities, providing feedback, and voting on significant matters such as budget approvals and constitutional changes. Their engagement ensures that the church remains dynamic and responsive to its members' needs.

Church leaders, including pastors, deacons, and trustees, are instrumental in guiding the church and managing its operations. The pastor serves as the primary spiritual leader, responsible for preaching, teaching, and providing pastoral care. Deacons assist with practical needs and support the pastor in various capacities, while trustees manage the church's property and handle legal affairs.

Auxiliaries and committees within the church focus on specific areas such as education, outreach, and social activities. These groups are responsible for planning and executing programs and initiatives that align with the church's mission. Their work helps to ensure that the church's programs run smoothly and effectively, supporting the overall goal of ministry and community service.

Importance of Church Composition

A well-defined church composition is essential for ensuring that all aspects of church life are managed effectively. Clear roles and responsibilities help the church operate efficiently, coordinate its ministries, and foster a strong sense of community among its members. Understanding the structure and composition of the church allows for better planning, execution, and fulfillment of the church's mission.

Conclusion

Church composition is fundamental to the effective governance and operation of a Baptist church. By understanding the different membership categories, roles, and responsibilities, the church can ensure that it functions efficiently and fulfills its mission. This chapter provides a foundational understanding of church composition, setting the stage for exploring other aspects of governance and church life in subsequent chapters.

CHAPTER THIRTY-NINE
CHURCH OFFICERS

Introduction

C hurch officers play a pivotal role in the governance and daily functioning of a Baptist church. Their responsibilities are crucial for maintaining the church's spiritual health, administrative efficiency, and overall effectiveness. This chapter explores the various church officer roles, their duties, and their importance within the Baptist tradition, providing a comprehensive understanding of how these roles contribute to the church's mission.

Biblical Foundation for Church Officers

The roles and responsibilities of church officers are deeply rooted in Scripture. The New Testament provides guidance on the qualifications and duties of church leaders. In 1 Timothy 3:1-13, the Apostle Paul outlines the qualifications for overseers (pastors) and deacons, emphasizing virtues such as integrity, wisdom, and leadership. Similarly, Titus 1:5-9 describes the attributes of elders and their role in teaching and leading the church. These passages establish a biblical framework for understanding the expectations and standards for church officers.

Roles and Responsibilities

Pastor

The Pastor is the primary spiritual leader of the church, responsible for preaching, teaching, and pastoral care. According to Ephesians 4:11-12, the pastor is given to equip the saints for ministry and to build up the body of Christ. The pastor's key responsibilities include delivering sermons, teaching Bible studies, and providing pastoral care, such as counseling and visiting members during times of crisis. The pastor also plays a crucial role in guiding the church's mission and vision, making strategic decisions, and leading worship and ministry activities.

Deacons

Deacons serve as assistants to the pastor and help manage the practical and spiritual needs of the congregation. Their role is based on the account in Acts 6:1-6, where the early church appointed deacons to address the distribution of food and other duties. Deacons are responsible for assisting with church functions such as communion, baptisms, and visitation of the sick. They also manage specific areas of church life, including benevolence programs and facility maintenance, providing essential support to the pastor and other church leaders.

Trustees

Trustees manage the church's property and legal affairs. Their role involves the stewardship of church assets and ensuring compliance with legal requirements. Trustees are responsible for overseeing the maintenance, repair, and improvement of church facilities. They handle legal matters such as contracts and insurance, and ensure compliance with local regulations. Trustees also assist with budgeting and financial planning related to property and facilities.

Clerk

The Clerk maintains the official records of the church, ensuring proper documentation of meetings and decisions. This role includes keeping minutes of church meetings, such as business meetings and congregational votes. The Clerk is also responsible for managing membership records, baptisms, and other important church documents, and facilitating communication between the church and external organizations.

Treasurer

The Treasurer oversees the church's finances, ensuring the proper handling of funds and financial reporting. Key responsibilities include managing the collection, disbursement, and accounting of church funds. The Treasurer provides regular financial reports to the church board and congregation and assists with preparing the church budget and financial planning.

Interactions and Collaboration

Effective collaboration among church officers is essential for the smooth operation of the church. Pastors, deacons, trustees, clerks, and treasurers each have distinct roles that must work in harmony to achieve the church's mission. Regular communication and coordination among officers ensure that the church's activities are well-managed and that its goals are met.

Best Practices for Church Officers

To fulfill their roles effectively, church officers should adhere to best practices that include a commitment to biblical principles, clear communication with other officers and the congregation, ongoing training and development, and maintaining accountability to the church board and congregation. These practices help ensure that church officers are well-equipped to perform their duties and support the church's mission.

Conclusion

Church officers are integral to the governance and functioning of a Baptist church. By understanding their roles and responsibilities, church members and leaders can ensure that the church operates efficiently and effectively. This chapter provides a comprehensive overview of key church officers, setting the stage for a deeper exploration of governance and administrative practices in the subsequent chapters.

CHAPTER FORTY
KEY RESPONSIBILITIES OF CHURCH BOARDS

Introduction

C hurch boards are essential components of governance in Baptist churches, playing a significant role in administration and oversight. This chapter explores the key responsibilities of various church boards, providing insight into their functions and best practices for effective governance.

Biblical Foundation for Board Responsibilities

The Bible offers guidance on the roles and responsibilities of church boards. 1 Timothy 3:1-13 highlights the qualifications for church leaders, emphasizing wisdom, integrity, and service. Acts 6:1-7 demonstrates the early church's approach to managing practical needs through deacons, illustrating the importance of delegation and effective oversight.

List of Common Church Boards

Board of Deacons: The Board of Deacons is responsible for serving the congregation's practical and spiritual needs. Their duties include visitation, caring for the sick, and assisting with church services.

This role is rooted in Acts 6:1-6, where deacons were appointed to manage the distribution of food, allowing apostles to focus on prayer and ministry.

Board of Trustees: The Board of Trustees oversees the church's property and legal affairs. They manage the maintenance, repairs, and legal compliance of church facilities. This board's responsibilities are supported by Matthew 25:14-30, which emphasizes the importance of stewardship and proper management of entrusted resources.

Administrative Board: The Administrative Board handles the day-to-day operations of the church, including staff management and operational policies. They ensure that church activities are conducted efficiently and align with the church's mission. This role is supported by 1 Corinthians 14:40, which advocates for orderly and effective church practices.

Mission Board: The Mission Board focuses on coordinating the church's outreach and mission activities, both locally and globally. They ensure that mission efforts align with the church's values and objectives. This board's work reflects Matthew 28:19-20, where Jesus commissions His followers to make disciples of all nations.

Building and Grounds Committee: The Building and Grounds Committee manages the maintenance and improvement of church facilities. They handle repairs, renovations, and ensure that the church's physical environment is well-maintained and welcoming. Their role is crucial for providing a functional and inviting space for worship and ministry.

Key Functions of Church Boards

1. Strategic Planning

Church boards play a key role in guiding the strategic direction of the church. They collaborate with church leaders to set long-term goals and develop strategies that align with the church's mission. This involves prioritizing initiatives and ensuring that the church remains focused on its vision.

2. Financial Oversight

While the Finance Committee is not included in this chapter, the responsibility for overseeing financial matters may still rest with the boards, especially in smaller churches. Boards review budgets, financial reports, and ensure proper management of church funds, maintaining transparency and accountability.

3. Policy Development

Boards are responsible for developing and implementing policies that govern church operations. These policies provide a framework for decision-making and ensure consistency in church activities. Regular review and updates of policies are necessary to address evolving needs and best practices.

4. Leadership and Staff Oversight

Boards oversee the hiring, evaluation, and support of church staff. They provide guidance and feedback to ensure that staff members fulfill their roles effectively and contribute to the church's mission. Creating a positive work environment is crucial for staff and volunteers.

5. Legal and Ethical Compliance

Boards ensure that the church operates in accordance with legal and ethical standards. This includes staying informed about relevant laws, maintaining proper documentation, and addressing any legal or ethical issues that arise.

6. Congregational Engagement

Boards engage with the congregation by ensuring clear communication about church activities and decisions, gathering feedback, and addressing concerns. Building trust and fostering a positive relationship between the church leadership and its members is essential.

7. Risk Management

Boards assess and manage potential risks related to church operations, finances, and programs. Developing strategies to mitigate risks and preparing for potential crises helps the church handle unforeseen challenges effectively.

Best Practices for Effective Church Boards

To operate effectively, church boards should adhere to several best practices. First, it is essential to define clear roles, ensuring that each board member fully understands their responsibilities and duties. Regular meetings should be scheduled to discuss important matters, review progress, and make necessary decisions to guide the church's direction. Open communication should be encouraged not only among board members but also with the congregation, fostering transparency and trust. Additionally, providing training and development opportunities is crucial for enhancing the skills and knowledge of board members. Lastly, regularly evaluating the board's performance and seeking feedback allows for continuous improvement and growth in church governance.

Conclusion

Understanding the roles and responsibilities of church boards is crucial for effective governance in Baptist churches. By fulfilling their key functions and following best practices, church boards contribute significantly to the church's overall health and success. This chapter provides an overview of common church boards and their functions, laying a foundation for effective governance in the Baptist context.

CHAPTER FORTY-ONE
CHURCH DISCIPLINE

Introduction

Church discipline is a vital aspect of maintaining the health and integrity of a Baptist church. It involves guiding and correcting members to ensure adherence to biblical principles and church standards. Effective church discipline fosters spiritual growth, accountability, and a loving community. This chapter explores the principles, processes, and practices of church discipline within the Baptist tradition, providing a framework for its implementation.

Biblical Basis for Church Discipline

The Bible provides clear instructions on the practice of church discipline. Matthew 18:15-17 outlines a process for addressing personal grievances within the church, emphasizing the importance of reconciliation and accountability. 1 Corinthians 5:1-13 addresses the need for discipline in cases of serious misconduct, urging the church to take action to preserve its purity and witness. Galatians

6:1 further instructs believers to restore those who have sinned with a spirit of gentleness.

Principles of Church Discipline

Restoration and Reconciliation: The primary goal of church discipline is to restore the individual to a right relationship with God and the church community. Discipline should be carried out with a spirit of love and compassion, aiming for reconciliation rather than punishment. 2 Corinthians 2:6-8 highlights the importance of forgiveness and restoration after a disciplinary action.

Transparency and Fairness: The process of church discipline should be transparent and fair, ensuring that all parties involved have the opportunity to be heard and understood. Proverbs 18:13 emphasizes the need for careful consideration before making judgments.

Confidentiality: While discipline must be transparent, confidentiality is also important to protect the dignity and privacy of the individuals involved. 1 Peter 4:8 reminds believers to cover a multitude of sins with love, avoiding unnecessary public exposure.

Processes of Church Discipline

Private Confrontation: The initial step in the discipline process involves a private conversation between the offended party and the offender. This approach aligns with Matthew 18:15, where Jesus instructs individuals to address conflicts directly and privately.

Witnesses and Mediation: If the issue is not resolved through private confrontation, the next step involves bringing one or two witnesses to mediate the situation. This step aims to provide additional perspectives and facilitate resolution, as outlined in Matthew 18:16.

Church Involvement: If the issue remains unresolved, the matter is brought before the church. This step involves a formal process where the church may take disciplinary action, such as suspension or exclusion from membership. Matthew 18:17 instructs the church to treat the unrepentant individual as a "Gentile and a tax collector," signifying a break in fellowship while leaving room for future reconciliation.

Restoration and Reconciliation: Following disciplinary action, the church should work towards the restoration and reconciliation of the individual. 2 Corinthians 2:6-8 encourages the church to reaffirm their love and forgiveness towards the repentant individual, facilitating their return to fellowship.

Best Practices for Implementing Church Discipline

Effective church discipline requires clear policies, training for church leaders, and a commitment to biblical principles. Churches should establish written guidelines for discipline, ensure that leaders are trained in the process, and approach discipline with a spirit of grace and humility. Regular review of disciplinary practices and feedback from the congregation can help maintain the effectiveness and fairness of the process.

Conclusion

Church discipline is an essential practice for maintaining the integrity and health of a Baptist church. By following biblical principles and implementing clear processes, churches can address issues effectively while fostering a loving and restorative environment. This chapter provides a foundational understanding of church discipline, setting the stage for exploring governance and decision-making in subsequent chapters.

CHAPTER FORTY-TWO
DEVELOPING AND IMPLEMENTING
EFFECTIVE POLICIES FOR CHURCH
AUXILIARIES

Introduction

Effective policies are essential for the smooth operation and governance of church auxiliaries. Policies provide clear guidelines and standards, ensuring consistency and accountability. This chapter explores the importance of developing and implementing policies for church auxiliaries and provides practical steps for creating policies that support their effective functioning.

Biblical Foundation for Policies

The Bible emphasizes the importance of order and accountability within the church. 1 Corinthians 14:40 instructs that all things should be done decently and in order, reflecting the need for structured policies. Proverbs 11:14 highlights the value of guidance and counsel, which policies provide to help navigate complex situations and decisions.

Importance of Policies for Church Auxiliaries

1. Establishing Clear Guidelines

Policies provide clear guidelines for the operation and conduct of auxiliary groups. They outline expectations, procedures, and responsibilities, reducing ambiguity and helping members understand their roles and duties. Proverbs 16:3 underscores the importance of committing plans to the Lord for success, which can be reflected in well-crafted policies.

2. Ensuring Consistency

Consistent policies help ensure that auxiliary activities are conducted uniformly, promoting fairness and equity. Consistency in policies helps prevent confusion and disputes among members and ensures that similar situations are handled in a similar manner. James 1:17 speaks to the unchanging nature of God, which can inspire consistent and reliable policies.

3. Enhancing Accountability

Policies establish accountability by defining roles, responsibilities, and procedures. They provide a framework for evaluating performance and addressing issues, which helps maintain integrity and transparency within auxiliaries. Matthew 18:15-17 provides a framework for addressing conflicts and promoting accountability.

4. Facilitating Effective Decision-Making

Having established policies in place helps streamline decision-making processes, providing a clear path for resolving issues and making informed choices. Proverbs 15:22 highlights the value of seeking counsel and advice, which can be reflected in the development of effective policies.

Developing Effective Policies

1. Identify Needs and Objectives

Start by identifying the needs and objectives of the auxiliary. Determine the specific areas where policies are required, such as financial management, meeting procedures, or conflict resolution. Nehemiah 2:12 illustrates the importance of assessing needs and planning accordingly.

2. Involve Key Stakeholders

Engage key stakeholders, including auxiliary members, church leaders, and legal advisors, in the policy development process. Their input ensures that policies are comprehensive, practical, and aligned with the church's mission. Proverbs 15:22 emphasizes the value of counsel and collaboration in decision-making.

3. Draft Policies

Create draft policies based on the identified needs and objectives. Ensure that policies are clear, concise, and specific. Include sections on purpose, scope, procedures, and responsibilities. Habakkuk 2:2 encourages writing down and making vision clear, which applies to drafting policies.

4. Review and Revise

Review the draft policies with key stakeholders to gather feedback and make necessary revisions. This review process helps ensure that policies are effective and applicable. Proverbs 27:17 speaks to the importance of mutual feedback and sharpening one another, relevant to refining policies.

5. Implement Policies

Once finalized, implement the policies by communicating them to all members of the auxiliary. Provide training and resources to ensure that everyone understands and follows the policies. Ephesians 6:7 encourages serving wholeheartedly, reflecting the importance of commitment to implemented policies.

6. Monitor and Evaluate

Regularly monitor the implementation of policies and evaluate their effectiveness. Make adjustments as needed to address any issues or changes in circumstances. 2 Corinthians 13:5 encourages self-examination and evaluation, applicable to assessing the effectiveness of policies.

7. Update Policies as Needed

Policies should be reviewed and updated periodically to remain relevant and effective. Changes in church needs, legal requirements, or best practices may necessitate updates. Ecclesiastes 3:1 acknowledges the times and seasons for change, supporting the need for periodic policy reviews.

Common Policy Areas

1. Financial Management

Policies related to financial management ensure that funds are handled responsibly and transparently. This includes budgeting, expense approval, and financial reporting.

2. Meeting Procedures

Policies governing meeting procedures outline how meetings are conducted, including scheduling, agendas, and record-keeping.

3. Conflict Resolution

Conflict resolution policies provide guidelines for addressing disputes and disagreements within the auxiliary.

4. Volunteer Management

Policies related to volunteer management cover recruitment, training, and recognition of volunteers.

5. Safety and Security

Safety and security policies address measures to protect members and church property, including emergency procedures and safeguarding protocols.

Conclusion

Developing and implementing effective policies for church auxiliaries is essential for ensuring their smooth operation and success. By establishing clear guidelines, promoting consistency, and enhancing accountability, policies support the effective functioning of auxiliaries and align their activities with the church's mission. This chapter has provided practical steps for creating and implementing policies, emphasizing the importance of ongoing evaluation and adaptation to meet the evolving needs of the church.

CHAPTER FORTY-THREE
CHURCH GOVERNANCE AND DECISION-MAKING

Introduction

C hurch governance and decision-making are fundamental to the effective functioning of a Baptist church. These processes ensure that decisions are made in a manner consistent with the church's mission, values, and biblical principles. This chapter examines the structures and practices of church governance, focusing on decision-making processes and the role of various church bodies in shaping the direction of the church.

Biblical Foundation for Governance and Decision-Making

The New Testament provides guidance on church governance and decision-making through examples of early church practices. Acts 15:1-29 illustrates how early church leaders convened to make significant decisions regarding doctrine and practice, emphasizing the importance of collective wisdom and consultation. 1 Corinthians 14:40 underscores the need for orderly and respectful decision-making processes within the church.

Governance Structures

Congregational Polity: Many Baptist churches operate under a congregational polity, where the entire membership has a voice in decision-making. This structure emphasizes democratic participation and accountability, with decisions made through congregational meetings and votes. Acts 6:3 highlights the role of the congregation in appointing leaders, reflecting the importance of collective decision-making.

Elder-Led Governance: Some Baptist churches use an elder-led model, where a group of elders oversees church affairs and makes decisions on behalf of the congregation. This model is based on the principle of 1 Timothy 5:17, which recognizes the role of elders in leading and teaching the church. Elders are responsible for spiritual oversight, while the congregation may still participate in significant decisions.

Board-Led Governance: In this model, various boards or committees are responsible for specific areas of church life, such as finance, property, and personnel. Boards make decisions within their areas of responsibility, with oversight and final approval by the congregation or senior leadership. This approach allows for specialized expertise and effective management of church affairs.

Decision-Making Processes

Consultative Decision-Making: Effective decision-making often involves seeking input and advice from various stakeholders. This approach ensures that decisions are well-informed and consider multiple perspectives. Proverbs 15:22 emphasizes the value of seeking counsel and advice in decision-making processes.

Consensus Building: Building consensus among church leaders and members can lead to more unified and effective decisions. This process involves open dialogue, negotiation, and compromise to achieve common agreement. Acts 15:22 reflects the early church's practice of reaching consensus on important issues.

Voting and Ratification: In congregationally governed churches, formal voting is often used to make decisions on significant matters. The voting process should be conducted transparently and in accordance with church bylaws. 1 Corinthians 14:40 underscores the need for order and clarity in decision-making processes.

Best Practices for Governance and Decision-Making

To ensure effective governance and decision-making, churches should establish clear policies and procedures, provide training for leaders, and foster a culture of transparency and accountability. Regular review of governance practices and feedback from the congregation can help improve decision-making processes and maintain alignment with the church's mission.

Conclusion

Church governance and decision-making are crucial for the effective functioning of a Baptist church. By understanding governance structures and implementing best practices, churches can ensure that decisions are made in a manner consistent with biblical principles and the church's mission. This chapter provides a foundational overview of governance and decision-making, setting the stage for further exploration of financial management and oversight in subsequent chapters.

CHAPTER FORTY-FOUR
FINANCIAL MANAGEMENT AND
OVERSIGHT

Introduction

Financial management and oversight are essential for maintaining the financial health and integrity of a Baptist church. Effective financial practices ensure that resources are used wisely and in alignment with the church's mission. This chapter explores the principles, practices, and best practices of financial management and oversight within the Baptist tradition.

Biblical Foundation for Financial Management

The Bible provides guidance on financial stewardship and management. 1 Timothy 5:17-18 highlights the importance of providing for church leaders and managing resources responsibly. Proverbs 3:9-10 encourages honoring God with one's wealth and ensuring that resources are used to support God's work. 2 Corinthians 9:6-7 underscores the principles of generosity and cheerful giving, which are central to financial stewardship.

Principles of Financial Management

Stewardship: Financial management in the church is a form of stewardship, recognizing that all resources belong to God and should be used in accordance with His purposes. This principle involves careful planning, budgeting, and monitoring of financial resources to ensure that they support the church's mission.

Transparency: Transparency in financial management involves clear and open reporting of financial activities and decisions. Regular financial reports, including income statements, balance sheets, and budget reports, should be shared with the congregation to ensure accountability and trust.

Accountability: Effective financial oversight requires accountability at all levels of financial management. This includes regular audits, adherence to financial policies and procedures, and oversight by church boards or committees. Accountability helps prevent misuse of funds and ensures that resources are used appropriately.

Financial Practices

Budgeting: Developing and managing a church budget is a key component of financial management. The budget should reflect the church's priorities and goals, allocating resources to various ministries and operational needs. Regular review and adjustment of the budget help ensure that financial resources are used effectively.

Record-Keeping: Accurate and comprehensive record-keeping is essential for tracking financial transactions and maintaining financial integrity. This includes documenting income, expenses, and investments, as well as maintaining records of financial decisions and approvals.

Fundraising and Stewardship: Fundraising efforts should align with the church's mission and values, promoting generosity and support for the church's work. Stewardship programs can help educate members about financial giving and encourage ongoing support.

Best Practices for Financial Oversight

To ensure effective financial management and oversight, churches should implement best practices such as regular financial audits, clear financial policies, and separation of financial duties. Training for financial officers and regular review of financial practices can also help maintain financial health and integrity.

Conclusion

Financial management and oversight are critical for the effective functioning of a Baptist church. By adhering to biblical principles and implementing best practices, churches can ensure that their financial resources are used wisely and in alignment with their mission. This chapter provides a foundational understanding of financial management, setting the stage for exploring legal and ethical considerations in subsequent chapters.

CHAPTER FORTY-FIVE
LEGAL AND ETHICAL CONSIDERATIONS

Introduction

Legal and ethical considerations are integral to the governance and operation of a Baptist church. Adhering to legal requirements and ethical standards ensures that the church operates within the bounds of the law and maintains integrity in its practices. This chapter examines the key legal and ethical issues facing Baptist churches and provides guidance on addressing these concerns.

Legal Considerations

Incorporation and Tax-Exempt Status: Many Baptist churches are incorporated as non-profit entities, which provides legal protection for church leaders and qualifies the church for tax-exempt status. This status requires compliance with federal and state regulations, including annual filings and adherence to non-profit guidelines. **IRS Code Section 501(c)(3)** outlines the requirements for maintaining tax-exempt status.

Employment Law: Churches must comply with employment laws, including those related to hiring practices, employee rights, and workplace safety. This includes adhering to regulations such as the

Fair Labor Standards Act (FLSA) and ensuring that employment practices are non-discriminatory and fair.

Property and Liability: Legal considerations also involve managing church property and addressing liability issues. Churches should ensure that property is properly insured and that liability risks are minimized through appropriate policies and procedures.

Ethical Considerations

Financial Integrity: Ethical financial practices are essential for maintaining trust and credibility. This includes avoiding conflicts of interest, ensuring transparency in financial reporting, and adhering to ethical fundraising practices. Proverbs 11:1 emphasizes the importance of honesty and fairness in financial dealings.

Confidentiality: Maintaining confidentiality in church matters, including counseling and personal information, is crucial for protecting the privacy and dignity of individuals. Ethical considerations involve handling sensitive information with care and ensuring that confidentiality is upheld.

Conflict of Interest: Church leaders should avoid conflicts of interest that could compromise their decision-making and integrity. This involves disclosing potential conflicts and recusing oneself from decisions where personal interests may interfere.

Best Practices for Legal and Ethical Compliance

Churches should implement best practices for legal and ethical compliance, including regular training for leaders, maintaining up-to-date policies and procedures, and seeking legal counsel when necessary. Regular reviews of legal and ethical practices can help ensure ongoing compliance and address potential issues proactively.

Conclusion

Legal and ethical considerations are fundamental to the governance and operation of a Baptist church. By adhering to legal requirements and ethical standards, churches can maintain integrity, protect their members, and fulfill their mission effectively. This chapter provides a comprehensive overview of legal and ethical issues, setting the stage for exploring future trends in church governance in the final chapter.

CHAPTER FORTY-SIX
RELATION TO OTHER BODIES

Introduction

The relationship between a Baptist church and other bodies—such as denominational organizations, local associations, and community groups—is a crucial aspect of church governance and ministry. Understanding these relationships helps a church align its activities with broader goals and collaborate effectively with external organizations. This chapter explores the various types of external relationships a Baptist church may have, their significance, and how these relationships can enhance the church's mission and operations.

Biblical Foundation for Church Relationships

The Bible encourages the church to engage with the broader body of Christ and the community. Acts 15:1-29 depicts the early church's interaction with other church leaders and communities to resolve theological and practical issues, highlighting the importance of cooperation and shared wisdom. Additionally, 1 Corinthians 12:12-27 illustrates the concept of the church as part of a larger body, emphasizing the interconnectedness of all believers and the importance of mutual support and collaboration.

Denominational Affiliation

Denominational Organizations play a significant role in the life of many Baptist churches. These organizations provide structure, support, and accountability, helping churches stay connected with a broader network of congregations. Denominations often offer resources such as training, theological education, and mission opportunities, which can aid churches in their ministry efforts.

Affiliation with a denomination provides several benefits, including shared resources, collective mission initiatives, and a sense of belonging to a larger community of faith. Denominations also offer a framework for resolving disputes, providing accountability, and maintaining doctrinal consistency across congregations. Churches that are part of a denomination may participate in denominational events, contribute to denominational missions, and adhere to denominational guidelines and policies.

Local Associations

Local Associations are networks of churches within a specific geographic area that come together for mutual support and collaboration. These associations often facilitate cooperative efforts such as joint missions, community outreach, and shared events. They provide a platform for churches to exchange ideas, resources, and encouragement, strengthening their collective impact on the community.

Local associations may also serve as a forum for addressing common challenges and working together to solve problems. They can offer training and support for church leaders, provide opportunities for shared worship and fellowship, and coordinate collective ministry efforts. Engaging with a local association helps churches build relationships with other congregations and work together to fulfill their mission in the local context.

Community Organizations

Community Organizations encompass a wide range of groups and agencies that operate within the local area, including social service agencies, non-profits, and civic organizations. Baptist churches often collaborate with these organizations to address community needs, support social justice initiatives, and promote the welfare of the community.

Partnerships with community organizations can enhance a church's outreach efforts and extend its impact beyond the walls of the church. For example, a church may work with local food banks, homeless shelters, or educational programs to provide support and resources to those in need. Engaging with community organizations also helps churches build relationships with local leaders and residents, fostering a positive presence in the community and demonstrating the church's commitment to service and outreach.

Interfaith and Ecumenical Relations

Interfaith and Ecumenical Relations involve collaborating with churches and faith communities from different traditions and denominations. These relationships can promote understanding, foster cooperation on shared goals, and address common social issues. Baptist churches may participate in interfaith dialogues, joint community service projects, and ecumenical worship services to build bridges and work together for the common good.

While maintaining theological distinctiveness, Baptist churches can benefit from engaging in respectful and constructive relationships with other faith communities. These interactions provide opportunities for learning, growth, and collaboration, contributing to a broader sense of unity within the Christian faith and the larger community.

Best Practices for Managing External Relationships

To manage relationships with external bodies effectively, churches should practice clear communication, mutual respect, and alignment of goals. Establishing formal agreements or memoranda of understanding can help clarify expectations and responsibilities in collaborative efforts. Regular evaluation of partnerships and ongoing dialogue with external organizations can ensure that relationships remain productive and beneficial for all parties involved.

Conclusion

The relationships between a Baptist church and other bodies—whether denominational organizations, local associations, community groups, or interfaith partners—play a crucial role in the church's governance and ministry. By understanding and managing these relationships effectively, churches can enhance their mission, broaden their impact, and foster a sense of unity and collaboration within the broader Christian community. This chapter provides a foundational overview of these relationships, setting the stage for further exploration of governance and administrative practices in subsequent chapters.

CHAPTER FORTY-SEVEN
FUTURE TRENDS IN CHURCH
GOVERNANCE

Introduction

As society and technology continue to evolve, Baptist churches must adapt to new trends and challenges in governance. Understanding future trends helps churches remain relevant and effective in their ministry. This chapter explores emerging trends in church governance, including technological advancements, demographic shifts, and changing societal expectations.

Technological Advancements

Technological advancements have revolutionized every aspect of life, and churches are no exception. The rapid evolution of digital communication, data management, and online ministry platforms is reshaping how churches operate, engage, and expand their reach.

First, *digital communication* tools have significantly changed how churches connect with their congregations and the broader community. Churches are now leveraging social media platforms like Facebook, Instagram, and Twitter to share sermons, provide updates, and promote upcoming events. Email newsletters, once a supplementary tool, have become primary means of outreach, providing direct and immediate communication with church members. The introduction of video conferencing platforms such as Zoom or Microsoft Teams has enabled virtual Bible studies, prayer meetings, and committee discussions, helping to bridge the gap for congregants unable to attend in person. In line with Acts 1:8, these technological tools facilitate the spreading of the gospel "to the ends of the earth," transcending physical limitations and reaching global audiences.

Next, *data management* and analytics tools are providing churches with a wealth of information previously difficult to capture and analyze. Churches can now track attendance trends, monitor giving patterns, and evaluate the effectiveness of various ministries. With tools like Church Management Software (ChMS), church leaders can maintain member databases, automate follow-ups with visitors, and identify pastoral care opportunities by analyzing data. This information helps churches make informed decisions, improve resource allocation, and tailor ministry efforts to the specific needs of their congregation. Data-driven strategies allow churches to remain connected with members while enhancing engagement and spiritual growth.

Additionally, *online worship and ministry* have experienced unprecedented growth, particularly in the wake of global events like the COVID-19 pandemic. Virtual church services, livestreamed sermons, and online worship gatherings have now become staples for many congregations. While some churches were already experimenting with online platforms, the pandemic accelerated this trend. Churches are creating innovative and interactive ways for members to participate in worship—from live chat features during sermons to virtual small groups and digital Sunday schools. These online platforms not only extend the reach of the church to those who cannot attend in person, but they also offer a new avenue for evangelism, allowing churches to connect with people worldwide.

Demographic Shifts

Churches are also adapting to significant demographic changes. Shifts in age, ethnicity, socio-economic status, and geographic location are influencing how churches develop ministry programs and engage their communities.

One key demographic trend is the *changing congregational composition* in terms of ethnicity and socio-economic status. As communities become increasingly diverse, churches must embrace this diversity within their congregations. This involves not only recognizing cultural differences but also offering ministries and programs that are relevant to various cultural and ethnic groups. Some churches are adopting multilingual services, hiring bilingual staff, and celebrating different cultural holidays to create an inclusive environment. In addition, socio-economic disparities within congregations are prompting churches to implement outreach programs that provide food, housing assistance, and financial literacy training to low-income families. By being attuned to these demographic changes, churches can ensure that their ministries reflect the diversity of the Kingdom of God.

Another significant demographic trend is the increasing importance of *intergenerational ministry.* Churches are increasingly recognizing the need to foster relationships and interactions between different age groups. Rather than separating ministries by age, churches are now creating spaces where older generations can mentor and guide younger members, fulfilling the exhortation in Titus 2:3-5, which encourages older believers to instruct the younger. By promoting intergenerational worship services, prayer groups, and fellowship events, churches can strengthen the bonds between generations and create a more cohesive, unified body of believers.

Urbanization and migration patterns are also influencing church dynamics. As more people move to urban centers, rural churches are seeing a decline in membership while city churches are experiencing growth. Additionally, migration patterns—both domestic and international—are leading to more culturally and ethnically diverse congregations. These shifts present both challenges and opportunities for churches. Rural congregations may need to explore new ways to attract members, such as focusing on community-based ministries, while urban churches might need to adapt to growing, diverse populations by expanding services and programs tailored to specific cultural or immigrant groups. By remaining flexible and responsive to these demographic shifts, churches can better serve their communities and fulfill their mission.

Changing Societal Expectations

As society evolves, so too do the expectations placed on churches by both their members and the wider public. In an age where transparency, social justice, and innovative ministry models are valued, churches must adjust their governance and outreach accordingly.

One of the most significant changes in recent years is the growing emphasis on *social justice and advocacy*. Churches are no longer seen as just spiritual centers but are increasingly expected to play a role in addressing societal issues like racial inequality, poverty, environmental degradation, and human rights abuses. Many congregations have embraced this role, engaging in community activism, forming partnerships with social justice organizations, and advocating for change from a biblical perspective. This aligns with the calling of Micah 6:8, which encourages believers to "act justly and to love mercy." Churches that respond to these calls for justice not only align themselves with biblical values but also gain the respect and trust of their communities.

The demand for *transparency and accountability* in church governance has also intensified. Members expect their church leaders to uphold ethical practices in financial management, decision-making, and pastoral care. Churches are increasingly implementing governance structures that ensure checks and balances, such as creating finance committees, conducting regular financial audits, and establishing clear protocols for addressing allegations of misconduct. Many congregations are also embracing open communication with their members, providing regular financial updates and making leadership decisions more transparent. This level of accountability fosters trust and enhances the credibility of the church, ensuring that it remains a trustworthy steward of its resources and mission.

Finally, churches are exploring *innovative ministry models* that adapt to the needs of contemporary society. Traditional models of church ministry—such as Sunday worship, Bible study, and prayer meetings—are now being supplemented by creative alternatives. Missional communities, for example, focus on outreach and evangelism outside of the church walls, encouraging members to serve in their neighborhoods and engage with local non-profits. Other churches are experimenting with collaborative partnerships, working with other religious and community organizations to pool resources and address broader social needs. Some churches are also adopting more decentralized forms of leadership, empowering lay members to take on significant roles in ministry and outreach. These innovative models reflect the church's adaptability and willingness to rethink how it fulfills its mission in an ever-changing world.

Conclusion

The trends of technological advancements, demographic shifts, and changing societal expectations are shaping the future of church governance. Baptist churches that recognize and respond to these trends will not only remain relevant but will also thrive in their ministry. By embracing digital communication tools, data management, and online ministry platforms, churches can reach a broader audience and engage their members more effectively. By understanding demographic changes and fostering intergenerational connections, churches can build stronger, more inclusive communities. And by addressing societal expectations for justice, transparency, and innovation, churches can serve as beacons of hope and transformation in a rapidly evolving world. This chapter provides a foundation for navigating these trends and looking ahead to a future where the church remains a vital force for good in society.

PART V. ORDINANCES OF THE CHURCH

CHAPTER FORTY-EIGHT
THE ROLE OF ORDINANCES IN BAPTIST IDENTITY

Introduction

Ordinances play a pivotal role in Baptist worship and identity. They are not mere rituals but are deeply embedded in the Baptist understanding of faith and practice. This chapter explores the significance of ordinances—baptism and the Lord's Supper—in shaping Baptist identity and community. We will delve into their historical origins, theological meanings, and how they reinforce the sense of belonging and adherence to Baptist principles.

Historical Background

Origins of Ordinances

The concept of ordinances has its roots in the early Christian church. Baptism and the Lord's Supper were instituted by Christ Himself, as seen in Matthew 28:19, where Jesus commands His followers to baptize all nations, and in Luke 22:19-20, where He institutes the Lord's Supper. These practices were integral to the early church's worship and have been maintained through the centuries.

Baptist Distinctions

Baptists have historically distinguished themselves from other Christian traditions through their particular understanding and practice of ordinances. Unlike some traditions that may emphasize sacraments as means of grace, Baptists view ordinances primarily as symbolic acts of obedience and public declaration of faith. This distinction is grounded in a commitment to Scripture as the sole authority for doctrine and practice.

Theological Significance

Biblical Foundations

Ordinances are firmly rooted in Scripture. Baptism is grounded in passages such as Acts 2:38, where Peter exhorts believers to be baptized for the remission of sins. The Lord's Supper is instituted in 1 Corinthians 11:23-26, where Paul recounts Jesus' words and actions during the Last Supper. These ordinances are seen not as means of earning salvation but as acts of obedience that affirm and publicly declare one's faith in Christ.

Symbolism and Meaning

In Baptist theology, ordinances are rich with symbolism. Baptism symbolizes the believer's identification with Christ's death, burial, and resurrection, as expressed in Romans 6:4. It is a public proclamation of faith and a step of obedience. The Lord's Supper represents Christ's sacrifice and serves as a means of spiritual nourishment and community unity. The elements of bread and wine symbolize Christ's body and blood, reminding believers of the new covenant established through His sacrifice.

Ordinances and Baptist Identity

Community and Identity

Ordinances play a crucial role in shaping Baptist identity and community. Baptism is often the first step in becoming a member of a Baptist church, marking the individual's entrance into the community of believers. It signifies a personal commitment to follow Christ and be part of a church that values individual and collective obedience to Scripture.

The Lord's Supper, on the other hand, is a regular act of worship that reaffirms the believer's connection to Christ and to fellow believers. It is a communal event that reflects the unity of the church and the shared commitment to the teachings of Christ. Through partaking in the Lord's Supper, Baptists express their collective identity and commitment to the covenant community.

Membership and Discipline

The practice of ordinances also ties closely to church membership and discipline. Baptism serves as a prerequisite for membership, affirming the individual's commitment to the church's teachings and practices. The Lord's Supper, while a means of grace, also functions within the context of church discipline. Participation is often reserved for members in good standing, reflecting a shared adherence to the church's doctrine and ethical standards.

Challenges and Controversies

Historical Disputes

Throughout history, Baptists have faced various controversies related to the practice of ordinances. One significant issue has been the debate over the mode of baptism. Baptists have historically rejected infant baptism and emphasized believer's baptism by immersion. This stance has led to disagreements with other

Christian traditions and has been a defining characteristic of Baptist identity.

Modern Issues

In contemporary settings, Baptists continue to navigate challenges related to the practice of ordinances. These challenges include differing interpretations of Scripture, variations in practice among Baptist churches, and evolving cultural attitudes toward religious rituals. Addressing these issues requires a careful examination of Scripture and a commitment to maintaining the integrity of Baptist practices while engaging with contemporary issues.

Case Studies

Examples from Different Churches

Examining how different Baptist churches observe ordinances can provide valuable insights into the diversity within the Baptist tradition. For example, some churches may have elaborate baptismal services with testimonies and celebrations, while others may have simpler ceremonies. Similarly, practices related to the Lord's Supper can vary, with some churches using traditional elements and others incorporating contemporary practices.

Impact on Community

The way ordinances are practiced can significantly impact the church community. For instance, a church's emphasis on baptism as a public declaration of faith can strengthen the sense of community and encourage new believers. Likewise, the observance of the Lord's Supper can foster a deep sense of unity and shared purpose among members.

Conclusion

Summary of Key Points

This chapter has explored the crucial role of ordinances in shaping Baptist identity. We have examined their historical origins, theological significance, and impact on community life. Ordinances are not merely rituals but are integral to the Baptist understanding of faith and practice.

Reflection on Baptist Future

Looking ahead, the practice of ordinances will continue to be a central element of Baptist worship and identity. As Baptists navigate contemporary challenges, it is essential to remain faithful to the Scriptural foundations of these practices while engaging thoughtfully with modern issues. The continued emphasis on baptism and the Lord's Supper will play a vital role in maintaining the integrity and vitality of Baptist faith and practice.

CHAPTER FORTY-NINE
ADMINISTRATION OF THE ORDINANCES

Introduction

In Baptist churches, the administration of ordinances—baptism and the Lord's Supper—holds profound significance, reflecting core beliefs and practices. Proper administration ensures these rites are performed in alignment with Baptist theology and maintain their sacred status. This chapter examines the procedures, roles, and best practices involved in administering these ordinances, emphasizing the importance of adhering to established practices, including the common practice of reserving the administration of ordinances for ordained ministers.

Administration of Baptism

Preparation for Baptism

The preparation process for baptism begins with thorough instruction for candidates. Typically, prospective candidates engage in classes or counseling sessions designed to impart the theological and practical significance of baptism. This period of instruction ensures candidates fully understand the meaning of their commitment. Additionally, candidates are required to make a public profession of faith, affirming their belief in Jesus Christ and their intention to follow Him. This profession is often expressed through a personal testimony shared with the congregation, which reinforces their readiness for baptism.

Scheduling and planning a baptismal service involves careful coordination. Baptisms are often integrated into regular worship services or held during special baptismal services. The timing and format can vary based on the church's traditions and schedule. The preparation of the baptistry—whether located within the church building or at a natural body of water—includes ensuring it is clean and accessible, which is crucial for a smooth and respectful baptismal experience.

Conducting the Baptism

During the baptismal service, the proceedings typically start with an introduction where the pastor or officiant explains the significance of baptism and introduces the candidates. Candidates may then recite baptismal vows or affirm their faith in response to questions posed by the pastor. The actual baptism is performed by immersion, consistent with Baptist practice, symbolizing the believer's identification with Christ's death, burial, and resurrection. The act involves submerging the candidate in water and then raising them, symbolizing their new life in Christ.

Following the baptism, new believers are welcomed into the church fellowship, often through a brief address or prayer celebrating their entry into the community. It is also essential to record the baptism in the church's membership records, noting details such as the candidate's name and the date of the baptism. This documentation is important for maintaining an accurate record of church ordinances.

Administration of the Lord's Supper

Preparation for the Lord's Supper

The preparation for the Lord's Supper involves several key steps. Scheduling typically occurs during regular worship services or special communion services, with frequency varying among Baptist churches. Preparing the elements—bread and wine or grape juice—requires ensuring that they are clean, fresh, and handled with reverence.

Participants are encouraged to engage in self-examination before partaking in the Lord's Supper, as outlined in 1 Corinthians 11:28. This self-examination helps ensure that participants approach the ordinance with a clear conscience and sincerity, fostering a meaningful and spiritually enriching experience.

Conducting the Lord's Supper

The communion service begins with an explanation of the significance of the Lord's Supper. The pastor or officiant provides a brief teaching or reflection on the meaning of the elements, based on passages such as 1 Corinthians 11:23-26. The elements are then distributed to the congregation, which may be done by passing trays or serving them individually. The act of partaking in the bread and wine serves as a reminder of Christ's sacrifice and a reaffirmation of the new covenant.

After the Lord's Supper, the service often includes a time of reflection and prayer, focusing on the ordinance's meaning and its implications for the faith community. Any remaining elements and materials are cleaned up and disposed of properly, maintaining the ordinance's reverence.

Roles in Administering Ordinances

Pastoral Role

The administration of ordinances is typically performed by ordained ministers, reflecting a common practice in Baptist churches. Ordained ministers are seen as having the theological training and authority necessary to administer these sacred rites properly. This practice underscores the importance of theological and spiritual oversight in the administration of ordinances.

The pastor plays a crucial role in providing spiritual leadership, including teaching about the significance of the ordinances, officiating their administration, and offering counseling and support to candidates. The pastor ensures that the ordinances are conducted in accordance with Baptist principles and Scripture, providing guidance and support throughout the process.

Deacons and Church Leaders

Deacons and other church leaders also contribute significantly to the administration of ordinances. In the context of baptism, they may assist with practical aspects such as preparing the baptistry and managing the logistics of the service. During the Lord's Supper, deacons or designated leaders may help with the distribution of elements and ensure the service proceeds smoothly. These leaders help maintain reverence and order, ensuring that the ordinances are conducted with the respect they deserve.

Best Practices and Considerations

Ensuring Consistency and Reverence

Adhering to Scripture and maintaining theological integrity are fundamental to the proper administration of ordinances. Churches should ensure their practices align with biblical teachings and reflect Baptist beliefs. The role of ordained ministers in administering ordinances emphasizes the importance of theological oversight and consistency.

Cultural sensitivity is also important. While adhering to Baptist principles, churches should be aware of and sensitive to cultural contexts and variations in practice. This helps ensure that the administration of ordinances remains meaningful and relevant to the congregation.

Training and Preparation

Training and preparation for church leaders are vital for effective administration. Implementing training programs ensures that pastors, deacons, and other leaders are well-prepared to administer ordinances. Ongoing education and resources support leaders in staying informed about best practices and theological developments. Regularly reviewing and evaluating the practices for administering ordinances helps maintain their effectiveness and relevance, while soliciting feedback provides valuable insights for continuous improvement.

Conclusion

The administration of baptism and the Lord's Supper is central to Baptist worship, reflecting the tradition's core values and beliefs. Proper administration involves careful preparation, adherence to theological principles, and the involvement of ordained ministers and church leaders. As Baptist churches continue to engage with contemporary issues, maintaining the integrity and reverence of these ordinances remains essential to preserving their significance and impact on the faith community.

CHAPTER FIFTY
BAPTISM

Introduction

Baptism stands as a foundational ordinance in the Baptist tradition, symbolizing the believer's entry into the faith community and their identification with Christ's death, burial, and resurrection. This chapter delves into the history, theology, and practice of baptism within the Baptist tradition, exploring its significance, practices, and the broader implications for church life and personal faith.

Historical Background

Early Christian Baptism

The practice of baptism traces its origins to the early Christian church, following the example set by Jesus Christ. In Matthew 3:16, Jesus Himself was baptized by John the Baptist, setting a precedent for His followers. Baptism was seen as a rite of initiation and repentance, as evidenced in Acts 2:38, where Peter calls on the people to "repent, and be baptized every one of you in the name of Jesus Christ for the remission of sins."

Development in Baptist Tradition

The Baptist tradition has a distinct understanding of baptism that developed during the Reformation. Early Baptists, such as John Smyth and Thomas Helwys, rejected infant baptism practiced by many other Christian denominations. They argued that baptism should only be administered to those who have made a personal profession of faith. This position is grounded in passages like Acts 8:36-38, where Philip baptizes the Ethiopian eunuch upon his profession of faith. This practice of believer's baptism by immersion has become a defining feature of Baptist identity.

Theological Significance

Scriptural Basis

Baptism is deeply rooted in Scripture. In Acts 2:41, those who accepted Peter's message were baptized, and "the same day there were added unto them about three thousand souls." This passage highlights baptism as a response to the gospel and an initiation into the Christian community. Romans 6:4 underscores the theological significance of baptism: "Therefore we are buried with him by baptism into death: that like as Christ was raised up from the dead by the glory of the Father, even so we also should walk in newness of life." This verse illustrates baptism as a symbol of the believer's identification with Christ's work of redemption.

Symbolism and Meaning

In Baptist theology, baptism symbolizes several key aspects of the Christian faith. It represents the believer's identification with Christ's death and resurrection, signifying a spiritual rebirth and the beginning of a new life in Christ. The immersion in water symbolizes the believer's death to sin and resurrection to a new life. This symbolism is reinforced by Colossians 2:12, which states, "Buried with him in baptism, wherein also ye are risen with him through the faith of the operation of God, who hath raised him from the dead."

Mode of Baptism

Immersion Practice

Baptists practice baptism by immersion, a method that aligns with the Greek word for baptism, "baptizo," which means "to immerse" or "to dip." This practice is based on the example of Jesus' baptism in Matthew 3:16, where He "went up straightway out of the water," indicating a full immersion. Immersion is also supported by passages such as John 3:23, which describes John the Baptist baptizing in Aenon near Salim "because there was much water there."

Historical and Theological Arguments

The emphasis on immersion over other modes, such as sprinkling or pouring, is rooted in theological and historical arguments. Baptists argue that immersion best represents the symbolism of burial and resurrection depicted in Romans 6:4. Additionally, historical records from early Christian practices and writings support immersion as the original mode of baptism.

Procedures and Practices

Baptismal Service

The baptismal service in Baptist churches typically involves several key elements. Candidates for baptism are often asked to give a brief testimony of their faith, affirming their belief in Christ and their readiness to follow Him. The actual act of baptism usually takes place in a baptistry or a body of water, where the candidate is fully immersed. The service may also include prayers, hymns, and a sermon focusing on the significance of baptism.

Preparation and Instruction

Preparation for baptism involves instruction in the meaning and implications of the ordinance. Candidates are often provided with classes or counseling sessions to understand the significance of baptism and the expectations of church membership. This instruction ensures that candidates are making an informed and meaningful commitment to their faith.

Case Studies and Reflections

Examples from Different Churches

Examining baptismal practices across various Baptist churches reveals some diversity in how the ordinance is observed. For example, some churches may incorporate elaborate ceremonies with testimonies and celebrations, while others may conduct simpler services. The context of the church and its cultural setting often influences these variations.

Personal Reflections

Personal experiences with baptism can provide valuable insights into its impact on individuals and communities. Many believers reflect on their baptism as a pivotal moment in their spiritual journey, marking a significant step in their commitment to Christ. These reflections highlight the profound personal and communal significance of the ordinance.

Conclusion

Summary of Key Points

This chapter has explored the practice of baptism within the Baptist tradition, examining its historical development, theological significance, and practical application. Baptism serves as a critical expression of faith, symbolizing the believer's identification with Christ and their entry into the Christian community.

Future Perspectives

Looking ahead, the practice of baptism will continue to be a central aspect of Baptist worship and identity. As Baptist churches engage with contemporary issues and cultural changes, the core principles of baptism—its symbolism, mode, and significance—will remain foundational to the Baptist understanding of faith and practice. The ongoing emphasis on believer's baptism by immersion will continue to shape the identity and witness of Baptist communities.

CHAPTER FIFTY-ONE
THE LORD'S SUPPER

Introduction

The Lord's Supper, also known as Communion, is a central ordinance in Baptist worship, deeply embedded in the practice and theology of the church. It serves as a profound expression of faith, a reminder of Christ's sacrifice, and a celebration of the new covenant. This chapter explores the history, theological significance, and practical aspects of the Lord's Supper within the Baptist tradition, examining its role in the life of the church and its impact on the faith community.

Historical Background

Origins and Early Practices

The Lord's Supper traces its origins to the Last Supper that Jesus shared with His disciples on the eve of His crucifixion. As recorded in Luke 22:19-20, Jesus took bread and wine, gave thanks, and instructed His disciples to "do this in remembrance of me." This act was instituted as a lasting memorial of His sacrifice and a means of spiritual nourishment for His followers.

Development in Baptist Tradition

In the Baptist tradition, the practice of the Lord's Supper has evolved while maintaining its core elements. Early Baptists, such as those in the 17th century, emphasized the ordinance's symbolic nature rather than viewing it as a sacrament that conveys grace. Baptists have historically rejected transubstantiation (the belief that the bread and wine become the actual body and blood of Christ) and instead view the elements as symbols that represent Christ's body and blood. This view aligns with passages such as 1 Corinthians 11:23-26, where Paul recounts the institution of the Lord's Supper and emphasizes its symbolic significance.

Theological Significance

Scriptural Basis

The theological foundation for the Lord's Supper is firmly rooted in Scripture. The primary passages include Luke 22:19-20, which details the institution of the ordinance, and 1 Corinthians 11:23-26, where Paul provides instructions for its observance. These passages highlight the importance of remembrance, proclamation, and participation in the Lord's Supper as acts of faith and devotion.

Symbolism and Meaning

In Baptist theology, the Lord's Supper is a symbolic act that represents several key aspects of the Christian faith. The bread symbolizes Christ's body, broken for believers, while the wine represents His blood, shed for the forgiveness of sins. This symbolism is reflected in 1 Corinthians 11:24-25, where Paul writes, "This is my body, which is broken for you: this do in remembrance of me" and "This cup is the new testament in my blood: this do ye, as oft as ye drink it, in remembrance of me."

The Lord's Supper serves as a reminder of Christ's sacrifice and a celebration of the new covenant established through His blood. It also functions as a means of spiritual nourishment and a way to express unity within the body of Christ, as emphasized in 1 Corinthians 10:16-17, which speaks of the communion of the body and blood of Christ and the unity it fosters among believers.

Practice and Procedures

Observance of the Lord's Supper

In Baptist churches, the Lord's Supper is typically observed regularly, though the frequency can vary from church to church. Some churches celebrate it weekly, while others do so monthly or quarterly. The observance usually involves a formal service where the elements of bread and wine (or grape juice) are distributed to the congregation.

Preparation and Participation

Preparation for the Lord's Supper often includes a period of self-examination and confession, as encouraged by 1 Corinthians 11:28, which states, "But let a man examine himself, and so let him eat of that bread, and drink of that cup." This preparation helps ensure that participants approach the ordinance with a clear conscience and a sincere heart.

During the service, the pastor or designated leader will typically offer a brief explanation of the elements and their significance, followed by the distribution and partaking of the bread and wine. The service may also include hymns, prayers, and a sermon that reflects on the meaning of the Lord's Supper.

Cultural Variations

Different Practices

Practices related to the Lord's Supper can vary among Baptist churches. Some churches use traditional elements of unleavened bread and wine, while others may opt for grape juice and various types of bread. The method of distribution can also differ, with some churches using individual cups and others employing a communal cup.

Impact on Worship

These variations reflect the diversity within the Baptist tradition and the adaptability of the ordinance to different cultural contexts. Regardless of the specific practices, the central focus remains on the symbolic meaning of the elements and the spiritual significance of the ordinance.

Personal Reflections and Observations

Personal Experiences

Personal experiences with the Lord's Supper can be deeply meaningful and transformative. Many believers reflect on the ordinance as a moment of spiritual renewal and a profound reminder of Christ's sacrifice. The communal aspect of the Lord's Supper also fosters a sense of unity and shared purpose among members of the church.

Case Studies

Examining different Baptist churches' practices can provide insights into how the Lord's Supper impacts the faith community. For example, some churches may emphasize the ordinance's role in fostering unity and reconciliation, while others may focus on its role in spiritual nourishment and personal reflection.

Conclusion

Summary of Key Points

This chapter has explored the significance of the Lord's Supper within the Baptist tradition, examining its historical origins, theological foundations, and practical observance. The Lord's Supper serves as a central ordinance that embodies key aspects of Baptist faith, including remembrance, proclamation, and unity.

Future Perspectives

As Baptist churches continue to engage with contemporary issues and cultural changes, the practice of the Lord's Supper will remain a vital aspect of worship and community life. The symbolic nature of the ordinance, its emphasis on remembrance and unity, and its role in spiritual nourishment will continue to shape Baptist worship and identity.

PART VI. A JOB FOR EVERYONE

CHAPTER FIFTY-TWO
INTRODUCTION TO CHURCH
COMMITTEES AND AUXILIARIES

Introduction

In Baptist churches, committees and auxiliaries are integral to maintaining an organized and effective ministry. Rooted in the belief of the priesthood of all believers, these groups facilitate shared responsibility and leadership within the church. This chapter explores the significance of committees and auxiliaries, grounded in biblical principles and Baptist tradition.

The Role of Committees and Auxiliaries in Baptist Churches

Committees: Committees in Baptist churches are essential for addressing various operational and ministry needs. They help manage the church's resources, provide oversight, and ensure effective functioning. The Bible supports the concept of organized leadership and delegation through several scriptures.

In Exodus 18:21, it is written, "But select capable men from all the people—men who fear God, trustworthy men who hate dishonest gain—and appoint them as officials over thousands, hundreds, fifties, and tens." This passage highlights the importance of selecting capable and trustworthy leaders to manage various responsibilities.

Similarly, 1 Corinthians 12:28 indicates that different roles and functions within the church are essential for its overall health and effectiveness: "And God has placed in the church first of all apostles, second prophets, third teachers, then miracles, then gifts of healing, of helping, of guidance, and of different kinds of tongues."

Auxiliaries: Auxiliaries focus on specialized areas of ministry and fellowship, providing targeted support and enhancing the church's outreach. Biblical principles support the role of specialized groups. Romans 12:4-8 underscores that every member has a unique role and contribution within the body of Christ: "For just as each of us has one body with many members, and these members do not all have the same function, so in Christ we, though many, form one body, and each member belongs to all the others... If it is serving, then serve; if it is teaching, then teach; if it is to encourage, then give encouragement; if it is giving, then give generously..."

Additionally, 1 Peter 4:10 encourages believers to use their gifts for the benefit of others: "Each of you should use whatever gift you have received to serve others, as faithful stewards of God's grace in its various forms."

Historical Context and Baptist Tradition

Baptist churches have a tradition of congregational governance and lay participation, reflecting a commitment to shared leadership and responsibility. This tradition is rooted in the biblical model of leadership and ministry.

Acts 6:2-4 illustrates the early church's approach to delegating responsibilities to ensure that all aspects of church life were managed effectively: "So the Twelve gathered all the disciples together and said, 'It would not be right for us to neglect the ministry of the word of God in order to wait on tables. Brothers and sisters, choose seven men from among you who are known to be full of the Spirit and wisdom. We will turn this responsibility over to them and will give our attention to prayer and the ministry of the word.'"

The Importance of Committees

Committees are vital for managing various aspects of church life, allowing pastors and leaders to focus on their primary responsibilities. Key committees in Baptist churches include the Finance Committee, which oversees budgeting and financial stewardship, supported by scriptures such as 1 Corinthians 4:2: "Now it is required that those who have been given a trust must prove faithful." The Property Committee manages church facilities, with Proverbs 24:3-4 emphasizing the importance of diligent management: "By wisdom a house is built, and through understanding it is established; through knowledge its rooms are filled with rare and beautiful treasures." The Personnel Committee handles hiring and supporting staff, with 1 Timothy 3:1-7 providing guidelines for church leaders, highlighting the importance of character and qualifications.

The Role of Auxiliaries

Auxiliaries enhance church life by focusing on specific groups or needs. Examples include the Women's Ministry, which supports the spiritual and practical needs of women, as instructed in Titus 2:3-5, where older women are encouraged to teach and guide younger women. The Men's Ministry engages men in spiritual growth and service, with Proverbs 27:17 underscoring the value of mutual encouragement and growth: "As iron sharpens iron, so one person sharpens another." The Youth Ministry provides for the spiritual development of young people, with 1 Timothy 4:12 encouraging the empowerment of youth within the church: "Don't let anyone look down on you because you are young, but set an example for the believers in speech, in conduct, in love, in faith, and in purity."

Best Practices for Effective Committees and Auxiliaries

To ensure effectiveness, Baptist churches should adopt several best practices. Clear objectives should be defined, as Proverbs 16:3 advises: "Commit to the Lord whatever you do, and he will establish your plans." Regular meetings should be scheduled to review progress and plan activities, in accordance with Hebrews 10:24-25, which emphasizes the importance of meeting together to encourage one another. Broad participation and leadership should be fostered, reflecting Ephesians 4:11-13, which describes how different roles contribute to the body of Christ's growth and unity.

Additionally, resources and training should be provided, as recommended in 2 Timothy 2:2: "And the things you have heard me say in the presence of many witnesses entrust reliable people who will also be qualified to teach others."

Conclusion

Committees and auxiliaries are crucial to the effective operation and ministry of Baptist churches. Grounded in biblical principles and Baptist tradition, these groups enable members to serve and lead in various capacities. By understanding their roles and implementing best practices, Baptist churches can enhance their ministry and better fulfill their mission.

CHAPTER FIFTY-THREE
UNDERSTANDING CHURCH
COMMITTEES

Introduction

In Baptist churches, committees are vital for managing various aspects of church life, ensuring that responsibilities are shared and tasks are handled efficiently. This chapter explores the nature and functions of church committees, their biblical foundations, and best practices for their operation.

Biblical Foundations for Church Committees

Committees are supported by biblical principles emphasizing shared leadership and delegation of responsibilities. Scriptures such as Exodus 18:21 and Acts 6:3 illustrate the importance of appointing capable individuals to manage different aspects of church life, allowing leaders to focus on their primary duties.

Types of Church Committees

Finance Committee: The Finance Committee is responsible for overseeing the church's financial matters, including budgeting, financial planning, and stewardship. This committee ensures that resources are managed effectively and transparently. Guided by 1 Corinthians 16:2, which emphasizes planned financial giving, the Finance Committee develops and monitors the church's budget, manages expenditures, and promotes financial integrity within the congregation.

Property Committee: Tasked with maintaining and improving the church's physical facilities, the Property Committee ensures that the church building and grounds are well-kept and functional. Proverbs 24:3-4 highlights the importance of diligent management and upkeep. This committee handles routine maintenance, repairs, and any necessary upgrades to ensure that the facilities support the church's mission and ministry.

Personnel Committee: The Personnel Committee manages the hiring, evaluation, and support of church staff. It plays a crucial role in ensuring that the church is staffed with qualified individuals who meet the biblical qualifications outlined in 1 Timothy 3:1-7. This committee addresses staff needs, conducts performance reviews, and provides support and development opportunities for church employees.

Outreach Committee: Focusing on community engagement and evangelism, the Outreach Committee works to extend the church's mission beyond its walls. Matthew 28:19-20 emphasizes the church's call to make disciples, and this committee develops and implements strategies for outreach and service projects that promote the gospel and meet community needs.

Worship Committee: The Worship Committee oversees the planning and execution of worship services. It collaborates with the pastor and worship leaders to ensure that services are spiritually enriching and aligned with biblical principles. Colossians 3:16 underscores the importance of teaching and admonishing one another through psalms, hymns, and spiritual songs, guiding the committee in creating meaningful worship experiences.

Education Committee: Responsible for the development and oversight of educational programs, the Education Committee ensures that Bible study, Sunday school, and other teaching activities are effective and spiritually enriching. This committee's work is supported by 2 Timothy 2:15, which encourages believers to present themselves as approved workers who handle the word of truth accurately.

Missions Committee: The Missions Committee focuses on supporting and organizing mission efforts both locally and globally. It plans mission trips, coordinates with missionaries, and supports outreach programs. Acts 1:8 highlights the church's role in being witnesses to the ends of the earth, guiding this committee's efforts in global and local missions.

Fellowship Committee: This committee is responsible for organizing events and activities that foster community and fellowship among church members. Hebrews 10:24-25 encourages believers to meet together and spur one another on toward love and good deeds. The Fellowship Committee plans events such as social gatherings, potlucks, and special celebrations to build relationships and strengthen the church community.

Technology Committee: The Technology Committee manages the church's technological needs, including audio-visual equipment, online presence, and digital communication. This committee ensures that technology supports the church's mission and enhances worship and ministry. While not directly referenced in scripture, the use of technology in ministry can be seen as a means to effectively reach and serve the congregation and community.

Health and Safety Committee: Focused on ensuring a safe and healthy environment for church activities, the Health and Safety Committee addresses issues such as emergency preparedness, health protocols, and building safety. While the specific role may not be detailed in scripture, principles of care and diligence can be found in 1 Corinthians 14:40, which advises that all things be done decently and in order.

Roles and Responsibilities of Committees

Each committee should have a clear structure with defined roles and responsibilities. The Chairperson leads meetings, sets agendas, and ensures that the committee fulfills its duties, as supported by 1 Timothy 3:1, which emphasizes the importance of responsible leadership. Committee members contribute to discussions, make decisions, and carry out tasks, reflecting the principle in Romans 12:4-5 that every member has a unique role within the body of Christ. The Secretary maintains records and keeps minutes of meetings, guided by Proverbs 25:2, which values accurate and diligent record-keeping.

Best Practices for Effective Committees

To ensure effectiveness, committees should establish clear objectives, schedule regular meetings, encourage member involvement, and provide training and support. Proverbs 16:3 encourages committing plans to the Lord for establishment, Hebrews 10:24-25 stresses the importance of regular meetings, 1 Corinthians 14:26 highlights the value of diverse contributions, and 2 Timothy 2:2 underscores the importance of training and equipping committee members.

Conclusion

Committees are essential for the effective operation and ministry of Baptist churches, enabling shared leadership and organized management of church functions. By understanding their roles, responsibilities, and best practices, Baptist churches can enhance their ministry and fulfill their mission more effectively.

CHAPTER FIFTY-FOUR
UNDERSTANDING CHURCH AUXILIARIES

Introduction

C hurch auxiliaries play a vital role in the life of Baptist churches, focusing on specialized areas of ministry and service. These groups support the overall mission of the church by addressing specific needs and enhancing the church's outreach and fellowship efforts. This chapter explores the nature of church auxiliaries, their functions, and their biblical foundations, providing insight into how they contribute to the church's mission.

Biblical Foundations for Church Auxiliaries

Auxiliaries are rooted in biblical principles that emphasize service, ministry, and the diversity of roles within the body of Christ. One key scripture, 1 Peter 4:10, calls on believers to "use whatever gift you have received to serve others, as faithful stewards of God's grace in its various forms." This verse underlines the importance of every church member utilizing their unique abilities to serve the broader community, forming a foundation for the purpose and work of auxiliaries.

Similarly, Romans 12:6-8 highlights the variety of gifts given to individuals, stressing that each person's contribution is vital to the life of the church. The passage states, "We have different gifts, according to the grace given to each of us. If your gift is prophesying, then prophesy in accordance with your faith... if it is serving, then serve; if it is teaching, then teach; if it is to encourage, then give encouragement." This scripture reflects the diversity of roles within the church, much like how auxiliaries serve distinct purposes, ensuring that the church operates as a unified, multifaceted body.

These verses underscore the biblical principle that auxiliaries function as extensions of the church's mission, mobilizing members to use their God-given talents for ministry and service. By adhering to these scriptural guidelines, auxiliaries ensure that each person's unique contributions help fulfill the broader mission of the church.

Types of Church Auxiliaries

Women's Ministry: The Women's Ministry focuses on the spiritual, emotional, and practical needs of women in the church. It organizes events, Bible studies, and support groups tailored to women's interests and needs. Titus 2:3-5 provides guidance for this ministry, instructing older women to teach and encourage younger women in various aspects of life, including faith, family, and personal conduct.

Men's Ministry: This auxiliary engages men in spiritual growth, fellowship, and service. It provides opportunities for men to connect, support one another, and participate in church activities. Proverbs 27:17 emphasizes the mutual sharpening and growth that occurs when men come together in fellowship and accountability.

Youth Ministry: The Youth Ministry is dedicated to the spiritual development and engagement of young people. It organizes activities, Bible studies, and service projects for youth. 1 Timothy 4:12 encourages young people to be examples in speech, conduct, love, faith, and purity, highlighting the importance of nurturing youth within the church.

Children's Ministry: Focused on the spiritual education and growth of children, this auxiliary provides age-appropriate teaching and activities. Matthew 19:14: "Jesus said, 'Let the little children come to me, and do not hinder them, for the kingdom of heaven belongs to such as these.'" This verse underscores the value of ministering to children and fostering their relationship with Christ.

Senior Adult Ministry: This ministry addresses the needs and interests of older adults in the congregation, offering fellowship, support, and activities tailored to their stage of life. Psalm 71:18: "Even when I am old and gray, do not forsake me, God, till I declare your power to the next generation, your mighty acts to all who are to come." This verse reflects the ongoing value and role of senior adults in the church.

Music Ministry: The Music Ministry focuses on enhancing worship through music. It involves choirs, bands, and soloists who lead and participate in worship services. Colossians 3:16 encourages the use of music to teach and admonish one another with psalms, hymns, and spiritual songs, reflecting the significance of music in worship.

Hospitality Ministry: This auxiliary is responsible for welcoming visitors and making them feel at home. It includes greeting new members, organizing receptions, and ensuring a warm atmosphere. Hebrews 13:2: "Do not forget to show hospitality to strangers, for by so doing some people have shown hospitality to angels without knowing it." This verse emphasizes the importance of hospitality in the church.

Prayer Ministry: The Prayer Ministry focuses on intercessory prayer, organizing prayer meetings, and supporting the congregation through prayer. 1 Thessalonians 5:16-18: "Rejoice always, pray continually, give thanks in all circumstances; for this is God's will for you in Christ Jesus." This passage highlights the importance of prayer in the life of the church.

Outreach Ministry: This auxiliary is involved in local and global outreach efforts, including evangelism, community service, and mission support. Acts 1:8: "But you will receive power when the Holy Spirit comes on you; and you will be my witnesses in Jerusalem, and in all Judea and Samaria, and to the ends of the earth." This verse guides the mission and outreach efforts of the church.

Roles and Responsibilities of Auxiliaries

Each church auxiliary operates with distinct roles and responsibilities that contribute to the overall mission of the church. Typically, an auxiliary has a leader or coordinator who oversees its activities. This individual is responsible for ensuring that the auxiliary's goals and efforts align with the church's mission. They often handle the planning of events, coordinating with church leadership, and managing the day-to-day operations of the auxiliary. Leadership within an auxiliary plays a crucial role in maintaining focus and driving the group's ministry forward.

Members of the auxiliary contribute by participating in the activities and initiatives of the ministry. They offer their ideas, talents, and time to support the auxiliary's work. Through their involvement, members bring life to the ministry, using their gifts to serve others and promote spiritual growth within the church community. As 1 Peter 4:10 reminds believers, their participation in such ministries is a way to faithfully steward God's grace.

Volunteers play an essential role in supporting auxiliaries by helping with specific tasks, events, and projects. Whether through assisting at events, coordinating logistics, or providing necessary support, volunteers ensure the smooth execution of the auxiliary's plans. Their willingness to offer their time and energy makes them an invaluable part of the success of the ministry.

Together, the leaders, members, and volunteers of church auxiliaries work in unity to advance the goals of the church and fulfill their shared mission of service and outreach.

Best Practices for Effective Auxiliaries

To ensure that church auxiliaries operate effectively and make a meaningful impact, Baptist churches should adopt several key best practices.

Establishing a clear mission and setting specific goals are foundational steps for each auxiliary. A well-defined mission helps align the auxiliary's activities with the broader objectives of the church, ensuring that its efforts are purposeful and intentional. Proverbs 16:3 underscores the importance of committing one's plans to the Lord, which is essential for successful ministry.

Regular meetings are another important practice for effective auxiliaries. These gatherings allow members to plan activities, assess progress, and address any challenges that may arise. Consistent communication fosters unity and ensures that everyone is aligned with the auxiliary's mission. Hebrews 10:24-25 highlights the value of regular fellowship and mutual encouragement, both of which are essential for ministry success.

Active participation from all members is crucial to an auxiliary's success. Every member is encouraged to contribute their gifts and talents, as 1 Corinthians 14:26 emphasizes the collective effort needed to build up the church. Engaging all members in the auxiliary's work fosters a sense of ownership and strengthens the ministry's impact.

Providing training and support to leaders and members is vital for maintaining an effective auxiliary. Equipping members with the necessary skills and knowledge ensures that they are prepared to carry out their responsibilities. As 2 Timothy 2:2 suggests, passing on knowledge and training to reliable individuals is critical for sustainable leadership and ministry development.

By adopting these practices, Baptist church auxiliaries can function more efficiently and contribute significantly to the church's mission, ensuring that their ministries flourish and remain aligned with biblical principles.

Conclusion

Auxiliaries are essential for the effective functioning and outreach of Baptist churches. By focusing on specialized areas of ministry and service, these groups enhance the church's ability to fulfill its mission. Understanding their roles, responsibilities, and best practices helps ensure that auxiliaries contribute positively to the church's overall mission and ministry.

CHAPTER FIFTY-FIVE
KEY RESPONSIBILITIES OF CHURCH AUXILIARIES

Introduction

Church auxiliaries play a crucial role in supporting the church's mission and ensuring that various aspects of ministry are effectively managed. Each auxiliary has specific responsibilities that align with its purpose and function. This chapter delves into the key responsibilities of different church auxiliaries, providing a comprehensive understanding of their roles and how they contribute to the church's overall mission.

Biblical Foundations for Responsibilities

The responsibilities of church auxiliaries are rooted in biblical principles that emphasize service, leadership, and stewardship within the church community. These responsibilities are guided by scriptures that highlight the diverse roles and the purpose of these roles in the body of Christ.

Diversity of Roles and Responsibilities

1 Corinthians 12:4-6 states, "There are different kinds of gifts, but the same Spirit distributes them. There are different kinds of service,

but the same Lord. There are different kinds of working, but in all of them and in everyone it is the same God at work." This passage emphasizes the diversity of roles and responsibilities within the church. Each auxiliary and its members are endowed with unique gifts and talents, all of which contribute to the overall functioning and health of the church. The variety of services and works reflects the multifaceted nature of the church's mission, where every role is vital and valued.

Equipping Believers for Service

Ephesians 4:11-12 highlights the purpose of various roles within the church: "So Christ himself gave the apostles, the prophets, the evangelists, the pastors and teachers, to equip his people for works of service, so that the body of Christ may be built up." This scripture underscores the objective of the different roles and responsibilities, which is to equip believers for service. Church auxiliaries play a crucial role in this equipping process, providing support and resources that enable members to actively participate in the ministry and contribute to the growth and strengthening of the church. The goal is to build up the body of Christ through service and leadership, ensuring that each member is empowered and prepared to fulfill their part in the church's mission.

Detailed Responsibilities of Church Auxiliaries

Women's Ministry: The Women's Ministry is dedicated to addressing the unique needs and interests of women within the church. It is responsible for organizing events and programs such as Bible studies, retreats, and fellowship activities tailored to women's spiritual growth and community building. This ministry also provides support and counseling to women facing life challenges, reflecting the biblical principle of mutual support. Additionally, the Women's Ministry leads service projects that benefit the community, using gifts in service to others as encouraged in 1 Peter 4:10.

Men's Ministry: The Men's Ministry focuses on fostering spiritual growth and fellowship among men. Its key responsibilities include facilitating Bible studies and fellowship meetings that promote mutual encouragement and accountability, in line with Proverbs 27:17. The ministry also plans outreach activities that advance the church's mission and provides support and accountability for men in their spiritual journeys. Through these activities, the Men's Ministry helps men grow in their faith and contribute to the church's work.

Youth Ministry: The Youth Ministry is tasked with the spiritual development of young people. Responsibilities include organizing youth events and activities such as retreats, Bible studies, and social gatherings that engage and inspire young members. The ministry provides mentorship and guidance to help youth navigate their spiritual and personal lives, in accordance with 1 Timothy 4:12. Additionally, the Youth Ministry involves young people in service and outreach projects, fostering a sense of mission and service as guided by Matthew 28:19-20.

Children's Ministry: The Children's Ministry focuses on teaching and nurturing children in their faith. This includes developing age-appropriate curriculum that teaches biblical truths in engaging ways, as emphasized in Deuteronomy 6:6-7. The ministry organizes activities and events such as Vacation Bible School and children's camps to provide fun and educational experiences. Ensuring a safe and nurturing environment for children is also a key responsibility, supported by Matthew 19:14, which highlights the importance of welcoming and nurturing children.

Senior Adult Ministry: The Senior Adult Ministry addresses the needs and interests of older adults in the church. Key responsibilities involve organizing fellowship and social events that foster community and engagement among senior adults, reflecting Psalm 71:18. The ministry provides support and resources for issues related to aging, such as health and financial planning. It also

300

UNAPOLOGETICALLY BAPTIST

encourages senior adults to remain actively involved in church life, recognizing their valuable contributions and experience.

Music Ministry: The Music Ministry is integral to worship, focusing on enhancing the worship experience through music. Responsibilities include planning and leading worship music, selecting and rehearsing songs that align with the church's worship goals. This role involves organizing and directing choirs and musical groups, providing leadership and support to enhance worship. Special musical events and programs are also planned to enrich the church's worship life, in line with Colossians 3:16, which encourages the use of music to teach and admonish.

Hospitality Ministry: The Hospitality Ministry ensures that visitors and members feel welcomed and valued. This includes greeting visitors and new members, organizing receptions and events such as welcome luncheons, and providing support during services. The ministry's role in making newcomers and members feel at home is supported by Hebrews 13:2, which emphasizes the importance of showing hospitality.

Prayer Ministry: The Prayer Ministry focuses on intercessory prayer and spiritual support for the congregation. Responsibilities include organizing prayer meetings and chains, providing prayer support for members facing various needs, and encouraging a culture of prayer throughout the church. 1 Thessalonians 5:16-18 underscores the importance of continual prayer in the life of the church.

Outreach Ministry: The Outreach Ministry is dedicated to extending the church's mission beyond its walls. This involves planning outreach events and programs such as community service projects, mission trips, and evangelistic activities. The ministry coordinates with missionaries and outreach partners to further the church's mission and develops strategies to engage with and serve the local community, as guided by Acts 1:8.

Conclusion

Church auxiliaries are essential for the effective functioning of Baptist churches, each with distinct responsibilities that support the church's mission and ministry. By understanding and fulfilling these responsibilities, auxiliaries contribute significantly to the overall health and effectiveness of the church. This chapter has provided an overview of the key responsibilities associated with various church auxiliaries, offering a framework for their effective operation and service.

CHAPTER FIFTY-SIX
EFFECTIVE MANAGEMENT AND COORDINATION OF CHURCH AUXILIARIES

Introduction

Effective management and coordination of church auxiliaries are essential for ensuring that these groups function efficiently and contribute positively to the overall mission of the church. This chapter explores strategies and best practices for managing and coordinating church auxiliaries, offering insights into how to foster effective teamwork, communication, and organizational structure.

Biblical Foundations for Management

The principles of effective management and coordination are deeply rooted in biblical teachings. Scriptures such as 1 Corinthians 14:40, which states, "But everything should be done in a fitting and orderly way," underscore the importance of order and structure in church activities. Proverbs 15:22 also highlights the value of planning and counsel: "Plans fail for lack of counsel, but with many advisers they succeed."

Strategies for Effective Management

1. Establish Clear Objectives and Goals

Each auxiliary should have clear objectives and goals aligned with the church's mission. Establishing these goals involves setting specific, measurable, achievable, relevant, and time-bound (SMART) objectives. This clarity ensures that each auxiliary understands its purpose and how its activities contribute to the broader mission of the church. Habakkuk 2:2 encourages writing down the vision so that it is clear and can be followed.

2. Develop a Structured Organizational Framework

A well-defined organizational framework is crucial for effective management. This includes creating roles and responsibilities for each member of the auxiliary, outlining reporting structures, and defining decision-making processes. A structured framework helps prevent confusion and ensures that tasks are completed efficiently. 1 Corinthians 12:18 reminds us that God has placed each part of the body in its proper place, emphasizing the importance of each member's role.

3. Promote Open and Effective Communication

Effective communication is key to managing church auxiliaries. Regular meetings should be held to discuss progress, address concerns, and plan future activities. Utilizing communication tools such as email, messaging apps, and newsletters can help keep everyone informed and engaged. Ephesians 4:29 advises: "Do not let any unwholesome talk come out of your mouths, but only what is helpful for building others up according to their needs."

4. Encourage Collaboration and Teamwork

Encouraging collaboration among members fosters a sense of unity and shared purpose. Creating opportunities for team-building activities, brainstorming sessions, and collaborative projects can enhance the effectiveness of the auxiliary. Ecclesiastes 4:9 states: "Two are better than one, because they have a good return for their labor," highlighting the benefits of working together.

5. Implement Training and Development Programs

Providing training and development opportunities helps members of auxiliaries enhance their skills and knowledge. This includes training in leadership, project management, and specific skills relevant to their roles. Investing in development not only improves the effectiveness of the auxiliary but also supports individual growth. Proverbs 1:5 says: "Let the wise hear and increase in learning, and the one who understands obtain guidance."

6. Establish Accountability and Evaluation Processes

Regular evaluation of the auxiliary's activities and performance is essential for continuous improvement. Establishing accountability measures and reviewing progress against goals can help identify areas for improvement and ensure that the auxiliary remains focused on its mission. 2 Corinthians 13:5 encourages self-examination and testing to ensure that one is living in accordance with faith.

7. Foster a Spirit of Service and Stewardship

A spirit of service and stewardship should permeate the work of church auxiliaries. Encouraging members to view their roles as a form of service to others and as a stewardship of their gifts can enhance their commitment and effectiveness. 1 Peter 4:10 encourages believers to use their gifts to serve others, as faithful stewards of God's grace.

Best Practices for Coordination

1. Coordination with Church Leadership

Auxiliaries should coordinate closely with church leadership to ensure alignment with the church's overall vision and goals. Regular updates and feedback sessions with pastors and church leaders can help maintain this alignment and address any issues that arise.

2. Integration with Church Activities

Auxiliaries should be integrated into the broader activities of the church. This involves coordinating with other ministries and auxiliaries to avoid duplication of efforts and to leverage resources effectively. 1 Corinthians 12:12 illustrates the interconnectedness of different parts of the body, emphasizing the importance of coordination.

3. Effective Use of Resources

Efficient use of resources, including time, money, and volunteers, is crucial for the effective functioning of auxiliaries. Budgeting, resource allocation, and planning should be done thoughtfully to maximize the impact of the auxiliary's activities. Matthew 25:14-30 (The Parable of the Talents) teaches the importance of using resources wisely and responsibly.

4. Conflict Resolution

Addressing conflicts within auxiliaries promptly and effectively is essential for maintaining a positive working environment. Implementing conflict resolution strategies and encouraging open dialogue can help resolve issues and prevent them from escalating. Matthew 18:15-17 provides guidance on resolving disputes in a manner that promotes reconciliation and understanding.

Conclusion

Effective management and coordination of church auxiliaries are critical for the success of their ministries and the overall mission of the church. By establishing clear objectives, promoting open communication, encouraging collaboration, and implementing best practices, church leaders can ensure that auxiliaries function effectively and contribute positively to the church's work. This chapter has provided a framework for managing and coordinating church auxiliaries, offering practical strategies and biblical principles to guide their operation.

CHAPTER FIFTY-SEVEN
CHALLENGES AND SOLUTIONS IN
MANAGING CHURCH AUXILIARIES

Introduction

Managing church auxiliaries presents unique challenges that can impact their effectiveness and the overall health of the church. Understanding these challenges and exploring practical solutions are crucial for maintaining vibrant and productive auxiliary ministries. This chapter addresses common issues faced by church auxiliaries and offers strategies to overcome them, ensuring that auxiliaries can fulfill their roles effectively and contribute to the church's mission.

Biblical Perspective on Overcoming Challenges

The Bible provides guidance and encouragement for overcoming challenges. James 1:2-4 teaches that facing trials with faith and perseverance leads to growth and maturity. Philippians 4:13 reminds us that with Christ's strength, we can overcome difficulties. These scriptures underscore the importance of relying on faith and seeking God's guidance in addressing challenges within church auxiliaries.

Common Challenges and Solutions

1. Volunteer Recruitment and Retention

One of the significant challenges for church auxiliaries is finding and retaining volunteers. Many churches struggle with having enough volunteers to fill roles and sustain programs. To address this challenge, it is important to actively recruit and engage members through targeted communication and outreach. Highlighting the impact and importance of auxiliary roles can inspire members to get involved. Offering flexible volunteer opportunities and recognizing the contributions of volunteers can also help with retention. Matthew 9:37-38 encourages prayer for more workers in the harvest, acknowledging the need for more volunteers and the role of prayer in addressing this need.

2. Limited Resources

Church auxiliaries often operate with limited financial and material resources, which can restrict their ability to carry out activities and projects. Effective resource management and creative problem-solving are key to overcoming this challenge. Auxiliaries can seek donations, fundraisers, and grants to supplement their budgets. Collaborating with other ministries and leveraging in-kind donations can also help maximize resources. 2 Corinthians 9:8 assures that God provides for every need, and churches can trust in His provision while using resources wisely.

3. Conflicts and Disagreements

Conflicts and disagreements among auxiliary members can disrupt harmony and hinder productivity. Implementing conflict resolution strategies and fostering a culture of open communication can help address conflicts constructively. Establishing clear guidelines for resolving disputes and providing mediation when necessary can also contribute to a positive working environment. Matthew 18:15-17 provides a biblical framework for addressing conflicts and promoting reconciliation.

4. Lack of Engagement and Motivation

Maintaining high levels of engagement and motivation among auxiliary members can be difficult, especially when members are balancing multiple responsibilities. Encouraging regular feedback and involving members in decision-making processes can help increase engagement. Providing opportunities for personal and spiritual growth, as well as recognizing and celebrating achievements, can also enhance motivation. Hebrews 10:24-25 emphasizes the importance of encouraging one another and meeting together, which can foster a sense of community and motivation.

5. Ineffective Communication

Poor communication within auxiliaries can lead to misunderstandings, inefficiencies, and lack of cohesion. Establishing clear communication channels and protocols is essential for effective management. Regular meetings, updates, and the use of communication tools can help ensure that everyone is informed and aligned. Proverbs 15:1 highlights the importance of a gentle answer and thoughtful communication in maintaining good relationships.

6. Resistance to Change

Auxiliaries may encounter resistance when implementing new initiatives or changes to existing processes. To manage resistance, involve members in the change process and provide clear explanations of the reasons for changes. Offering training and support to help members adapt can also ease the transition. Isaiah 43:19 speaks of God doing new things, encouraging a positive view of change and progress.

7. Balancing Multiple Responsibilities

Members of auxiliaries often juggle multiple responsibilities, leading to potential burnout or neglect of auxiliary duties. Encouraging members to prioritize their responsibilities and providing support can help manage this challenge. Delegating tasks and offering assistance when needed can also alleviate the burden on individual members. Galatians 6:2 encourages carrying each other's burdens, reflecting the importance of mutual support and shared responsibilities.

Conclusion

Managing church auxiliaries involves navigating various challenges that can impact their effectiveness and the overall health of the church. By understanding these challenges and implementing practical solutions, church leaders and auxiliary members can work together to overcome obstacles and achieve their goals. This chapter has explored common challenges and provided strategies for addressing them, emphasizing the importance of faith, communication, and collaboration in maintaining vibrant and effective auxiliary ministries.

CHAPTER FIFTY-EIGHT
EVALUATING AND IMPROVING THE EFFECTIVENESS OF CHURCH AUXILIARIES

Introduction

C ontinuous evaluation and improvement are crucial for ensuring that church auxiliaries remain effective and aligned with the church's mission. Regular assessment helps identify strengths and areas for improvement, enabling auxiliaries to enhance their contributions and better serve the congregation. This chapter outlines strategies for evaluating the effectiveness of church auxiliaries and offers practical steps for implementing improvements.

Biblical Foundations for Evaluation and Improvement

The Bible encourages self-examination and continual growth. 2 Corinthians 13:5 urges believers to examine themselves to ensure they are in the faith, reflecting the importance of self-assessment. Proverbs 27:17 highlights the value of mutual feedback and accountability, emphasizing that evaluation leads to growth and improvement.

Strategies for Evaluating Effectiveness

1. Define Clear Metrics and Objectives

To evaluate the effectiveness of auxiliaries, it is essential to define clear metrics and objectives. These should align with the church's mission and the specific goals of the auxiliary. Metrics may include participation rates, the impact of programs, member satisfaction, and achievement of set objectives. Habakkuk 2:2 encourages writing down and making vision clear, which helps in setting and measuring goals.

2. Conduct Regular Reviews and Assessments

Regular reviews and assessments provide opportunities to evaluate progress and address any issues. This can be done through surveys, feedback forms, and performance reviews. Scheduled evaluations, such as quarterly or annual reviews, help maintain focus and address concerns proactively. 1 Timothy 4:15 advises giving attention to one's progress and growth, which can be applied to assessing the effectiveness of auxiliaries.

3. Gather Feedback from Members

Collecting feedback from auxiliary members and the broader congregation is crucial for understanding the impact and effectiveness of the auxiliary's activities. This feedback can be gathered through surveys, focus groups, and one-on-one conversations. Proverbs 15:22 emphasizes the importance of seeking counsel and feedback for successful planning and decision-making.

4. Evaluate Impact on the Church's Mission

Assessing how well an auxiliary's activities contribute to the church's mission is essential. This involves reviewing whether the auxiliary's programs and efforts align with the overall goals of the church and support its mission. Matthew 28:19-20 calls for making disciples and fulfilling the Great Commission, which can guide the evaluation of an auxiliary's impact.

5. Identify Strengths and Areas for Improvement

A thorough evaluation should identify both strengths and areas for improvement. Recognizing strengths allows for the reinforcement of successful practices, while identifying areas for improvement provides opportunities for growth and development. Philippians 1:6 assures that God completes the good work He begins, encouraging ongoing efforts to enhance effectiveness.

6. Implement Action Plans for Improvement

Based on evaluation results, developing and implementing action plans for improvement is essential. These plans should address identified areas for improvement and include specific steps, timelines, and responsibilities. James 2:14-26 underscores the importance of action in faith, which can be applied to taking steps towards improvement.

7. Provide Training and Support

Ongoing training and support for auxiliary members can enhance their skills and effectiveness. Offering workshops, seminars, and mentorship opportunities helps members develop the competencies needed for their roles. Ephesians 4:11-12 speaks to equipping the saints for the work of ministry, which aligns with providing training and support.

8. Celebrate Achievements and Successes

Recognizing and celebrating achievements and successes boosts morale and encourages continued effort. Acknowledging the contributions and accomplishments of auxiliary members fosters a positive environment and motivates ongoing participation. 1

Thessalonians 5:11 encourages encouraging and building each other up, which includes celebrating successes.

Steps for Continuous Improvement

1. Set Regular Evaluation Dates

Establish a schedule for regular evaluations to ensure ongoing assessment and improvement. This could include quarterly reviews, annual evaluations, or periodic check-ins depending on the auxiliary's activities and goals.

2. Foster a Culture of Feedback

Create an environment where feedback is welcomed and valued. Encourage open communication and constructive criticism to support continuous improvement and growth.

3. Encourage Innovation and Adaptability

Promote a culture of innovation and adaptability within auxiliaries. Encourage members to explore new ideas and approaches, and be open to making changes that enhance effectiveness.

4. Monitor Progress and Adjust Strategies

Continuously monitor progress towards goals and adjust strategies as needed. Regularly review action plans and make necessary adjustments to stay aligned with the church's mission and objectives.

5. Involve Members in the Improvement Process

Involve auxiliary members in the evaluation and improvement process. Engaging members in identifying issues and developing solutions fosters a sense of ownership and commitment to the auxiliary's success.

Conclusion

Evaluating and improving the effectiveness of church auxiliaries is essential for their ongoing success and contribution to the church's mission. By defining clear metrics, conducting regular reviews, gathering feedback, and implementing action plans, auxiliaries can enhance their impact and effectiveness. This chapter has outlined strategies for evaluation and improvement, emphasizing the importance of ongoing assessment and growth in maintaining vibrant and productive auxiliary ministries.

CHAPTER FIFTY-NINE
CASE STUDIES AND BEST PRACTICES IN CHURCH MANAGEMENT

Introduction

Case studies and best practices provide valuable insights into the effective management of church committees, boards, and auxiliaries. By examining real-world examples and successful strategies, church leaders can learn from the experiences of others and apply proven methods to their own contexts. This chapter explores notable case studies and highlights best practices that exemplify effective church management within the Baptist tradition.

Biblical Foundation for Learning from Examples

The Bible encourages learning from examples and experiences to gain wisdom and understanding. Proverbs 27:17 reflects this principle with the statement, "As iron sharpens iron, so one person sharpens another," underscoring the value of learning from others. Additionally, 1 Corinthians 10:11 reminds us that "these things happened to them as examples and were written down as warnings for us," emphasizing the importance of examining past experiences for guidance.

Case Study 1: The Transformation of Community Outreach Programs

A mid-sized Baptist church in Texas revitalized its community outreach programs by reorganizing its committees and enhancing collaboration among auxiliaries. Facing declining participation and ineffective outreach efforts, the church established a Community Outreach Committee composed of representatives from various auxiliaries, such as the Women's Missionary Society and the Youth Ministry.

They conducted a needs assessment and aligned their outreach initiatives with the community's most pressing needs. This revitalization led to increased community engagement, improved attendance at outreach events, and stronger partnerships with local organizations. The collaborative approach fostered a sense of shared purpose and effectiveness.

Key takeaways include involving multiple auxiliaries in planning and implementing outreach programs, conducting regular needs assessments to ensure relevance, and fostering collaboration to leverage diverse skills and resources.

Case Study 2: Streamlining Financial Management through Effective Policies

A large Baptist church in Georgia faced challenges with financial transparency and accountability due to inconsistent financial practices among its various boards and committees. To address this, the church implemented a comprehensive financial management policy that included clear procedures for budgeting, expense approvals, and reporting.

They provided training for board members and auxiliary leaders on financial best practices and established regular audits. These measures improved financial transparency, reduced errors, and enhanced accountability. The church experienced greater trust from the congregation and more efficient financial operations.

Key takeaways are developing and enforcing clear financial management policies, providing training and resources to ensure adherence, and conducting regular audits to maintain transparency.

Case Study 3: Enhancing Volunteer Engagement through Strategic Leadership

A Baptist church in Florida struggled with low volunteer engagement in its various ministries and auxiliaries. Recognizing the need to enhance volunteer recruitment and retention, the church established a Volunteer Coordination Committee to oversee recruitment, training, and recognition.

They implemented a structured onboarding process and created a volunteer recognition program to acknowledge contributions. This strategic approach led to increased volunteer participation, higher satisfaction among volunteers, and more effective ministry operations. The church experienced a more vibrant and engaged volunteer base.

Key takeaways include creating a dedicated committee to manage volunteer engagement, implementing structured onboarding and training processes, and recognizing and appreciating volunteers to boost morale.

Best Practices for Effective Church Management

To enhance church management, several best practices have emerged. First, fostering collaboration across auxiliaries can leverage diverse skills and resources, enhancing the effectiveness of church ministries. Second, developing clear policies and procedures for various aspects of church management—such as finance, governance, and volunteer management—helps ensure transparency and accountability. Third, investing in regular training and development opportunities for church leaders and members, including leadership training, financial management, and effective communication skills, is crucial.

Fourth, emphasizing transparency and accountability through regular reporting, audits, and open communication contributes to trust and effective management. Fifth, utilizing technology and innovative solutions, such as management software, digital communication tools, and online resources for training and outreach, can enhance church operations. Lastly, regularly evaluating the effectiveness of church programs and management practices, being open to feedback, and adapting strategies to meet changing needs and circumstances are essential for continuous improvement.

Conclusion

Case studies and best practices offer valuable lessons for managing church committees, boards, and auxiliaries. By learning from successful examples and implementing proven strategies, church leaders can enhance the effectiveness of their ministries and support the church's mission more effectively. This chapter has highlighted key takeaways from real-world experiences and provided practical recommendations for achieving excellence in church management.

CHAPTER SIXTY
FUTURE TRENDS AND INNOVATIONS IN
CHURCH MANAGEMENT

Introduction

As the landscape of church management evolves, it is essential for Baptist churches to stay informed about emerging trends and innovations that can enhance their operations and ministry effectiveness. This chapter explores future trends and technological advancements that are shaping church management, providing insights into how these developments can be integrated into Baptist church practices.

Biblical Foundation for Embracing Change

The Bible acknowledges the importance of being adaptable and wise in response to changing circumstances. Ecclesiastes 3:1 reflects the need for adaptability with the statement, "There is a time for everything, and a season for every activity under the heavens." Additionally, Matthew 9:17 notes that new wine requires new wineskins, suggesting that new methods may be necessary for new circumstances.

Emerging Trends in Church Management

Digital transformation is reshaping how churches operate and engage with their congregations. This trend includes the adoption of digital tools for communication, financial management, and worship services. Churches are increasingly using platforms for online giving, virtual meetings, and live streaming services. Key considerations include implementing online platforms for giving, communication, and service streaming to expand outreach and increase engagement. Additionally, utilizing digital tools for managing church records, communications, and analytics can streamline operations and enhance decision-making.

The use of data analytics is becoming more prevalent in church management, allowing churches to make informed decisions based on insights from congregational data. This includes tracking attendance, giving patterns, and engagement levels to improve ministry effectiveness. Important considerations involve implementing systems to collect and analyze data related to church operations and congregational engagement, and using these insights to make strategic decisions, set goals, and evaluate the impact of various programs and initiatives.

With the rise of digital technology, many churches are offering hybrid worship services that combine in-person and online experiences. This approach allows churches to reach a broader audience and accommodate diverse preferences for worship. Key considerations for this trend include investing in technology to support hybrid services, such as audio-visual equipment and streaming software, and ensuring that both in-person and online worship experiences are engaging and inclusive for all participants.

Churches are increasingly focusing on community engagement through innovative outreach programs and partnerships. This includes collaborating with local organizations, using social media for outreach, and developing programs that address specific community needs. To enhance community impact and outreach, building relationships with local organizations is essential. Additionally, utilizing social media platforms to connect with the community, share information, and promote events is becoming increasingly important.

Sustainability is becoming a key focus for many churches, with efforts to reduce their environmental impact and promote stewardship of resources. This includes implementing green practices in church operations and encouraging environmental responsibility among members. Key considerations include adopting green initiatives such as energy efficiency, waste reduction, and sustainable building design, as well as educating congregants about environmental stewardship and encouraging participation in sustainable practices.

Innovations in Church Management

Virtual Reality (VR) and Augmented Reality (AR) technologies are beginning to be explored for immersive worship experiences, virtual tours, and interactive Bible studies. These technologies offer new ways to engage with congregants and provide innovative learning opportunities. Considerations for these technologies include exploring how VR and AR can enhance worship experiences and educational programs, and ensuring that these technologies are accessible to all members, including those with limited technological resources.

Artificial Intelligence (AI) and automation are being used to streamline administrative tasks, manage communications, and analyze data. Chatbots, automated scheduling, and AI-driven insights can improve efficiency and reduce the burden on church staff. Key considerations involve identifying areas where AI and automation can enhance efficiency, such as scheduling, communication, and data analysis, while also considering the ethical implications and ensuring that technology supports rather than replaces human interactions.

Online learning platforms are increasingly used for Bible studies, leadership training, and discipleship programs. These platforms offer flexible and accessible options for spiritual growth and education. Important considerations include selecting user-friendly online learning platforms that provide engaging content, and ensuring that online resources are accessible to all members, including those with varying levels of technological proficiency.

Preparing for Future Trends

To prepare for future trends, it is important to invest in training and development for church leaders and members. This includes staying informed about new technologies, best practices, and emerging trends in church management. Key considerations involve providing ongoing education opportunities for leaders to learn about new technologies and management practices and fostering a culture of adaptability and openness to change within the church.

Incorporating future trends into the church's strategic planning process is also crucial. Developing long-term goals and strategies that align with emerging trends and innovations will be important. Considerations include developing a vision that embraces new technologies and trends, and setting specific, measurable goals related to integrating innovations into church operations.

Conclusion

Future trends and innovations are shaping the landscape of church management, offering new opportunities for engagement, efficiency, and impact. By staying informed about emerging trends and integrating innovative practices, Baptist churches can enhance their operations and ministry efforts. This chapter has provided insights into key trends and innovations, offering practical recommendations for preparing for and embracing the future of church management.

PART VII. KEY OBSERVANCES AND TRADITIONS

CHAPTER SIXTY-ONE
THE RICH TRADITION OF BAPTIST OBSERVANCES

Introduction

The Baptist Church is characterized by a rich tapestry of traditions that reflect both its historical faith and current practices. Among these traditions, various observances play a pivotal role in shaping the church's life and rhythm. These observances are far more than mere rituals; they are deeply rooted in biblical principles, historical developments, and communal significance. They offer unique opportunities for reflection, celebration, and spiritual growth within the church community. By engaging in these observances, members connect with their faith and heritage, reinforcing the church's sense of identity and purpose.

Traditions and Their Significance

Traditions within the Baptist Church serve as markers of its faith journey, linking present-day practices with the historical experiences of its forebears. Each tradition, including the various observances, acts as a living expression of the church's identity, mission, and spiritual heritage. They are designed to foster a sense of continuity and purpose, connecting the congregation to its past and its future. Through these observances, the church maintains a link to its history while looking forward to its continued growth and impact.

Observances as Expressions of Faith

Observances in the Baptist Church embody profound spiritual truths and communal values. They are crafted to engage the church community in meaningful ways, grounded in biblical teachings and shaped by historical practices. These observances are integral to the church's worship life, reinforcing its commitment to Scripture and providing opportunities for collective growth and celebration. They serve not only as acts of worship but also as key moments for the congregation to reflect on and deepen their spiritual journey.

Biblical and Historical Foundations

The observances practiced in Baptist churches are deeply rooted in both biblical and historical contexts. The New Testament provides examples of communal worship and special observances that continue to inform Baptist practices today. For instance, the early church, as described in Acts 2:42-47, exemplified the importance of communal worship, shared meals, and prayer, which are central to Baptist practices like Church Anniversaries and Fellowship Events. These observances reflect the early church's model of unity and communal faith, emphasizing the importance of coming together to celebrate and support one another in the faith.

Similarly, Paul's instructions in 1 Corinthians 14:26-33 provide guidance on the conduct of worship and the use of spiritual gifts within the church. Paul emphasizes the need for order and edification in worship, where every participant contributes to the building up of the church. This principle guides practices such as Choir Anniversaries and Minister Ordinations, ensuring that these observances are conducted in a manner that is orderly, respectful, and focused on the edification of the congregation.

The Old Testament offers a rich heritage of annual festivals and sacred assemblies, as outlined in Leviticus 23. These festivals, including Passover, the Feast of Weeks, and the Feast of Tabernacles, served as occasions for communal worship, remembrance, and celebration. Baptist observances, such as Church Anniversaries and Revival Services, echo these practices by creating regular opportunities for the congregation to remember and celebrate God's work in their lives and in the church's history.

Echoing Biblical Themes

Observances like Church Anniversaries are designed to reflect themes of gratitude and remembrance. Just as the annual festivals in the Old Testament served to remind Israel of God's faithfulness and provision, Church Anniversaries provide Baptist congregations with an opportunity to reflect on and give thanks for God's faithfulness throughout the church's history. These observances help cultivate a spirit of thanksgiving and acknowledgment of God's continued presence and blessings.

The practice of ordaining ministers and installing pastors is grounded in the New Testament teachings on spiritual leadership and authority. Passages such as 1 Timothy 3:1-13 and Titus 1:5-9 outline the qualifications and responsibilities of church leaders, emphasizing the importance of appointing individuals who are called and equipped for ministry. Baptist practices of Minister Ordination and Pastoral Installation honor these biblical principles by publicly recognizing and setting apart individuals for leadership roles within the church.

Revival Services in Baptist churches are rooted in the biblical call to repentance and spiritual renewal. The Old Testament prophets frequently called Israel to return to God with repentance and a renewed commitment to His ways (e.g., Joel 2:12-13, Isaiah 55:6-7). Similarly, New Testament passages such as 2 Corinthians 7:10 emphasize the transformative power of repentance and godly sorrow. Baptist revivals provide a focused time for the church to seek spiritual renewal, deepen their commitment to God, and experience His transformative work in their lives.

The Bible as Foundation and Guide

The Bible serves not just as a reference point but as the foundational guide that shapes and informs Baptist observances. Each observance is designed to align with biblical teachings and principles, ensuring that they remain true to the faith and purpose of the church. As Jude 1:3 exhorts, the faith once delivered to the saints is the standard by which these observances are measured, ensuring their authenticity and spiritual significance. By grounding their practices in Scripture, Baptist churches ensure that their observances are both meaningful and faithful to the tradition of biblical worship.

Cultural and Historical Context

While the biblical foundations of these observances are clear, their expression within Baptist churches has also been shaped by cultural and historical factors. The African American Baptist tradition, in particular, has enriched these observances with its own distinctive practices and emphases. For instance, the tradition of the Church Anniversary is deeply intertwined with the history of African American communities, where the church has often been a central hub of social, cultural, and spiritual life.

Similarly, events like the Pastor's and Musician's Appreciation services have developed in response to the unique needs and dynamics of Baptist congregations. These observances reflect a deep respect for leadership and a recognition of the vital role that music and worship play in the life of the church. Understanding the historical and cultural context of these observances helps appreciate their significance more fully and reveals how they continue to evolve in response to the church's needs.

An Overview of Key Observances

In the chapters that follow, we will explore seventeen key observances that are widely practiced in Baptist churches:

1. **Church Anniversary:** A celebration of the church's founding, growth, and ongoing mission.
2. **Pastor's Anniversary (Appreciation):** An opportunity to honor and recognize the pastor's leadership and ministry.
3. **Musician's Appreciation:** A recognition of the musicians who contribute to the church's vibrant worship life.
4. **Choir Anniversary:** A celebration of the choir's ministry and its crucial role in leading worship.
5. **Church Picnic:** A time of fellowship and relaxation, promoting community and connection among members.
6. **Family & Friends Day:** Encourages the inclusion of family and friends in church life, celebrating their role in the community.
7. **Homecoming:** Welcomes back former members and celebrates the church's ongoing mission.
8. **Men's and Women's Day:** Honors the distinct roles and contributions of men and women in the church.
9. **Installation of Church Officers:** Recognizes the formal appointment of church leaders and officers.
10. **Missionary Day:** Highlights the church's commitment to missions and outreach, celebrating missionary efforts.
11. **Minister Ordination:** The setting apart of individuals for pastoral ministry, marking their formal entry into service.
12. **Deacon Ordination:** The commissioning of deacons to serve and support the church's ministry.
13. **Pastoral Installation:** A formal recognition of a pastor's call and responsibility to lead a specific congregation.
14. **Revival Services:** Focused periods of spiritual renewal and evangelism.
15. **Youth and Children's Day:** Celebrates the involvement and contributions of young members, emphasizing their role in the church community.

16. **Easter Sunrise Service**: A special worship service held early on Easter Sunday to celebrate the resurrection of Jesus Christ.
17. **Watch Night Service**: Observed on New Year's Eve, it is a time for reflection, prayer, and anticipation as believers mark the transition from one year to the next.

Each of these observances will be examined in detail, including their biblical foundations, historical development, and practical outlines for implementation. Scripture references will anchor each observance in the Word of God, ensuring that these practices are not only meaningful but also theologically sound.

Conclusion

As we delve into each observance, we uncover their profound impact on the spiritual vitality of the Baptist Church. These observances are not merely traditions passed down through generations; they are vital components of the church's worship life, teaching ministry, and community-building efforts. Each observance serves a distinct purpose, yet collectively, they contribute to the overall health and vibrancy of the church.

Observances such as Communion, Baptism, and Revivals are deeply embedded in the worship practices of Baptist churches. They provide structured opportunities for members to engage in acts of worship that honor God and reflect the core tenets of their faith. For example, Communion serves as a regular reminder of Christ's sacrifice and a celebration of His covenant with His people. Similarly, Revivals offer a focused period for repentance, renewal, and spiritual awakening, reinvigorating the church's commitment to God. These observances elevate worship from routine to profound, allowing congregants to experience and express their faith in transformative ways.

Many observances are designed to reinforce biblical teaching and doctrinal instruction. For instance, Pastor's Anniversaries and Minister Ordinations provide opportunities to reflect on the biblical qualifications and roles of church leaders, drawing from Scriptures that outline their responsibilities and significance. These occasions offer platforms for teaching about leadership within the church and the importance of following biblical principles in ministry. By integrating teaching with practice, these observances ensure that the church's teachings are lived out in the context of real-life ministry.

Observances such as Church Anniversaries, Choir Anniversaries, and Church Picnics play crucial roles in fostering community and strengthening relationships within the church. These events create spaces for fellowship, celebration, and mutual support, reinforcing the sense of belonging and shared purpose among members. A Church Picnic, for example, provides a relaxed setting for members to interact and build connections outside the formal worship environment. This sense of community and mutual support is essential for the church's health and growth.

As we examine each observance, it becomes clear that they are more than just rituals—they are expressions of the church's faith, values, and mission. They offer tangible ways for congregations to live out their beliefs, celebrate their heritage, and engage with their community. By understanding and embracing these observances, Baptist churches can continue to enrich their worship life, deepen their spiritual commitment, and strengthen their role in the broader community.

CHAPTER SIXTY-TWO
THE CHURCH ANNIVERSARY

Introduction

The Church Anniversary is a profound observance in the life of a Baptist church, marking the passage of time and celebrating God's enduring faithfulness. It is more than a mere commemoration; it is a sacred occasion for reflection, celebration, and renewal. This chapter explores the Church Anniversary's significance, its biblical and historical roots, and provides a comprehensive guide for planning and executing this pivotal observance.

Biblical Foundations

Celebrating anniversaries and milestones is deeply rooted in Scripture. The Old Testament emphasizes the importance of remembering and commemorating significant events in communal life. For instance, Leviticus 23 outlines various festivals and feasts, such as Passover and the Feast of Weeks, which were instituted to commemorate God's faithfulness and provision. These celebrations served as a means to remember God's deeds and reinforce communal identity.

In the New Testament, early church practices reflect similar themes of regular gatherings for reflection and celebration. Acts 2:42-47 describes the early believers' dedication to communal worship, fellowship, and the breaking of bread. The Apostle Paul's instructions in 1 Corinthians 14:26-33 highlight the importance of orderly worship and mutual edification, guiding the Church Anniversary to build up the congregation in faith and unity.

Historical Development

The tradition of celebrating a Church Anniversary has evolved significantly over the centuries, mirroring the growth and development of Christian communities. Early Christians commemorated pivotal milestones such as the establishment of a church or notable occurrences in its history, reinforcing both God's faithfulness and the community's spiritual identity.

In the Baptist tradition, the Church Anniversary has become a more formalized observance, characterized by structured services, celebratory events, and historical reflections. This evolution reflects the church's role as a cornerstone of faith and community life. Baptist churches have adapted this practice to fit their context, emphasizing the celebration of past achievements and a renewed commitment to future ministry.

Typically, Baptist Church Anniversaries involve recounting the church's history, honoring past and present leaders, and celebrating the congregation's achievements. This reflection highlights the church's growth and impact while inspiring the congregation to continue their mission with renewed vigor.

Theological Significance

Theologically, the Church Anniversary is a time to acknowledge God's continued presence and faithfulness. It is an opportunity for the congregation to reflect on the church's journey, celebrate its achievements, and renew its commitment to the mission. The anniversary serves as a reminder of God's guidance and the collective efforts of the church community in advancing God's kingdom. It provides a moment to express gratitude and reinforce the church's identity and purpose.

Planning the Church Anniversary

Effective planning is crucial for a successful Church Anniversary. Begin by selecting a date and theme that align with the church's calendar and the celebration's purpose. Whether marking a milestone, reflecting on God's faithfulness, or renewing the church's mission, ensure the theme reflects the focus of the anniversary.

Assemble a dedicated planning committee to manage the event. This team should include individuals skilled in event planning, worship coordination, and administration. Develop a comprehensive budget to cover expenses such as decorations, catering, and special guests. Seek resources and donations from the congregation to support the event financially.

Promotion and communication are vital. Announce the event well in advance through various channels—church announcements, newsletters, and social media—to ensure broad awareness and engagement.

Service Outline

1. **Opening Worship**: Begin the service with a time of praise and worship, setting a tone of celebration and gratitude. Include hymns and worship songs that reflect the theme of the anniversary.
2. **Historical Reflection**: Share a reflection on the church's history, highlighting key milestones and achievements. This could include a multimedia presentation, testimonials, or a narrative delivered by a prominent church member or historian.

3. **Sermon**: The sermon should focus on the biblical and theological aspects of the Church Anniversary. Emphasize God's faithfulness, the church's mission, and the call to continue pursuing God's work in the future.
4. **Special Presentations**: Include special moments such as recognition of long-standing members, awards, or special performances. These presentations should align with the anniversary's theme and celebrate the contributions of individuals and groups within the church.
5. **Communion and Prayer**: Incorporate Communion or a special prayer of dedication to reflect on the significance of the anniversary in the context of the church's faith and mission.
6. **Fellowship and Celebration**: Conclude the service with a time of fellowship, such as a meal or social event. This provides an opportunity for members to connect, celebrate, and strengthen their bonds.

Practical Considerations

Address all logistical aspects, including seating arrangements, audio-visual equipment, and transportation for special guests. Recruit and coordinate volunteers to assist with setup, guest services, and clean-up. After the anniversary, gather feedback from attendees to assess the event's impact and identify areas for improvement, ensuring future observances can be even more successful.

Reflections and Impact

The Church Anniversary is a powerful occasion that reinforces the church's sense of identity and mission. It fosters unity, celebrates achievements, and renews the congregation's commitment to its purpose. By reflecting on the church's journey and acknowledging God's faithfulness, the anniversary strengthens the community's bonds and encourages members to continue their work in advancing God's kingdom.

Conclusion

The Church Anniversary offers a rich opportunity for reflection, celebration, and renewal. By understanding its biblical foundations, historical development, and theological significance, and by planning thoughtfully and executing effectively, the church can honor God's faithfulness and strengthen its mission. This observance serves as a meaningful reminder of the church's journey and a call to continue faithfully in its work and worship.

CHAPTER SIXTY-THREE
PASTOR'S ANNIVERSARY

Introduction

The Pastor's Anniversary is a significant observance within many Baptist congregations, providing an opportunity to honor and recognize the pastor's leadership, dedication, and ministry. This annual celebration acknowledges the pastor's contributions to the church, reflects on their impact, and fosters a sense of gratitude and appreciation within the congregation. This chapter explores the biblical foundations, historical development, theological significance, and practical aspects of organizing a Pastor's Anniversary celebration.

Biblical Foundations

The Bible underscores the importance of honoring and appreciating those who lead and shepherd the church. Scripture encourages respect and recognition for pastoral leaders, as seen in 1 Timothy 5:17, which states, "The elders who direct the affairs of the church well are worthy of double honor, especially those whose work is preaching and teaching." This passage highlights the importance of honoring those who diligently serve in pastoral roles.

Additionally, Hebrews 13:17 emphasizes the need for support and respect for church leaders: "Have confidence in your leaders and submit to their authority, because they keep watch over you as those who must give an account. Do this so that their work will be a joy, not a burden, for that would be of no benefit to you." This verse reflects the mutual respect and support that should characterize the relationship between pastors and their congregations.

In 1 Thessalonians 5:12-13, Paul instructs, "But we request of you, brethren, that you appreciate those who diligently labor among you, and have charge over you in the Lord and give you instruction, and that you esteem them very highly in love because of their work." This encouragement to show appreciation aligns with the purpose of Pastor's Anniversary, affirming the value of the pastor's role in the spiritual life of the church.

Historical Development

The tradition of celebrating a Pastor's Anniversary has evolved over time, reflecting a long-standing practice of recognizing and appreciating pastoral leadership. Historically, these celebrations often involved special services, sermons, and communal gatherings focused on honoring the pastor's contributions to the church.

In many Baptist traditions, the Pastor's Anniversary has become an annual event, marked by a series of activities including sermons, testimonials, and fellowship meals. These events serve to celebrate the pastor's tenure, acknowledge their achievements, and express gratitude for their service.

The evolution of this observance has seen increased emphasis on including various elements such as special presentations, gifts, and recognition of the pastor's family, highlighting the broader impact of the pastor's ministry on the entire church community.

Theological Significance

The Pastor's Anniversary serves to reinforce the theological understanding of pastoral leadership as a vital and ordained role within the church. It acknowledges the pastor's role as a shepherd, teacher, and leader, entrusted with the responsibility of guiding and nurturing the congregation. The celebration provides an opportunity to reflect on the pastor's role in advancing the church's mission and fostering spiritual growth.

Recognizing and honoring the pastor aligns with biblical teachings about the respect and support due to those who lead and serve in ministry. It serves as a reminder of the collaborative nature of church leadership, where the pastor's efforts are supported and valued by the congregation.

Planning and Implementation

Organizing a Pastor's Anniversary requires careful planning to ensure that the celebration reflects the significance of the occasion and appropriately honors the pastor. The planning process typically begins with selecting a date for the celebration, often aligning it with the anniversary of the pastor's arrival at the church or a significant milestone in their ministry.

The planning committee should consider organizing a series of events to mark the occasion. This may include a special worship service featuring a sermon of appreciation, testimonials from congregation members, and special presentations. Additional elements might include a banquet or fellowship meal, where the pastor is honored with speeches, awards, and gifts.

Coordination with the church's music ministry to include special music or choir performances that reflect the theme of gratitude and celebration can enhance the event. It is also important to involve the congregation in the planning process, encouraging participation and contributions to make the celebration meaningful and memorable.

Promotion of the Pastor's Anniversary should be handled through various channels, including church bulletins, social media, and personal invitations. Providing clear information about the schedule of events and ways to contribute to the celebration helps ensure broad participation and engagement.

Service Outline

A typical Pastor's Anniversary service includes several key components. The service often begins with a time of worship and praise, setting the tone for a celebratory and reflective atmosphere. This is followed by a special sermon or message focused on honoring the pastor's contributions and reflecting on their impact on the church.

Testimonies from congregation members, highlighting personal experiences and expressions of gratitude, form a central part of the service. These testimonies offer a personal and heartfelt recognition of the pastor's influence and leadership.

The service may also include special music or choir performances, with selections chosen to reflect themes of gratitude and celebration. The presentation of gifts, awards, or tokens of appreciation is typically a highlight of the service, providing a tangible expression of the congregation's gratitude.

Practical Considerations

When organizing a Pastor's Anniversary, several practical considerations should be addressed to ensure a successful celebration. Securing a suitable venue and arranging for necessary logistics, such as seating, sound equipment, and decorations, is important to create an appropriate and welcoming environment.

Volunteers play a key role in the success of the event, with responsibilities including event setup, coordination of activities, and guest management. Clear communication and delegation of tasks help ensure that all aspects of the celebration are handled efficiently.

Budgeting for the anniversary celebration involves accounting for expenses related to special services, meals, gifts, and any additional activities. Providing guidelines for contributions and managing the budget effectively helps ensure that the celebration remains within financial limits while achieving its objectives.

Reflections and Impact

The Pastor's Anniversary often leaves a lasting impact on both the pastor and the congregation. For the pastor, the celebration provides a sense of affirmation and recognition, reinforcing the significance of their ministry and the support of the congregation. It can serve as a time of personal reflection and encouragement, strengthening the pastor's commitment to their role.

For the congregation, the Pastor's Anniversary fosters a deeper appreciation for their leader and a greater sense of community. It provides an opportunity to reflect on the pastor's contributions and the overall journey of the church under their leadership, enhancing the sense of unity and shared purpose within the congregation.

Conclusion

The Pastor's Anniversary is a meaningful observance that acknowledges and celebrates the vital role of pastoral leadership within the church. Rooted in biblical principles and enriched by historical traditions, the celebration offers a platform for expressing gratitude, reflecting on the pastor's impact, and fostering a sense of community. By understanding the significance of this observance and carefully planning its implementation, churches can effectively honor their pastors and strengthen their commitment to the shared mission of the church.

CHAPTER SIXTY-FOUR
MUSICIAN'S APPRECIATION

Introduction

Musician's Appreciation is a meaningful observance in Baptist churches, recognizing the essential role that musicians play in worship and community life. This chapter delves into the Biblical foundations, historical development, and practical aspects of Musician's Appreciation, shedding light on its significance and offering guidance on how to implement such a celebration effectively.

Biblical Foundations

The Bible provides a rich foundation for the role of music in worship. In Psalm 33:3, we are instructed to "Sing unto him a new song; play skilfully with a loud noise," emphasizing the importance of skillful and heartfelt music in our worship practices. Similarly, Psalm 150:4-5 encourages a variety of musical expressions to praise God, reflecting the diverse ways in which music can enhance our worship experience.

The organization and dedication of musical ministry are highlighted in 1 Chronicles 25:6-7, where we see the structured and dedicated nature of musical service in the Old Testament temple. This historical precedent underscores the value of a well-organized musical ministry in worship.

Music is also portrayed as a means of spiritual encouragement. Ephesians 5:19 encourages us to "Speak to yourselves in psalms and hymns and spiritual songs," emphasizing music's role in fostering spiritual connection and devotion. Similarly, Colossians 3:16 underscores the educational and encouraging aspects of music, highlighting its impact on spiritual growth and community.

Finally, 1 Chronicles 16:23-25 reminds us of music's role in proclaiming God's greatness and fostering unity among believers. Music in worship serves not only as an expression of praise but also as a unifying force within the faith community.

Historical Development

The tradition of honoring musicians has evolved significantly over time. Initially, recognition of musical contributions in Baptist churches was informal, with no specific events dedicated to celebrating musicians. However, as the role of music in worship became increasingly valued, the practice of formally acknowledging musicians gained prominence.

Musician's Appreciation serves several purposes. It provides an opportunity to acknowledge and thank musicians for their dedication and service, fosters encouragement, and strengthens community bonds. By celebrating musicians, churches not only express gratitude but also inspire continued excellence and commitment within the music ministry.

Theological Significance

Theologically, Musician's Appreciation reflects the value placed on each member's contribution to the worship and life of the church. It acknowledges that musical talents are gifts from God, meant to be used for His glory and the edification of the church. Recognizing musicians aligns with the broader Biblical principle of valuing and honoring the diverse gifts within the body of Christ, as seen in 1 Corinthians 12:4-7, which speaks to the variety of gifts but the same Spirit.

Planning and Implementation

Effective planning for Musician's Appreciation involves several key steps. Coordination with the music ministry team is essential to schedule the event and determine its format. Recognizing musicians with appropriate gifts or awards adds a personal touch to the celebration. Promoting the event ensures good attendance and participation from the congregation, enhancing the overall impact of the observance.

Service Outline

A typical Musician's Appreciation service may include the following elements:

- **Opening**: Welcome and opening prayer, emphasizing the theme of gratitude and celebration.
- **Musical Performances**: Special performances by the musicians being honored, showcasing their talents and contributions.
- **Testimonies**: Personal testimonies from congregation members and leaders, sharing how the musicians have impacted their worship experience.
- **Acknowledgment**: Presentation of gifts or tokens of appreciation, such as plaques or certificates, to the musicians.
- **Congregational Participation**: Hymns or songs performed by the congregation, highlighting the collective appreciation for the musicians.
- **Closing**: Final remarks and a closing prayer, reinforcing the church's gratitude and commitment to supporting its music ministry.

Practical Considerations

When planning Musician's Appreciation, it is important to allocate a budget that covers expenses for recognition gifts, special music, and other needs. Working with the church's financial team can help manage resources effectively. Involving the congregation in the planning process can also enhance the event's success. Encouraging feedback on the format, engaging volunteers, and promoting the event will contribute to a well-attended and meaningful celebration.

Reflections and Impact

Musician's Appreciation has a profound impact on the music ministry. It not only provides recognition and encouragement but also fosters a culture of support and appreciation within the church. These celebrations enhance the quality and dedication of musical contributions, reinforcing the role of music in worship.

Many individuals find Musician's Appreciation to be a deeply meaningful experience. It serves as a moment to reflect on the importance of music in worship and to recognize the hard work and dedication of those who contribute to the church's musical life.

Conclusion

Musician's Appreciation is an important observance that highlights the significance of music in worship. Rooted in Biblical principles, this event honors the contributions of musicians and reinforces their role in fostering spiritual growth and community unity. As Baptist churches continue to evolve, Musician's Appreciation will remain a vital aspect of church life, reflecting the ongoing value of honoring those who enhance worship through their musical talents.

CHAPTER SIXTY-FIVE
CHOIR ANNIVERSARY

Introduction

Choir Anniversaries are significant events in Baptist churches that celebrate the contributions of the church choir. This observance acknowledges the choir's role in enhancing worship, fostering community spirit, and supporting the church's mission. This chapter explores the Biblical foundations, historical development, and practical aspects of Choir Anniversaries, offering guidance on planning and executing these important celebrations.

Biblical Foundations

The Bible highlights the importance of music and choirs in worship through various passages. In 2 Chronicles 5:13-14, we see the role of choirs in the dedication of the temple, where the singing of the choir leads to the manifestation of God's glory. This passage underscores the significant role that organized musical groups play in worship.

Psalm 100:2 calls us to "Serve the Lord with gladness: come before his presence with singing." This verse reinforces the Biblical call to engage in joyful and spirited worship through music, reflecting the choir's role in leading and enhancing this aspect of worship.

Moreover, Nehemiah 12:24 describes the roles of choir leaders in the post-exilic restoration of Jerusalem, highlighting the structured and essential nature of choirs in the religious and communal life of the people.

Historical Development

The tradition of celebrating Choir Anniversaries has evolved from informal recognitions to more structured events. Initially, there were no dedicated celebrations for choirs; however, as their role in worship became more appreciated, churches began to formalize these observances.

Choir Anniversaries serve to honor the dedication and service of the choir members, acknowledge their contributions to the church's worship life, and encourage continued participation and excellence. These celebrations often include musical performances, testimonies from congregation members, and presentations of gifts or tokens of appreciation.

The historical development of Choir Anniversaries reflects a growing recognition of the choir's vital role in church life and worship, providing an opportunity to express gratitude and reinforce the importance of musical ministry.

Theological Significance

Theologically, Choir Anniversaries reflect the value placed on collective worship and the diverse gifts within the body of Christ. The choir, as a collective group, exemplifies the Biblical principle of unity and diversity in worship. In 1 Corinthians 12:12-14, the Apostle Paul speaks of the church as one body with many parts, each contributing to the whole. This principle applies to the choir, where each member's contribution enhances the worship experience and supports the church's mission.

Recognizing the choir through an anniversary celebration aligns with the Biblical call to honor those who serve faithfully. It acknowledges that the musical gifts of choir members are intended to glorify God and build up the church community.

Planning and Implementation

Planning a Choir Anniversary involves several key steps. Coordination with the choir is essential to schedule the event and decide on the format. This may include special musical performances, rehearsals, and the selection of appropriate recognition gifts or awards.

Promotion of the event is crucial to ensure good attendance and participation from the congregation. Effective communication about the event's purpose and details helps build excitement and support within the church community.

Involving the choir in the planning process allows for their input and ensures that the celebration reflects their contributions and preferences.

Service Outline

A typical Choir Anniversary service might include the following elements:

- **Opening**: Welcome and opening prayer, setting the tone for celebration and gratitude.
- **Musical Performances**: Special performances by the choir, showcasing their talents and contributions over the year.

- **Testimonies**: Sharing of personal testimonies from congregation members and church leaders about the impact of the choir's music.
- **Acknowledgment**: Presentation of gifts or tokens of appreciation to choir members, recognizing their dedication and service.
- **Congregational Participation**: Hymns or songs performed by the congregation, highlighting collective appreciation and participation.
- **Closing**: Final remarks and a closing prayer, reinforcing the church's gratitude and commitment to supporting its choir.

Practical Considerations

When planning a Choir Anniversary, several practical considerations should be addressed. Budgeting for recognition gifts, special music, and event logistics is crucial. Working with the church's financial team can help manage resources effectively.

Engaging the congregation in the planning process can enhance the event's success. Soliciting feedback, involving volunteers, and promoting the event will contribute to a well-organized and meaningful celebration.

Reflections and Impact

A well-executed Choir Anniversary has a profound impact on the choir and the church community. It not only provides recognition and encouragement for choir members but also fosters a culture of appreciation and support within the church. These celebrations reinforce the role of music in worship and strengthen the bond between the choir and the congregation.

Many individuals find Choir Anniversaries to be a deeply meaningful experience, reflecting on the significance of the choir's contributions to the church's worship and life.

Conclusion

Choir Anniversaries are an important observance in Baptist churches that highlight the essential role of music in worship. Rooted in Biblical principles and historical development, these events honor the dedication and service of choir members and reinforce their importance in the church community. As Baptist churches continue to celebrate and appreciate their choirs, these observances will remain a vital part of church life, reflecting the ongoing value of musical contributions to worship and community unity.

CHAPTER SIXTY-SIX
CHURCH PICNIC

Introduction

T he Church Picnic is a cherished tradition that provides an opportunity for fellowship and community-building outside of the formal worship setting. This chapter explores the Biblical foundations, historical development, and practical aspects of organizing and celebrating a Church Picnic, offering guidance on how to make this event a meaningful and enjoyable experience for all participants.

Biblical Foundations

While the Bible does not explicitly mention church picnics, it does emphasize the importance of fellowship and community. In Acts 2:46, we read that the early Christians "broke bread in their homes and ate together with glad and sincere hearts." This verse highlights the significance of shared meals and community bonding in the life of the early church.

Hebrews 10:24-25 encourages believers to "consider how we may spur one another on toward love and good deeds, not giving up meeting together, as some are in the habit of doing, but encouraging one another." This passage underscores the importance of regular gatherings and mutual encouragement, which can be enhanced through informal events like picnics.

Historical Development

The tradition of Church Picnics has evolved over time, from simple gatherings to more elaborate events. Initially, church picnics were informal and often held in local parks or church grounds, providing a casual setting for fellowship and relaxation.

As the tradition developed, churches began to organize more structured picnics with planned activities, games, and shared meals. This evolution reflects the growing emphasis on fostering community and strengthening relationships among church members.

Theological Significance

Theologically, the Church Picnic aligns with the Biblical principles of fellowship and community. It provides a setting for believers to connect with one another outside of the formal worship environment, reinforcing the bonds of Christian love and support.

By coming together in a relaxed and informal setting, church members have the opportunity to build deeper relationships and encourage one another in their faith journey, reflecting the Biblical call to mutual support and unity.

Planning and Implementation

Effective planning for a Church Picnic involves several key steps. Selecting a suitable location, such as a park or church grounds, and coordinating logistics, such as food, activities, and transportation, are essential for a successful event.

Engaging volunteers and church members in the planning process helps ensure that all aspects of the picnic are well-organized.

Promoting the event and encouraging participation will enhance the overall experience and foster a sense of community.

Service Outline

A typical Church Picnic may include the following elements:

- **Welcome and Opening Remarks**: Brief welcome and introduction to the picnic, setting the tone for a relaxed and enjoyable time.
- **Shared Meal**: A communal meal where participants can enjoy food and fellowship together.
- **Activities and Games**: Planned activities and games for all ages, designed to foster interaction and enjoyment.
- **Fellowship Time**: Informal time for conversation and connection among church members.
- **Closing**: Final remarks and a closing prayer, expressing gratitude for the time spent together and reinforcing the sense of community.

Practical Considerations

When planning a Church Picnic, it is important to allocate a budget for food, activities, and any other expenses. Collaborating with the church's financial team can help manage resources effectively.

Involving volunteers and church members in the planning and execution of the picnic will contribute to its success. Promoting the event through various channels, such as announcements and social media, will help ensure good attendance and participation.

Reflections and Impact

The Church Picnic has a significant impact on the church community, providing an opportunity for fellowship and relationship-building in a relaxed setting. It fosters a sense of belonging and strengthens the bonds among church members.

Many individuals find Church Picnics to be a deeply meaningful experience, as they offer a chance to connect with one another outside of the formal worship environment and build lasting friendships.

Conclusion

The Church Picnic is an important observance that highlights the value of fellowship and community within the church. Rooted in Biblical principles and historical development, this event provides a setting for informal interaction and relationship-building. As Baptist churches continue to celebrate and nurture their communities, the Church Picnic will remain a cherished tradition, reflecting the ongoing commitment to fostering Christian love and support.

CHAPTER SIXTY-SEVEN
FAMILY & FRIENDS DAY

Introduction

F amily & Friends Day is a special observance dedicated to celebrating and recognizing the importance of family and friends within the church community. This chapter explores the Biblical foundations, historical development, and practical aspects of Family & Friends Day, offering guidance on how to plan and implement this meaningful event effectively.

Biblical Foundations

The Bible emphasizes the importance of family and community relationships. In Ephesians 6:1-4, Paul instructs children to "obey your parents in the Lord, for this is right" and encourages fathers to "bring them up in the training and instruction of the Lord." This passage highlights the significance of family relationships and the role of the church in supporting and nurturing them.

In Proverbs 27:17, we read, "As iron sharpens iron, so one person sharpens another." This verse underscores the importance of mutual support and encouragement among friends and family, reflecting the value of strong relationships within the church community.

Acts 2:44-47 describes the early church's commitment to community and fellowship, where believers "had everything in common" and "broke bread in their homes and ate together with glad and sincere hearts." This passage illustrates the importance of gathering together and supporting one another in faith.

Historical Development

Family & Friends Day has evolved from simple gatherings to more structured celebrations that emphasize the importance of family and social connections. Initially, churches might have had occasional family-focused events, but the concept of a dedicated day grew to highlight the value of family and friends in church life.

Over time, Family & Friends Day has become an opportunity for church members to invite their loved ones and celebrate their role within the church community. This evolution reflects the growing recognition of the importance of familial and social relationships in nurturing a vibrant and supportive faith community.

Theological Significance

Theologically, Family & Friends Day aligns with the Biblical principles of community and mutual support. It provides a setting for celebrating the importance of family and friends and reinforcing the church's commitment to supporting these relationships.

By coming together to celebrate family and friends, the church reflects the Biblical call to build strong, supportive relationships and to foster a sense of belonging within the faith community.

Planning and Implementation

Effective planning for Family & Friends Day involves several key steps. Coordinating with church members to schedule the event, plan activities, and prepare for guests are essential for a successful celebration.

Promoting the event and encouraging members to invite their family and friends will enhance the overall experience and foster a sense of community. Engaging volunteers in the planning and execution of the event will contribute to its success.

Service Outline

A typical Family & Friends Day service may include the following elements:

- **Welcome and Opening Remarks**: Brief welcome and introduction to the day's events, highlighting the importance of family and friends.
- **Special Service**: A worship service that may include special music, testimonies, or messages focused on family and relationships.
- **Recognition**: Acknowledgment of families and friends, including any special presentations or awards.
- **Fellowship Time**: Time for conversation and connection among church members and their guests.
- **Closing**: Final remarks and a closing prayer, expressing gratitude for the time spent together and reinforcing the value of family and friends.

Practical Considerations

When planning Family & Friends Day, it is important to allocate a budget for event expenses, such as refreshments, decorations, and any special materials. Collaborating with the church's financial team can help manage resources effectively.

Involving volunteers and church members in the planning and execution of the event will contribute to its success. Promoting the event through announcements, social media, and personal invitations will help ensure good attendance and participation.

Reflections and Impact

Family & Friends Day has a significant impact on the church community, providing an opportunity to celebrate and strengthen relationships with family and friends. It fosters a sense of belonging and reinforces the importance of these connections within the church.

Many individuals find Family & Friends Day to be a deeply meaningful experience, as it offers a chance to connect with loved ones and celebrate the role of family and friends in their lives.

Conclusion

Family & Friends Day is a vital observance that highlights the significance of familial and social relationships within the church. Rooted in Biblical principles and historical development, this event provides an opportunity to celebrate and support these important connections. As Baptist churches continue to nurture their communities, Family & Friends Day will remain an important aspect of church life, reflecting the ongoing commitment to fostering strong and supportive relationships.

CHAPTER SIXTY-EIGHT
HOMECOMING SERVICE

Introduction

Homecoming is a special event that celebrates the return of former members, alumni, and friends of the church. This chapter explores the Biblical foundations, historical development, and practical aspects of Homecoming, providing guidance on how to plan and execute this meaningful event effectively.

Biblical Foundations

The Bible does not explicitly mention Homecoming, but it does emphasize the importance of welcoming and celebrating those who return. In Luke 15:11-32, the Parable of the Prodigal Son illustrates the joy and celebration that accompany the return of someone who was lost but is now found. This story reflects the Biblical principle of rejoicing in the return and reconciliation of individuals.

In 1 Thessalonians 5:11, Paul encourages believers to "encourage one another and build each other up," which aligns with the spirit of Homecoming as a time to reconnect and support one another.

Historical Development

The tradition of Homecoming has evolved from informal gatherings of former members and friends to more structured events that celebrate the church's history and heritage. Initially, Homecoming might have been a simple occasion for reconnecting with former members, but over time, it has grown to include various activities and celebrations.

Homecoming has become an opportunity to honor the contributions of past members, reflect on the church's history, and strengthen connections with those who have moved away or been away from the church community.

Theological Significance

Theologically, Homecoming aligns with the Biblical principles of reconciliation and celebration. It provides an opportunity to celebrate the return of individuals and acknowledge their contributions to the church community.

By coming together for Homecoming, the church reflects the Biblical call to welcome and support one another, fostering a sense of unity and continuity within the faith community.

Planning and Implementation

Effective planning for Homecoming involves several key steps. Coordinating with former members and alumni, scheduling activities, and preparing for the event are essential for a successful celebration.

Promoting the event through various channels, such as newsletters, social media, and personal invitations, will help ensure good attendance and participation. Engaging volunteers in the planning and execution of the event will contribute to its success.

Service Outline

A typical Homecoming service may include the following elements:

- **Welcome and Opening Remarks**: Brief welcome and introduction to the day's events, highlighting the significance of Homecoming.
- **Special Service**: A worship service that may include special music, testimonies, or messages focused on the church's history and heritage.
- **Recognition**: Acknowledgment of former members and alumni, including any special presentations or awards.
- **Fellowship Time**: Time for conversation and connection among church members, former members, and friends.
- **Closing**: Final remarks and a closing prayer, expressing gratitude for the time spent together and reinforcing the sense of unity and community.

Practical Considerations

When planning Homecoming, it is important to allocate a budget for event expenses, such as refreshments, decorations, and any special materials. Collaborating with the church's financial team can help manage resources effectively.

Involving volunteers and church members in the planning and execution of the event will contribute to its success. Promoting the event through various channels will help ensure good attendance and participation.

Reflections and Impact

Homecoming has a significant impact on the church community, providing an opportunity to reconnect with former members and celebrate the church's history. It fosters a sense of belonging and reinforces the importance of maintaining connections with those who have been part of the church community.

Many individuals find Homecoming to be a deeply meaningful experience, as it offers a chance to reflect on the church's history and reconnect with people who have played a significant role in their lives.

Conclusion

Homecoming is a vital observance that highlights the importance of celebrating and reconnecting with former members and friends of the church. Rooted in Biblical principles and historical development, this event provides an opportunity to honor the church's heritage and strengthen relationships within the faith community. As Baptist churches continue to celebrate their history and welcome back former members, Homecoming will remain an important aspect of church life, reflecting the ongoing commitment to unity and connection.

CHAPTER SIXTY-NINE
MEN'S AND WOMEN'S DAY

Introduction

Men's and Women's Day is a special observance dedicated to celebrating and recognizing the contributions of men and women within the church community. This chapter explores the Biblical foundations, historical development, and practical aspects of Men's and Women's Day, providing guidance on how to plan and implement these important events effectively.

Biblical Foundations

The Bible acknowledges the important roles and contributions of both men and women within the faith community. In Proverbs 31:10-31, the virtues of a capable wife are celebrated, highlighting the value of women's contributions to the household and community.

In 1 Corinthians 12:4-7, Paul describes the diverse gifts and roles within the church, emphasizing that "there are different kinds of gifts, but the same Spirit distributes them." This passage underscores the importance of recognizing and valuing the contributions of all members, regardless of gender.

1 Timothy 2:8-10 provides instructions for men and women to conduct themselves in ways that honor God. It emphasizes the importance of character and conduct in both men and women, reflecting the Biblical call to live lives of integrity and service.

Historical Development

Historically, Men's and Women's Day has evolved from simple acknowledgments of the contributions of men and women to more structured and celebratory events. Initially, these observances might have been informal gatherings or services, but over time they have developed into more organized and recognized events.

Men's and Women's Day provides an opportunity to celebrate the achievements and contributions of men and women within the church, reflecting a growing recognition of the importance of their roles and contributions.

Theological Significance

Theologically, Men's and Women's Day aligns with the Biblical principles of recognizing and valuing the diverse gifts and contributions within the church. It provides a setting for celebrating the unique roles and contributions of men and women, reinforcing the idea that all members have valuable roles in the church's mission and ministry.

By celebrating Men's and Women's Day, the church reflects the Biblical call to honor and support all members, recognizing their contributions and fostering a sense of unity and appreciation.

Planning and Implementation

Effective planning for Men's and Women's Day involves several key steps. Coordinating with church leaders and members to schedule the events, plan activities, and prepare for the celebration are essential for a successful observance.

Promoting the events and encouraging participation from both men and women will enhance the overall experience. Engaging volunteers in the planning and execution of the events will contribute to their success.

Service Outline

A typical Men's and Women's Day service may include the following elements:

- **Welcome and Opening Remarks**: Brief welcome and introduction to the day's events, highlighting the significance of Men's and Women's Day.
- **Special Service**: A worship service that may include special music, testimonies, or messages focused on the contributions and roles of men and women within the church.
- **Recognition**: Acknowledgment of the achievements and contributions of men and women, including any special presentations or awards.
- **Fellowship Time**: Time for conversation and connection among church members, focusing on the contributions of men and women.
- **Closing**: Final remarks and a closing prayer, expressing gratitude for the contributions of men and women and reinforcing the sense of unity and appreciation.

Practical Considerations

When planning Men's and Women's Day, it is important to allocate a budget for event expenses, such as refreshments, decorations, and any special materials. Collaborating with the church's financial team can help manage resources effectively.

Involving volunteers and church members in the planning and execution of the events will contribute to their success. Promoting the events through announcements, social media, and personal invitations will help ensure good attendance and participation.

Reflections and Impact

Men's and Women's Day has a significant impact on the church community, providing an opportunity to celebrate and recognize the contributions of both men and women. It fosters a sense of unity and appreciation, reinforcing the importance of valuing and supporting all members.

Many individuals find Men's and Women's Day to be a deeply meaningful experience, as it offers a chance to acknowledge the unique roles and contributions of men and women within the church.

Conclusion

Men's and Women's Day is a vital observance that highlights the significance of celebrating and recognizing the contributions of men and women within the church community. Rooted in Biblical principles and historical development, this event provides an opportunity to honor the diverse roles and contributions within the church. As Baptist churches continue to celebrate the achievements of their members, Men's and Women's Day will remain an important aspect of church life, reflecting the ongoing commitment to unity and appreciation.

CHAPTER SEVENTY
INSTALLATION OF CHURCH OFFICERS

Introduction

The Installation of Church Officers is a significant event in the life of a church, marking the formal appointment and commissioning of individuals to serve in various leadership roles. This chapter explores the Biblical foundations, historical development, and practical aspects of the Installation of Church Officers, providing guidance on how to conduct this important event effectively.

Biblical Foundations

The Bible provides a model for the appointment and installation of church leaders. In Acts 6:1-6, the early church appointed deacons to serve the needs of the congregation, demonstrating the importance of selecting and commissioning leaders for specific roles within the church.

1 Timothy 3:1-13 and Titus 1:5-9 offer qualifications and guidelines for church leaders, including bishops (overseers) and deacons. These passages emphasize the importance of choosing individuals who are spiritually qualified and capable of fulfilling their roles with integrity and dedication.

The Installation of Church Officers aligns with the Biblical principles of leadership and service, providing a formal recognition of individuals who are called to serve the church community in specific capacities.

Historical Development

Historically, the Installation of Church Officers has evolved from informal appointments to more structured and ceremonial events. Initially, the process of appointing leaders might have been relatively simple, but over time it has developed into a formalized ceremony that includes prayers, blessings, and affirmations of commitment.

The tradition of installing church officers reflects the growing recognition of the importance of leadership within the church and the need to formally acknowledge and support those who are called to serve.

Theological Significance

Theologically, the Installation of Church Officers aligns with the Biblical principles of leadership and service. It provides an opportunity to recognize and affirm the call of individuals to serve in specific roles within the church.

By conducting a formal installation ceremony, the church acknowledges the significance of leadership and the responsibilities that come with these roles, reinforcing the Biblical call to serve and lead with integrity and dedication.

Planning and Implementation

Effective planning for the Installation of Church Officers involves several key steps. Coordinating with church leaders to schedule the event, prepare the service, and communicate with the individuals being installed are essential for a successful ceremony.

Promoting the event to the congregation and involving church members in the planning and execution will contribute to the overall success of the installation. Ensuring that the service includes meaningful elements, such as prayers, blessings, and affirmations, will enhance the significance of the event.

Service Outline

A typical Installation of Church Officers service may include the following elements:

- **Welcome and Opening Remarks**: Brief welcome and introduction to the day's events, highlighting the significance of the installation.
- **Special Service**: A worship service that may include special music, readings, and a message focused on the role and responsibilities of church officers.
- **Installation Ceremony**: Formal installation of the officers, including the administration of vows or commitments, prayers, and blessings.
- **Recognition**: Acknowledgment of the newly installed officers, including any special presentations or affirmations.
- **Fellowship Time**: Time for conversation and connection among church members, focusing on the new officers and their roles.
- **Closing**: Final remarks and a closing prayer, expressing gratitude for the service of the officers and reinforcing the sense of unity and commitment.

Practical Considerations

When planning the Installation of Church Officers, it is important to allocate a budget for event expenses, such as refreshments, decorations, and any special materials. Collaborating with the church's financial team can help manage resources effectively.

Involving volunteers and church members in the planning and execution of the event will contribute to its success. Promoting the event through announcements, social media, and personal invitations will help ensure good attendance and participation.

Reflections and Impact

The Installation of Church Officers has a significant impact on the church community, providing an opportunity to formally recognize and support individuals who are called to serve in leadership roles. It fosters a sense of unity and commitment, reinforcing the importance of leadership and service within the church.

Many individuals find the installation ceremony to be a deeply meaningful experience, as it offers a chance to celebrate the call and commitment of the new officers and to support them in their roles.

Conclusion

The Installation of Church Officers is a vital observance that highlights the importance of recognizing and affirming the leadership roles within the church community. Rooted in Biblical principles and historical development, this event provides an opportunity to honor and support those who are called to serve. As Baptist churches continue to celebrate and support their leaders, the Installation of Church Officers will remain an important aspect of church life, reflecting the ongoing commitment to leadership and service.

CHAPTER SEVENTY-ONE
MISSIONARY DAY

Introduction

Missionary Day is a special observance dedicated to celebrating and supporting the work of missionaries and mission work. This chapter explores the Biblical foundations, historical development, and practical aspects of Missionary Day, providing guidance on how to plan and implement this significant event effectively.

Biblical Foundations

The Bible emphasizes the importance of missions and spreading the Gospel. In Matthew 28:19-20, Jesus commands His followers to "go and make disciples of all nations," reflecting the Biblical mandate for evangelism and mission work. This passage underscores the call to reach out to others and share the message of Christ.

Acts 1:8 also highlights the importance of missions, as Jesus instructs His followers to be "witnesses in Jerusalem, and in all Judea and Samaria, and to the ends of the earth." This verse emphasizes the global scope of the church's mission and the need to support and engage in mission work.

Historical Development

Missionary Day has evolved from informal acknowledgments of missionary work to more structured and celebrated events. Initially, churches might have had occasional missionary-focused services or events, but over time, Missionary Day has developed into a dedicated observance that highlights the work of missionaries and the importance of missions.

Historically, Missionary Day has become an opportunity to recognize the efforts of missionaries, raise awareness about mission work, and encourage support for missions both locally and globally.

Theological Significance

Theologically, Missionary Day aligns with the Biblical principles of evangelism and mission work. It provides a setting for celebrating and supporting the work of missionaries, reflecting the church's commitment to fulfilling the Great Commission.

By observing Missionary Day, the church emphasizes the importance of missions and reinforces the Biblical call to spread the Gospel and support those who are actively engaged in mission work.

Planning and Implementation

Effective planning for Missionary Day involves several key steps. Coordinating with missionaries and mission organizations, scheduling activities, and preparing for the event are essential for a successful observance.

Promoting the event and encouraging participation from the congregation will enhance the overall experience. Engaging volunteers in the planning and execution of the event will contribute to its success.

Service Outline

A typical Missionary Day service may include the following elements:

- **Welcome and Opening Remarks**: Brief welcome and introduction to the day's events, highlighting the significance of Missionary Day.
- **Special Service**: A worship service that may include special music, testimonies from missionaries, and messages focused on mission work and the importance of supporting missionaries.
- **Recognition**: Acknowledgment of missionaries and mission organizations, including any special presentations or awards.
- **Fellowship Time**: Time for conversation and connection among church members, focusing on mission work and ways to support missionaries.
- **Closing**: Final remarks and a closing prayer, expressing gratitude for the work of missionaries and reinforcing the church's commitment to missions.

Practical Considerations

When planning Missionary Day, it is important to allocate a budget for event expenses, such as refreshments, decorations, and any special materials. Collaborating with the church's financial team can help manage resources effectively.

Involving volunteers and church members in the planning and execution of the event will contribute to its success. Promoting the event through announcements, social media, and personal invitations will help ensure good attendance and participation.

Reflections and Impact

Missionary Day has a significant impact on the church community, providing an opportunity to celebrate and support the work of missionaries. It fosters a sense of unity and commitment to missions, reinforcing the importance of evangelism and mission work.

Many individuals find Missionary Day to be a deeply meaningful experience, as it offers a chance to engage with the mission work and support the efforts of missionaries.

Conclusion

Missionary Day is a vital observance that highlights the importance of supporting and celebrating the work of missionaries and mission work. Rooted in Biblical principles and historical development, this event provides an opportunity to honor those engaged in mission work and reinforce the church's commitment to evangelism. As Baptist churches continue to engage in and support missions, Missionary Day will remain an important aspect of church life, reflecting the ongoing commitment to spreading the Gospel and supporting mission efforts.

CHAPTER SEVENTY-TWO
MINISTER ORDINATION

Introduction

Minister Ordination is a critical and solemn observance in Baptist churches, marking the official recognition and setting apart of individuals for pastoral and ministerial roles. This chapter explores the Biblical foundations, historical development, and practical aspects of Minister Ordination, offering guidance on how to conduct and celebrate this significant event effectively.

Biblical Foundations

The Biblical basis for Minister Ordination is rooted in several key passages that emphasize the importance of setting apart individuals for ministry. In Acts 6:1-6, the apostles appointed seven men to serve the early church, laying hands on them to commission them for their roles. This passage highlights the practice of ordination as a way to officially recognize and empower individuals for ministry.

Another foundational passage is found in 1 Timothy 4:14, where Paul advises Timothy to "not neglect the gift you have, which was given you by prophecy when the council of elders laid their hands on you." This verse underscores the role of ordination in affirming and encouraging the gifts and callings of individuals within the church.

Additionally, Titus 1:5 reveals Paul's instruction to Titus to appoint elders in every town, which reflects the structured approach to leadership and ordination within the early church.

Historical Development

The practice of ordaining ministers has evolved over time, reflecting the growth and changes in church structure and theology. Initially, ordination practices were simple and focused on the recognition of spiritual gifts and calling. As the church developed, ordination became more formalized, with established procedures and rituals to set individuals apart for ministry.

Historically, ordination ceremonies have varied, but they commonly include the laying on of hands, prayers of blessing, and the presentation of symbols of office, such as a Bible or certificate. These ceremonies serve to formally recognize the individual's calling and commitment to ministry.

The development of ordination practices reflects the church's ongoing commitment to ensuring that individuals are properly equipped and supported in their ministerial roles.

Theological Significance

Theologically, Minister Ordination signifies the church's acknowledgment of an individual's call to serve in a leadership role. It reflects the Biblical principle that ministry is a communal and spiritual responsibility, as seen in Ephesians 4:11-12, where different roles are given to equip the saints for ministry and build up the body of Christ.

Ordination also emphasizes the importance of accountability and support within the church. By ordaining ministers, the church affirms their role and provides a framework for their ministry, ensuring that they are aligned with Biblical teachings and supported by the church community.

Planning and Implementation

Planning a Minister Ordination involves several important steps. Coordination with the candidate and the church leadership is essential to set a date and plan the details of the ceremony. This includes preparing the order of service, selecting participants for prayers and laying on of hands, and arranging for any symbolic presentations.

Promoting the event within the church helps ensure good attendance and participation. Effective communication about the significance of the ordination and the role of the new minister can enhance the impact of the ceremony.

Involving the candidate in the planning process allows for their input and ensures that the ceremony reflects their personal journey and commitment to ministry.

Service Outline

A typical Minister Ordination service may include the following elements:

- **Opening**: Welcome and opening prayer, setting the tone for the ceremony and acknowledging the significance of the ordination.
- **Scripture Reading**: Reading of Biblical passages related to ordination and ministry, highlighting the Biblical foundations of the ceremony.

- **Sermon or Charge**: A message from a senior pastor or church leader, offering guidance and encouragement to the candidate.
- **Laying on of Hands**: The laying on of hands by the ordaining ministers and church leaders, accompanied by prayers of blessing and empowerment.
- **Presentation**: Presentation of symbols of office, such as a Bible or certificate, symbolizing the candidate's new role.
- **Congregational Participation**: Hymns or songs performed by the congregation, reflecting the communal support and affirmation of the new minister.
- **Closing**: Final remarks and a closing prayer, reinforcing the church's commitment to supporting the new minister in their role.

Practical Considerations

Effective planning for Minister Ordination includes budgeting for ceremony expenses, such as certificates, gifts, and other needs. Working with the church's financial team ensures that resources are managed effectively.

Engaging the congregation in the planning process can enhance the event's success. Soliciting feedback, involving volunteers, and promoting the event will contribute to a meaningful and well-attended ceremony.

Reflections and Impact

Minister Ordination has a profound impact on both the individual being ordained and the church community. For the candidate, it represents the fulfillment of a calling and the beginning of a new chapter in their ministerial journey. For the church, it reinforces the importance of leadership and the collective responsibility to support and uphold those called to serve.

Many individuals find Minister Ordination to be a deeply significant and encouraging experience. It serves as a moment to reflect on the seriousness of the ministerial call and the support of the church community.

Conclusion

Minister Ordination is a vital observance in Baptist churches that highlights the significance of recognizing and setting apart individuals for ministry. Rooted in Biblical principles and historical development, this ceremony affirms the call to serve and supports the individual in their new role. As Baptist churches continue to celebrate and honor those called to ministry, Minister Ordination will remain a central and impactful aspect of church life, reflecting the ongoing commitment to spiritual leadership and community support.

CHAPTER SEVENTY-THREE
DEACON ORDINATION

Introduction

Deacon Ordination is a significant observance in Baptist churches, marking the formal recognition and commissioning of individuals to serve in the role of deacon. This chapter explores the Biblical foundations, historical development, theological significance, and practical aspects of Deacon Ordination, providing guidance on how to conduct and celebrate this important event effectively.

Biblical Foundations

The role of deacon is deeply rooted in Scripture, with several key passages providing the foundation for this ministry. Acts 6:1-6 describes the appointment of the first deacons to address the needs of the early church, emphasizing their role in serving and supporting the church's mission. The apostles instructed the congregation to select men of good reputation, full of the Spirit and wisdom, to oversee the distribution of food and care for widows, highlighting the practical and spiritual dimensions of the deacon's role.

1 Timothy 3:8-13 offers detailed qualifications for deacons, including integrity, self-control, and faithfulness. This passage

outlines the character and responsibilities expected of deacons, underscoring their role in supporting the church's ministry and serving the congregation with humility and diligence.

Additionally, Philippians 1:1 refers to deacons alongside bishops (elders), indicating their integral role in church leadership and governance. This inclusion reflects the collaborative nature of church leadership and the importance of deacons in upholding the church's mission.

Historical Development

The practice of ordaining deacons has evolved from its origins in the early church to the contemporary Baptist context. Initially, deacon appointments were made to address specific needs within the church community, such as caring for the poor and overseeing practical matters. Over time, the role of deacon became more formalized, with established procedures for ordination and duties.

Historically, deacon ordination ceremonies have included the laying on of hands, prayers of blessing, and the commissioning of deacons to their service roles. These ceremonies serve to officially recognize and empower individuals for their responsibilities within the church.

The development of deacon ordination reflects the church's commitment to ensuring that deacons are equipped and supported in their roles, contributing to the overall health and functioning of the church community.

Theological Significance

Deacon Ordination highlights the importance of service and leadership within the church. Theologically, it affirms the principle that ministry involves both spiritual and practical dimensions, as seen in 1 Timothy 3:8-13. Deacons are called to serve with integrity and wisdom, supporting the church's mission and facilitating its various ministries.

The ordination of deacons also emphasizes the communal and collaborative nature of church leadership. By ordaining deacons, the church acknowledges their role in upholding the church's mission and serving the congregation, reflecting the Biblical principle of shared responsibility and mutual support.

Planning and Implementation

Effective planning for Deacon Ordination involves several key steps. Coordination with the deacon candidates and church leadership is essential to schedule the event and plan its details. This includes preparing the order of service, selecting participants for the laying on of hands and prayers, and arranging for any symbolic presentations.

Promoting the event within the church ensures good attendance and participation. Effective communication about the significance of the ordination and the role of the new deacons can enhance the ceremony's impact.

Involving the candidates in the planning process allows for their input and ensures that the ceremony reflects their personal journey and commitment to service.

Service Outline

A typical Deacon Ordination service may include the following elements:

- **Opening**: Welcome and opening prayer, setting the tone for the ceremony and acknowledging the significance of the ordination.
- **Scripture Reading**: Reading of Biblical passages related to deacon ordination and service, highlighting the Biblical foundations of the ceremony.
- **Sermon or Charge**: A message from a senior pastor or church leader, offering guidance and encouragement to the deacon candidates.

- **Laying on of Hands**: The laying on of hands by the ordaining ministers and church leaders, accompanied by prayers of blessing and empowerment.
- **Presentation**: Presentation of symbols of office, such as a certificate or Bible, symbolizing the deacons' new roles.
- **Congregational Participation**: Hymns or songs performed by the congregation, reflecting the collective support and affirmation of the new deacons.
- **Closing**: Final remarks and a closing prayer, reinforcing the church's commitment to supporting the new deacons in their roles.

Practical Considerations

When planning Deacon Ordination, it is important to allocate a budget for ceremony expenses, such as certificates, gifts, and other needs. Working with the church's financial team ensures effective management of resources.

Engaging the congregation in the planning process can enhance the event's success. Soliciting feedback, involving volunteers, and promoting the event will contribute to a meaningful and well-attended ceremony.

Reflections and Impact

Deacon Ordination has a significant impact on both the deacons and the church community. For the candidates, it represents the official recognition of their call to serve and the beginning of a new chapter in their ministry. For the church, it reinforces the importance of leadership and the collective responsibility to support and uphold those called to serve.

Many individuals find Deacon Ordination to be a deeply meaningful experience. It serves as a moment to reflect on the seriousness of the deacon's role and the support of the church community.

Conclusion

Deacon Ordination is a vital observance in Baptist churches that highlights the significance of recognizing and setting apart individuals for service. Rooted in Biblical principles and historical development, this ceremony affirms the call to serve and supports the individuals in their new roles. As Baptist churches continue to celebrate and honor those called to serve as deacons, Deacon Ordination will remain a central and impactful aspect of church life, reflecting the ongoing commitment to spiritual leadership and community support.

CHAPTER SEVENTY-FOUR
PASTORAL INSTALLATION

Introduction

Pastoral Installation is a significant event in the life of a Baptist church, marking the formal introduction and commissioning of a new pastor. This chapter explores the Biblical foundations, historical development, theological significance, and practical aspects of Pastoral Installation, offering guidance on how to conduct and celebrate this important observance effectively.

Biblical Foundations

The Biblical basis for Pastoral Installation is found in various passages that highlight the role and responsibilities of pastors. In Acts 14:23, the apostles appointed elders in each church, a practice that underscores the importance of formal recognition and commissioning of church leaders. This passage reflects the early church's commitment to establishing and supporting spiritual leaders.

1 Timothy 3:1-7 provides detailed qualifications for church leaders, including pastors. This passage emphasizes the character, integrity, and ability required for pastoral leadership, reinforcing the need for careful selection and public affirmation of those called to this role.

Additionally, Titus 1:5-9 outlines the responsibilities and qualifications of elders (pastors), stressing the importance of appointing individuals who are sound in doctrine and exemplary in their conduct. This reinforces the need for a thorough and thoughtful process in installing a new pastor.

Historical Development

Historically, the practice of Pastoral Installation has evolved from the early church's informal practices to a more formalized process in contemporary Baptist churches. In the early church, pastoral roles were often established through the laying on of hands and prayer, reflecting the early church's focus on spiritual authority and communal support.

Over time, Pastoral Installation ceremonies have become more structured, incorporating specific elements such as ordination, commissioning, and the presentation of symbols of office. These ceremonies serve to officially recognize the new pastor's role and responsibilities, as well as to affirm the church's commitment to supporting their leadership.

The development of Pastoral Installation reflects the church's ongoing commitment to ensuring that pastors are equipped and supported in their roles, contributing to the overall health and mission of the church.

Theological Significance

Theologically, Pastoral Installation underscores the importance of leadership in the church and the principle of recognizing and affirming those called to serve. It aligns with the Biblical understanding of pastoral ministry as a calling that requires both spiritual and practical preparation.

The installation ceremony also emphasizes the communal aspect of church leadership. By publicly affirming the new pastor, the church acknowledges the role of pastoral leadership in guiding and nurturing the congregation, reflecting the Biblical principle of mutual support and accountability.

Planning and Implementation

Effective planning for Pastoral Installation involves several key steps. Coordination with the new pastor and church leadership is essential to schedule the event and plan its details. This includes preparing the order of service, selecting participants for the installation, and arranging for any symbolic presentations.

Promoting the event within the church ensures good attendance and participation. Effective communication about the significance of the installation and the role of the new pastor can enhance the ceremony's impact.

Involving the new pastor in the planning process allows for their input and ensures that the ceremony reflects their personal journey and vision for the church.

Service Outline

A typical Pastoral Installation service may include the following elements:

- **Opening**: Welcome and opening prayer, setting the tone for the ceremony and acknowledging the significance of the installation.
- **Scripture Reading**: Reading of Biblical passages related to pastoral leadership and installation, highlighting the Biblical foundations of the ceremony.

- **Sermon or Charge**: A message from a senior pastor or church leader, offering guidance and encouragement to the new pastor.
- **Installation Ceremony**: The formal installation of the new pastor, including the laying on of hands and prayers of blessing and commissioning.
- **Presentation**: Presentation of symbols of office, such as a Bible or certificate, symbolizing the new pastor's role.
- **Congregational Participation**: Hymns or songs performed by the congregation, reflecting the collective support and affirmation of the new pastor.
- **Closing**: Final remarks and a closing prayer, reinforcing the church's commitment to supporting the new pastor in their ministry.

Practical Considerations

When planning Pastoral Installation, it is important to allocate a budget for ceremony expenses, such as certificates, gifts, and other needs. Working with the church's financial team ensures effective management of resources.

Engaging the congregation in the planning process can enhance the event's success. Soliciting feedback, involving volunteers, and promoting the event will contribute to a meaningful and well-attended ceremony.

Reflections and Impact

Pastoral Installation has a significant impact on both the new pastor and the church community. For the pastor, it represents the official recognition of their call to serve and the beginning of a new chapter in their ministry. For the church, it reinforces the importance of pastoral leadership and the collective responsibility to support and uphold their new pastor.

Many individuals find Pastoral Installation to be a deeply meaningful experience. It serves as a moment to reflect on the importance of pastoral leadership and the church's commitment to supporting its leaders.

Conclusion

Pastoral Installation is a vital observance in Baptist churches that highlights the significance of recognizing and setting apart individuals for pastoral leadership. Rooted in Biblical principles and historical development, this ceremony affirms the call to serve and supports the new pastor in their role. As Baptist churches continue to celebrate and honor those called to lead, Pastoral Installation will remain a central and impactful aspect of church life, reflecting the ongoing commitment to spiritual leadership and community support.

CHAPTER SEVENTY-FIVE
REVIVALS

Introduction

Revival services are a pivotal aspect of church life, embodying a period of intense spiritual renewal, evangelism, and communal worship. Historically significant in many Baptist congregations, revivals focus on rekindling faith, deepening spiritual commitment, and reaching out to the community with the message of the Gospel. This chapter explores the biblical foundations, historical development, theological significance, and practical aspects of organizing revival services, with a particular focus on the Evangelistic Appeal and the Mourners' Bench.

Biblical Foundations

The concept of revival is deeply rooted in Scripture, emphasizing renewal and spiritual awakening. Key biblical passages include 2 Chronicles 7:14, which calls for repentance and prayer for God to heal the land: "If my people, who are called by my name, will humble themselves and pray and seek my face and turn from their wicked ways, then I will hear from heaven, and I will forgive their sin and will heal their land." This verse underscores the essence of revival as a response to spiritual need and a divine promise of restoration.

Additionally, passages like Acts 3:19 emphasize the need for repentance and renewal: "Repent, then, and turn to God, so that your sins may be wiped out, that times of refreshing may come from the Lord." The New Testament accounts of the early church experiencing revival, such as in Acts 2:1-4, illustrate the outpouring of the Holy Spirit and the resulting growth and transformation within the church community.

Historical Development

Revival meetings have a rich history within the Baptist tradition and broader Christian context. The Great Awakenings in the 18th and 19th centuries, particularly in America, were significant periods of revival that profoundly impacted the church and society. Figures like Jonathan Edwards and George Whitefield were instrumental in these movements, preaching messages of repentance and salvation that led to widespread conversions and renewed spiritual fervor.

In the Baptist tradition, revival services have often been characterized by dynamic preaching, fervent prayer, and an emphasis on personal conversion and renewal. These services are typically held over several days and include special meetings, evangelistic outreach, and a focus on deepening the spiritual life of both believers and non-believers.

Theological Significance

Theologically, revivals represent a period of spiritual awakening and renewal. They highlight the church's need for ongoing revival and transformation, reflecting the Biblical call for continual growth in faith and holiness. Revivals also serve as a reminder of God's power to transform lives and communities, emphasizing His sovereignty and grace.

The revival experience often brings to light the church's role in evangelism and mission. It reinforces the necessity of a vibrant faith that actively reaches out to the lost and seeks to revive the spiritual life of the congregation. Revivals also emphasize the importance of repentance, prayer, and the transformative work of the Holy Spirit in the life of the believer.

Evangelistic Appeal

Definition and Purpose

The Evangelistic Appeal, often referred to as "Searching the House," is a crucial element in revival services aimed at encouraging thorough self-examination and spiritual renewal. It involves a call for individuals to search their hearts and lives for areas of sin, complacency, or unmet spiritual needs. The purpose of this appeal is to prompt personal repentance, enhance spiritual sensitivity, and prepare participants for a deeper experience of revival.

Implementation in Revival Services

The Evangelistic Appeal is typically introduced through preaching that emphasizes the need for personal introspection and repentance. Preachers challenge attendees to examine their lives and consider areas where they may need to make changes or seek forgiveness. This appeal is designed to create a sense of urgency and reflection, encouraging participants to confront and address spiritual shortcomings.

Following the appeal, opportunities are provided for individuals to respond publicly or privately. This might include coming forward for prayer, writing down specific confessions or commitments, or participating in guided reflection sessions. These responses are aimed at facilitating genuine repentance and fostering a deeper spiritual renewal.

Examples and Impact

Many historic revivals have featured strong Evangelistic Appeals, such as those seen in the Great Awakenings. These appeals led to significant numbers of conversions and spiritual awakenings, demonstrating their effectiveness in revival contexts. The Evangelistic Appeal can lead to profound personal transformations, as individuals confront their spiritual state and make commitments to grow in their faith. It fosters a sense of urgency and earnestness in seeking God's work in their lives.

The Mourners' Bench

Historical Background

The Mourners' Bench, also known as the "Penitent Bench," has a storied history in revival practices. Originating in the 19th century, it is a specific place in the church where individuals come forward to express their sorrow for sin and seek spiritual renewal. This practice reflects a deep sense of repentance and a desire for personal transformation.

Significance in Revival Practices

The Mourners' Bench serves as a tangible representation of repentance and humility. By coming forward to this designated area, individuals publicly acknowledge their need for God's grace and demonstrate a willingness to engage in the revival process. It emphasizes the importance of personal response and commitment in the revival experience.

The use of the Mourners' Bench provides a dedicated space for individuals to receive prayer, counseling, and support as they seek to reconcile with God. It symbolizes the process of repentance and renewal, offering a visible and practical way for participants to express their spiritual commitments.

Modern Applications

While the traditional Mourners' Bench may not always be used in modern revivals, the principles behind it remain relevant.

Contemporary practices may include alternative forms of public response, such as designated prayer areas or counseling sessions, to facilitate personal renewal and repentance. The concept of the Mourners' Bench continues to influence revival practices by underscoring the importance of personal engagement and response, reminding participants of the need for genuine repentance and commitment in their spiritual journey.

Planning and Implementation

Organizing a revival requires careful planning and coordination to ensure its effectiveness and impact. The process typically begins with setting a date and determining the duration of the revival, which can range from several days to a week or more. Selecting a theme that resonates with the needs of the congregation and the community helps to focus the revival services.

Securing speakers and preachers who are spiritually prepared and capable of delivering impactful messages is crucial. These individuals should align with the revival's theme and bring a sense of urgency and inspiration to the services. Additionally, organizing music and worship that complement the revival's focus enhances the spiritual atmosphere.

Promotion and communication are vital to ensuring good attendance and engagement. Utilizing church bulletins, social media, and community outreach can help to raise awareness and encourage participation. Providing materials such as brochures or flyers with details about the revival, including the schedule and theme, supports effective communication.

Service Outline

A typical revival service includes several key components. The services generally begin with a time of worship and praise, setting the tone for a spiritually enriching experience. This is followed by the preaching of the Word, which is central to revival, focusing on themes of repentance, renewal, and salvation.

Testimonies from individuals who have experienced personal transformation or renewed faith often form an integral part of the service, providing tangible evidence of the revival's impact. Prayer meetings, both corporate and individual, are emphasized, with a focus on seeking God's intervention and guidance.

The revival may also include special events such as outreach activities, community service projects, and counseling sessions to support individuals in their spiritual journey. The closing of the revival typically involves a call to action, encouraging attendees to make personal commitments and engage actively in their faith.

Practical Considerations

Several practical aspects should be considered when organizing a revival. Ensuring that the venue is adequately prepared to accommodate the expected number of attendees is important, including seating arrangements, sound equipment, and lighting.

Volunteers play a crucial role in the success of a revival. Assigning tasks such as greeting, registration, and providing support during services helps to ensure a smooth experience for all participants. Additionally, preparing for potential logistical challenges, such as unexpected weather conditions or technical issues, is important.

Budgeting for the revival, including expenses for speakers, materials, and promotional efforts, should be carefully planned. Providing clear guidelines and support for volunteers and staff involved in the revival helps to ensure that everyone is aligned with the event's goals and objectives.

Reflections and Impact

Revival services often leave a profound impact on both individuals and the church community. They provide a time for spiritual renewal and growth, fostering a deeper commitment to faith and a greater sense of community among believers. Many participants reflect on the revival experience as a pivotal moment in their spiritual journey, marked by renewed fervor and a clearer sense of purpose.

The impact of revival extends beyond the church walls, influencing the broader community through outreach and service. The spiritual awakening experienced during a revival often leads to ongoing efforts in evangelism, missions, and community engagement, reflecting the revival's lasting effect on the church's mission.

Conclusion

Revival services are a vital component of the Christian faith, offering a period of intense spiritual renewal and communal worship. Rooted in biblical principles and enriched by a rich historical tradition, revivals continue to play a significant role in fostering spiritual growth and reaching out to the community. By understanding the historical context, theological significance, and practical aspects of revival services, including the Evangelistic Appeal and the Mourners' Bench, churches can effectively plan and implement revivals that inspire and transform both individuals and congregations.

CHAPTER SEVENTY-SIX
YOUTH AND CHILDREN'S DAY

Introduction

Youth and Children's Day is a special observance dedicated to recognizing and celebrating the contributions and growth of the younger members of the church. This chapter explores the Biblical foundations, historical development, and practical aspects of Youth and Children's Day, providing guidance on how to effectively plan and implement this important event.

Biblical Foundations

The Bible underscores the value and importance of children and youth within the faith community. In Matthew 19:14, Jesus says, "Let the little children come to me and do not hinder them, for the kingdom of heaven belongs to such as these," highlighting the significance of nurturing and valuing young members of the church.

Proverbs 22:6 advises, "Start children off on the way they should go, and even when they are old they will not turn from it." This verse emphasizes the role of the church in guiding and supporting the spiritual development of children.

In 1 Timothy 4:12, Paul encourages Timothy to "set an example for the believers in speech, in conduct, in love, in faith, and in purity," which is particularly relevant for older youth and young adults as they lead and inspire the younger generation.

Historical Development

Historically, Youth and Children's Day has evolved from simple acknowledgments of young members to more structured and celebratory events. Initially, churches might have had occasional children's services or activities, but the concept of a dedicated day grew to emphasize the importance of youth and children in church life.

Over time, the observance has become a platform for youth to participate in worship, share their talents, and be recognized for their contributions. This evolution reflects the growing recognition of the importance of engaging young members in the life of the church and supporting their spiritual growth.

Theological Significance

Theologically, Youth and Children's Day aligns with the Biblical principle of valuing and nurturing the younger generation. It reinforces the idea that children and youth are integral to the church's mission and community life. Recognizing their contributions and providing opportunities for their growth reflects a commitment to fostering a vibrant and inclusive faith community.

Planning and Implementation

Effective planning for Youth and Children's Day involves several key steps. Coordination with youth leaders and educators is essential to schedule the event and plan its activities. Engaging children and youth in the planning process ensures their participation and investment in the celebration.

Promoting the event within the church helps ensure good attendance and participation. Consider incorporating special activities, performances, or services that highlight the talents and contributions of young members.

Service Outline

A typical Youth and Children's Day service may include the following elements:

- **Opening**: Welcome and opening prayer, setting the tone for the celebration and emphasizing the value of young members.
- **Youth and Children's Participation**: Involvement of young members in various aspects of the service, such as leading worship, performing skits, or delivering messages.
- **Special Presentations**: Recognition of achievements, talents, and contributions of youth and children, including awards or certificates.
- **Congregational Participation**: Hymns or songs performed by the congregation, with a focus on celebrating and supporting young members.
- **Closing**: Final remarks and a closing prayer, reinforcing the church's commitment to nurturing and valuing its younger members.

Practical Considerations

When planning Youth and Children's Day, it is important to allocate a budget for event expenses, such as awards, materials, and refreshments. Collaborating with the church's financial team can help manage resources effectively.

Involving parents and volunteers in the planning process can enhance the event's success. Encouraging feedback from youth and children, and promoting the event effectively will contribute to a meaningful and well-attended celebration.

Reflections and Impact

Youth and Children's Day has a profound impact on the younger members of the church, providing them with recognition and encouragement. It fosters a sense of belonging and importance, reinforcing their role within the church community.

Many individuals find Youth and Children's Day to be a deeply meaningful experience. It serves as a moment to reflect on the importance of nurturing and supporting young members and celebrating their contributions to the church.

Conclusion

Youth and Children's Day is a vital observance that highlights the significance of young members in the life of the church. Rooted in Biblical principles and historical development, this event provides an opportunity to recognize and celebrate the contributions of youth and children. As Baptist churches continue to support and engage their younger members, Youth and Children's Day will remain an important aspect of church life, reflecting the ongoing commitment to nurturing the next generation.

CHAPTER SEVENTY-SEVEN
THE EASTER SUNRISE SERVICE

Introduction

The Easter Sunrise service is a cherished tradition in many Baptist congregations, celebrated in the early hours of Easter Sunday to commemorate the resurrection of Jesus Christ. This special service begins before dawn, symbolizing the moment when Jesus' followers discovered the empty tomb, signifying His victory over death. The service offers a unique way to start Easter Sunday with spiritual renewal and communal worship.

Biblical Foundations

The practice of the Easter Sunrise service is deeply rooted in the biblical accounts of Jesus' resurrection. According to the Gospels, Jesus rose from the dead early on the first day of the week, and the first witnesses to this event were Mary Magdalene and other women who visited the tomb at dawn. Key passages include John 20:1-18 and Matthew 28:1-10, which describe the discovery of the empty tomb and the angelic announcement of Christ's resurrection. These scriptures underscore the significance of the resurrection as the cornerstone of Christian faith and provide the basis for the Sunrise service's timing and focus.

Historical Development

The Easter Sunrise service has evolved over centuries from early Christian traditions that celebrated the resurrection at dawn. The practice became more formalized in the 19th century among various Christian denominations, including Baptists. Early celebrations often involved gathering outdoors to greet the sunrise, reflecting the biblical narrative of the women visiting the tomb at dawn. Over time, this tradition became a symbol of renewal and hope, embodying the triumph of light over darkness.

Theological Significance

Theologically, the Easter Sunrise service highlights the profound significance of Christ's resurrection. It serves as a celebration of the victory over sin and death, affirming the promise of eternal life. The early morning setting symbolizes the new beginning and the dawning of a new era in Christian history. By gathering before the sun rises, believers physically and spiritually align themselves with the resurrection narrative, embracing the hope and renewal that Easter represents.

Planning and Implementation

Planning an Easter Sunrise service requires careful consideration and preparation. The choice of location is crucial, as the service is traditionally held outdoors to symbolize the sunrise, though indoor settings can also be adapted to capture the early morning atmosphere. Ensuring that the venue is prepared for the service involves arranging seating and sound equipment, as well as considering lighting needs if the service is held outside.

Timing is another essential factor; the service should begin before sunrise to allow ample time for worship and reflection as the sun rises. Coordinating with local weather forecasts is important to manage any potential weather-related issues, especially if the service is planned for an outdoor setting. Safety and accessibility are also key considerations, ensuring that the location is accessible to all attendees, including those with mobility issues, and implementing any necessary safety measures.

Effective communication about the service is vital. Announcements should be made well in advance through church bulletins, social media, and community flyers to encourage participation. The planning process should also include preparing any materials needed for the service, such as hymnals and Scripture readings, and coordinating the involvement of volunteers for various aspects of the service, from setup to cleanup.

Service Outline

A typical Easter Sunrise service may include several key elements to foster a meaningful worship experience. The service usually begins with a warm welcome and an introduction to its significance, followed by the reading of Scripture passages that recount the resurrection story. Traditional Easter hymns are often sung, celebrating the resurrection with joy and reverence.

A sermon is typically delivered, focusing on the significance of the resurrection and its implications for believers' lives. This is followed by a time of prayer, offering thanks and reflection, and sometimes includes the celebration of the Lord's Supper, symbolizing the new covenant through Christ's resurrection. The service often concludes with a blessing and a call to carry the message of the resurrection into the new day.

Practical Considerations

When organizing the Easter Sunrise service, several practical aspects must be addressed. For outdoor services, preparing for varying weather conditions is essential. Having a backup plan for adverse weather, such as an indoor alternative or covered area, can help ensure the service proceeds smoothly. Accessibility needs should be considered, making sure that the location is suitable for attendees with different mobility requirements.

Safety is a significant concern, particularly for early morning services, which may involve navigating dimly lit areas or dealing with inclement weather. Ensuring that the venue is safe and well-lit, and that any potential hazards are addressed, is important for the safety of all participants. Effective communication about the service is key to ensuring good attendance and participation. Promoting the event through various channels and providing clear information about the time, location, and any special instructions can help attract a larger congregation.

Reflections and Impact

The Easter Sunrise service often leaves a lasting impact on participants. It provides a profound sense of connection to the resurrection story and fosters a spirit of renewal and hope. Many attendees reflect on the significance of starting Easter with a service that embodies the light and joy of the resurrection. Personal testimonies frequently highlight the service's ability to enhance their celebration of Easter and deepen their faith.

Conclusion

The Easter Sunrise service is a meaningful tradition that embodies the essence of Easter: the triumph of life over death and the promise of new beginnings. By aligning with the biblical narrative and celebrating the resurrection at dawn, the service offers a profound start to Easter Sunday. Its rich history, theological depth, and communal impact continue to make it a cherished observance in many Baptist congregations.

CHAPTER SEVENTY-EIGHT
WATCH NIGHT SERVICE

Introduction

Watch Night services, observed on New Year's Eve, hold a special place in many Baptist congregations, particularly within the African American community. These services are a time for reflection, prayer, and anticipation as believers gather to mark the transition from one year to the next. Watch Night combines elements of celebration and solemn reflection, making it a unique and meaningful observance that reflects on both the past year and the year ahead.

Biblical Foundations

While the Watch Night service itself is not explicitly outlined in the Bible, its practices are rooted in biblical principles of reflection, prayer, and renewal. The tradition of gathering to watch and pray can be linked to scriptures that emphasize staying vigilant and seeking God's guidance. For instance, Matthew 26:41 highlights the importance of watching and praying, "Watch and pray so that you will not fall into temptation. The spirit is willing, but the flesh is weak." This verse underscores the spiritual vigilance that Watch

Night encourages as believers reflect on the past and seek God's direction for the future.

Historical Development

The origins of Watch Night are intertwined with African American history. The tradition became prominent in the 19th century, particularly during the era of slavery in America. On the night of December 31, 1862, as the Emancipation Proclamation was set to take effect, many African American congregations held Watch Night services to celebrate the anticipated end of slavery and to pray for freedom and deliverance. This historical context imbued the service with a profound sense of hope and liberation.

Over the years, Watch Night services have evolved, but they continue to serve as a powerful symbol of transition and renewal. The practice of gathering to bid farewell to the old year and welcome the new one reflects a broader Christian tradition of marking time with spiritual reflection and thanksgiving.

Theological Significance

Theologically, Watch Night is a time for spiritual renewal and introspection. It offers believers an opportunity to reflect on the past year's experiences, acknowledge God's faithfulness, and seek His guidance for the coming year. The transition from one year to the next symbolizes the potential for new beginnings and spiritual growth. By gathering in prayer and reflection, believers embrace the biblical call to be vigilant and to renew their commitment to God.

Watch Night also serves as a reminder of God's sovereignty over time and history. The service reflects a deep trust in God's plan and providence, acknowledging both the trials and triumphs of the past year while looking forward to the opportunities and challenges of the year ahead.

Planning and Implementation

Planning a Watch Night service involves several considerations to ensure a meaningful and impactful observance. The choice of venue is important; the service can be held in the church or, for a more communal experience, at an outdoor location. Preparing the venue involves arranging for seating, sound equipment, and any necessary lighting, particularly if the service extends into the late evening.

Timing is crucial for Watch Night services. The service should start well before midnight to allow ample time for worship, reflection, and prayer. Coordinating with local weather conditions is important if the service is held outdoors, and having a backup plan for inclement weather is advisable.

Effective communication about the service is key to ensuring good attendance. Announcements should be made through church bulletins, social media, and community flyers to encourage participation. Additionally, preparing any materials needed for the service, such as hymnals and Scripture readings, and organizing volunteers to assist with various aspects of the service, from setup to cleanup, is essential.

Service Outline

A typical Watch Night service may include several key elements to create a meaningful worship experience. The service generally begins with a warm welcome and an introduction to the significance of the night. This is followed by a time of prayer and reflection, where attendees are invited to share their experiences and express gratitude for the past year.

Scripture readings that reflect themes of renewal and hope, such as Lamentations 3:22-23 or Isaiah 43:18-19, are often included. The sermon typically focuses on the significance of the new year and encourages believers to seek God's guidance and strength for the future.

The service may also include testimonies from congregants, sharing personal reflections and resolutions. Communion is sometimes offered, symbolizing renewal through the new covenant. The evening often culminates with a joyous celebration as the clock strikes midnight, marking the beginning of the new year with a sense of hope and anticipation.

Practical Considerations

Several practical aspects should be considered when organizing a Watch Night service. For outdoor services, weather conditions can impact the event, so having a contingency plan is crucial. Ensuring the location is accessible to all attendees, including those with mobility challenges, is important for inclusivity.

Safety measures should be in place, especially for late-night events, to ensure the well-being of all participants. Effective communication about the service details, including start time, location, and any special instructions, is essential for encouraging attendance and participation.

Volunteers play a key role in the smooth execution of the service. Assigning tasks such as greeting, setup, and cleanup helps ensure that the service runs efficiently and that attendees have a positive experience.

Reflections and Impact

Watch Night services often leave a lasting impact on participants. They provide a profound opportunity for communal reflection and renewal, fostering a sense of unity and shared purpose. Many attendees reflect on the significance of transitioning from one year to the next with a focus on spiritual growth and divine guidance.

Personal testimonies frequently highlight the emotional and spiritual benefits of the service. Participants often express appreciation for the chance to gather with fellow believers, reflect on the past year, and look forward to the future with renewed hope and commitment.

Conclusion

The Watch Night service is a meaningful tradition that encapsulates the themes of reflection, renewal, and anticipation. By gathering to bid farewell to the old year and welcome the new one, believers engage in a profound act of spiritual renewal and communal worship. Its rich history, theological depth, and lasting impact continue to make Watch Night a cherished observance in many Baptist congregations. Through its practices, Watch Night remains a testament to the enduring faith and hope of the Christian community.

APPENDICES

LIST OF NATIONAL BAPTIST CONVENTIONS

This is a list of prominent National Baptist conventions in the United States today. These conventions play crucial roles in their communities and the broader Baptist movement, each with its own unique emphasis and historical background.

National Baptist Convention, USA, Inc. (NBCUSA)
Founding Year: 1880
Description: One of the largest and oldest Black Baptist conventions in the U.S., focusing on evangelism, education, and social justice.
Headquarters: Nashville, Tennessee
Website: nationalbaptist.com

National Baptist Convention of America International, Inc. (NBCA)
Founding Year: 1915
Description: Promotes spiritual and educational growth of Baptist churches with an emphasis on evangelism, education, and church development.
Headquarters: Houston, Texas
Website: nbcainc.com

Progressive National Baptist Convention (PNBC)
Founding Year: 1961
Description: Emphasizes social justice and the progressive role of the church in addressing contemporary issues.
Headquarters: Washington, D.C.
Website: pnbc.org

Southern Baptist Convention (SBC)
Founding Year: 1845
Description: The largest Protestant denomination in the U.S., focusing on evangelism, church planting, missions, and conservative theological perspectives.
Headquarters: Nashville, Tennessee
Website: sbc.net

American Baptist Churches USA (ABCUSA)
Founding Year: 1907 (as the Northern Baptist Convention; renamed in 1972)
Description: A diverse group of Baptist churches with a focus on mission work, social justice, and inclusivity.
Headquarters: Valley Forge, Pennsylvania
Website: abc-usa.org

National Primitive Baptist Convention, Inc.
Founding Year: 1907
Description: Represents Primitive Baptists, focusing on traditional practices and beliefs with a conservative approach to worship and doctrine.
Headquarters: Greensboro, North Carolina
Website: npbci.org

National Missionary Baptist Convention of America (NMBCA)
Founding Year: 1919
Description: Focuses on missionary work and church growth with an emphasis on evangelism and education.
Headquarters: Memphis, Tennessee
Website: nmbca.org

National Association of Free Will Baptists (NAFWB)
Founding Year: 1935
Description: Part of the Free Will Baptist tradition, emphasizing evangelism, missions, and free will in salvation matters.
Headquarters: Nashville, Tennessee
Website: nafwb.org

National Association of Baptist Churches (NABC)
Founding Year: 1968
Description: Supports local churches with resources for ministry and cooperative missions.
Headquarters: Atlanta, Georgia
Website: nabchurches.org

American Baptist Association (ABA)
Founding Year: 1950
Description: Emphasizes cooperative missions, doctrinal education, and fellowship among member churches.
Headquarters: Texarkana, Texas
Website: abaptist.org

National Baptist Evangelical Life and Soul Winning Council (NBELSWC)
Founding Year: 1967
Description: Promotes evangelism and effective outreach strategies within Baptist churches.
Headquarters: Washington, D.C.
Website: nbelswc.org

National Association of Black Baptist Churches (NABBC)
Founding Year: 1976
Description: Advocates for Black Baptist churches and addresses social and community issues from a faith-based perspective.
Headquarters: Baltimore, Maryland
Website: nabbc.org

Additional Resources

Books

"Baptist History and Heritage" by William H. Brackney
A comprehensive overview of Baptist history and heritage, covering various Baptist conventions and their impact.
ISBN: 978-0914025896

"The Baptist Way: Distinctives of a Baptist Church" by Michael L. Haykin and C. Jeffrey Robinson Sr.
Explores the theological and historical distinctives of Baptist churches and conventions.
ISBN: 978-0805447830

"The Southern Baptist Convention and Its People, 1607-2007" by William H. Brackney
A detailed history of the Southern Baptist Convention, focusing on its development and influence over time.
ISBN: 978-0827229180

"The Rise of the Baptist Movement in America" by Walter B. Shurden
Discusses the growth and development of the Baptist movement in the United States, including various conventions.
ISBN: 978-0817007511

"Baptists and the American Revolution: 1776-1800" by David L. McCullough
Examines the role of Baptists in the American Revolution and their influence on early American society.
ISBN: 978-0820422714

"The Baptists: A History" by Thomas S. Kidd and Barry Hankins
> Provides a comprehensive overview of Baptist history from its origins to the present day.
> ISBN: 978-0631206648

"The Baptist Church: A History of Its Origins and Development" by E.E. Hoss
> Details the origins and development of the Baptist Church, covering key historical events and figures.
> ISBN: 978-0817007574

"A History of the Baptists" by William H. Brackney
> Offers an extensive history of Baptist movements and conventions, with an emphasis on their evolution and impact.
> ISBN: 978-0817012370

"Baptist Theology" by James Leo Garrett Jr.
> Examines the theological underpinnings and development of Baptist beliefs and practices.
> ISBN: 978-0805416362

Journals and Articles

"Baptist Quarterly"
> Scholarly articles on Baptist history, theology, and practice.
> Publisher: Baptist Historical Society
> Website Address: www.baptisthistory.org.uk

"Journal of Baptist Studies"
> Research and scholarship related to Baptist history, theology, and contemporary issues.
> Publisher: Center for Baptist Studies
> Website Address: www.baptiststudiesonline.org

"Christianity Today"

Includes articles and resources on various Baptist conventions and their influence on contemporary Christian life.
Website Address: www.christianitytoday.com

"The Baptist History and Heritage Journal"

Scholarly articles on the history and heritage of Baptists.
Publisher: Baptist History and Heritage Society
Website Address: www.baptistheritage.org

"The Journal of Southern Religion"

Scholarly research on religion in the American South, including Baptist history and practice.
Publisher: University of North Carolina Press
Website Address: www.jsreligion.org

"Baptist History and Heritage"

Journal dedicated to the history and heritage of Baptists.
Publisher: Baptist History and Heritage Society
Website Address: www.baptistheritage.org

Organizations and Associations

Baptist World Alliance

Connects Baptist conventions worldwide, offering resources and support for global Baptist missions.
Website Address: www.baptistworld.org

Baptist Joint Committee for Religious Liberty

Provides resources on religious liberty issues from a Baptist perspective and advocates for religious freedom.
Website Address: www.bjconline.org

The Center for Baptist Studies
Offers research materials and resources on Baptist history, including conventions and key figures.
Website Address: www.baptiststudiesonline.org

Glossary of Baptist Terminology

A

Arminianism: The belief in conditional election and the possibility of falling away from grace, contrasting with Calvinistic views of predestination and eternal security.

Autonomy of the Local Church: The principle that each Baptist church governs itself independently, free from external control or oversight.

Association: A group of Baptist churches organized for fellowship, cooperation, and mutual support in ministry and mission efforts.

B

Baptism: The Christian sacrament of initiation and adoption, often involving immersion in water, symbolizing purification and regeneration. In Baptist practice, baptism is typically reserved for believers who make a personal confession of faith.

Believer's Baptism: The practice of baptizing individuals who have made a personal profession of faith in Jesus Christ, as opposed to infant baptism.

Baptist Faith and Message: The statement of faith adopted by the Southern Baptist Convention outlining key Baptist beliefs and doctrines.

Benevolent: Pertaining to acts of charity and kindness, often directed toward helping those in need within the church and the community.

Building Fund: A designated fund within a church for the purpose of raising money to construct, renovate, or maintain church buildings.

C

Calvinism: A theological system associated with John Calvin, emphasizing the sovereignty of God, the total depravity of humanity, and predestination.

Church Covenant: A formal agreement among church members outlining their commitment to live according to Christian principles and to support one another in their spiritual journey.

Clerk: A church officer responsible for maintaining church records, including minutes of meetings and membership rolls.

Congregationalism: The form of church government where decisions are made by the entire congregation rather than a hierarchy of church leaders.

Convention: A gathering of Baptist churches or organizations for fellowship, worship, and cooperative ministry. Examples include the National Baptist Convention of America, Southern Baptist Convention.

D

Deacon: An elected or appointed church officer responsible for serving the church and its members, including tasks like visiting the sick, assisting in worship, and caring for church property.

Dispensation: A distinct period in God's plan for humanity, according to dispensationalist theology.

Dispensationalism: A theological framework that divides history into distinct periods or dispensations, each characterized by different ways God interacts with humanity.

E

Elder: A church leader responsible for teaching, preaching, and providing spiritual oversight. In some Baptist traditions, elders may also be referred to as pastors or ministers.

Evangelism: The act of preaching or sharing the message of Jesus Christ with the goal of converting others to Christianity.

F

Free Will: The belief in the ability of individuals to make choices that are not predetermined, often contrasted with predestination.

G

Grace: The unmerited favor and love of God toward humanity, essential for salvation and spiritual growth.

Great Commission: The instruction given by Jesus to his disciples to spread the gospel and make disciples of all nations (Matthew 28:19-20).

M

Mission: The work of spreading the gospel and serving others in the name of Jesus Christ, often involving local, national, and international efforts.

Missionary Baptist: A Baptist church or denomination focused on spreading the gospel and supporting missionary work.

Mourner's Bench: A place at the front of the church where individuals come to pray and seek spiritual comfort, often associated with a period of intense personal or communal seeking of God's help.

O

Ordinance: A practice or ritual established by Jesus Christ that is to be observed by the church. In Baptist tradition, the two ordinances are Baptism and the Lord's Supper (Communion).

P

Predestination: The doctrine that God has eternally chosen those who will be saved and those who will not, often debated in Baptist circles concerning free will and divine sovereignty.

R

Revival: A series of Christian meetings aimed at renewing spiritual fervor, often characterized by preaching, prayer, and an emphasis on personal conversion and recommitment.

S

Sanctification: The process of becoming more holy or Christ-like through the work of the Holy Spirit in the life of a believer.

Sola Scriptura: The doctrine that the Bible alone is the supreme authority in all matters of faith and practice.

Soul Freedom: The belief that each individual has the right to interpret Scripture and make personal decisions regarding their faith without coercion.

T

Tithing: The practice of giving one-tenth of one's income to the church or for religious purposes.

Trustee: A church officer responsible for managing church property, finances, and other administrative matters.

BIBLIOGRAPHY

Alcorn, Randy. *Managing God's Money: A Biblical Guide.* Tyndale House Publishers, 2011.

Alcorn, Randy. *The Treasure Principle.* Multnomah Books, 2001.

Beale, G.K. *The Book of Revelation: A Commentary.* Eerdmans, 1999.

Bolton, Samuel. *The Lord's Day: A Theological Study.* Banner of Truth, 2020.

Bridges, Jerry. *The Pursuit of Holiness.* NavPress, 1978.

Bruce, F.F. *Resurrection and the Life: The New Testament Hope.* Eerdmans, 1977.

Buchanan, James. *The Doctrine of Justification.* Banner of Truth Trust, 1867.

Bunyan, John. *Grace Abounding to the Chief of Sinners.* Penguin Classics, 1987.

Carey, William. *The Great Commission: A Call to Global Evangelism.* Crossway, 2002.

Carson, D.A. *The Sabbath and the Lord's Day.* Baker Academic, 1982.

Chandler, Diane J. *To Know Him and Make Him Known: A Guide to Christian Education.* Wipf & Stock Publishers, 2009.

Chester, Tim. *Compassion and Justice: The Christian's Role in Social Service.* IVP Books, 2007.

Dever, Mark. *Polity: A Practical Guide to Church Government.* 9Marks, 2001.

deSilva, David A. *The Lord's Supper: A Theological Introduction.* InterVarsity Press, 2008.

Forster, Greg. *God and Government: A Christian Perspective.* Crossway, 2012.

Fee, Gordon D., and Douglas Stuart. *How to Read the Bible for All Its Worth.* Zondervan, 2014.

Greear, J.D. *Gaining by Losing: Why the Future Belongs to Churches That Send.* B&H Publishing Group, 2015.

Grudem, Wayne. *Systematic Theology: An Introduction to Biblical Doctrine.* Zondervan, 1994.

Habermas, Gary R., and Michael R. Licona. *The Case for the Resurrection of Jesus.* Kregel Publications, 2004.

Hammett, John S. *Stewardship: A Biblical Approach.* B&H Publishing Group, 2002.

Hiscox, Edward T. *Standard Manual for Baptist Churches.* Revised by William E. Tucker, The American Baptist Publication Society, 1993.

Holy Bible. *King James Version.* Thomas Nelson, 2016.

Holy Bible. *New King James Version.* Thomas Nelson, 2019.

Holy Bible. *New International Version.* Zondervan, 2011.

Hodge, Charles. *The Whole Counsel of God: A Survey of the Bible's Doctrine of Redemption.* Banner of Truth Trust, 2002.

Johnson, Andy. *Missions: How the Local Church Goes Global.* Crossway, 2017.

King, Martin Luther Jr. *The Autobiography of Martin Luther King, Jr.* Edited by Clayborne Carson, Warner Books, 2001.

LaHaye, Tim. *The Return of the King: The Bible's Last Words on the End Times.* Tyndale House, 2002.

Leiter, Charles. *Justification and Regeneration.* Granted Ministries Press, 2007.

Lisle, George. "The Impact of African American Baptist Leaders." *Journal of Baptist History,* vol. 10, no. 2, 2023, pp. 45-67.

MacArthur, John. *The Doctrine of Scripture.* Crossway, 2005.

MacArthur, John. *The Gospel According to Jesus.* Zondervan, 2008.

Murray, John. *Regeneration and Conversion.* P&R Publishing, 1961.

Owen, John. *The Christian Sabbath: A Biblical and Historical Study.* Banner of Truth Trust, 1972.

Owen, John. *The Meaning of the Lord's Supper.* Christian Focus Publications, 1988.

Owen, John. *The Righteousness of God: An Introduction to the Doctrine of Justification.* Banner of Truth Trust, 2006.

Packer, J.I. *Evangelism and the Sovereignty of God.* InterVarsity Press, 1961.

Packer, J.I. *Knowing God.* InterVarsity Press, 1973.

Packer, J.I. *The Church: The Body of Christ in the World.* Crossway, 1985.

Pink, A.W. *The New Birth.* Baker Books, 2003.

Pratt, Richard L., Jr. *Sanctification: A Biblical Theology.* Third Millennium Ministries, 2001.

Prior, Karen Swallow. *Serving with Compassion: Practical Guidelines for Christian Social Service.* Baker Books, 2018.

Rawlings, Harold. *Basic Baptist Beliefs.* Broadman Press, 1992.

Ryrie, Charles C. *Jesus Is Coming Again: A Study of the Second Coming of Christ.* Moody Publishers, 1974.

Ryrie, Charles C. *The Holy Spirit: A Comprehensive Study of the Person and Work of the Holy Spirit.* Moody Publishers, 1997.

Schaeffer, Francis. *How Should We Then Live? The Rise and Decline of Western Thought and Culture.* Crossway, 1976.

Smyth, John. *The True Christian's Faith.* Edited by Howard D. Williams, The Baptist History and Heritage Society, 2000.

Spurgeon, Charles H. *The Grace of God.* Pilgrim Publications, 1970.

Spurgeon, Charles H. *The Law and the Gospel.* Sovereign Grace Publishers, 1999.

Sproul, R.C. *Chosen by God.* Tyndale House Publishers, 1986.

Sproul, R.C. *Faith Alone.* Baker Books, 1995.

Sproul, R.C. *The Fall of Man and the Foundations of Grace.* Ligonier Ministries, 2012.

Stott, John. *The Christian's Role in Society.* IVP Books, 1979.

Stott, John. *The Church and Social Justice: A Biblical Perspective.* IVP Books, 1980.

Stott, John. *Christ and the Law: A Biblical Study of the Relationship between Old Testament Law and New Testament Grace.* InterVarsity Press, 1984.

Stott, John. *The Doctrine of Man: A Study of Human Nature and Its Consequences.* InterVarsity Press, 2008.

Stott, John. *The Cross of Christ.* InterVarsity Press, 1986.

Spooner, Bernard M. (General Editor). *Handbook for Baptists.* The Baptist Standard Press, 1987.

Torbet, Robert G. *A History of the Baptists (3rd Edition).* Judson Press, 1995.

Turner, Nat. *The Confessions of Nat Turner.* Edited by Benjamin P. Thomas, The University of North Carolina Press, 1968.

Vlach, Michael J. *The Future of Everything: Essential Truths About the End Times.* Moody Publishers, 2012.

Walvoord, John F. *The Second Coming of Christ.* Zondervan, 1979.

Warren, Rick. *The Purpose Driven Church: Growth Without Compromising Your Message & Mission.* Zondervan, 1995.

Washer, Paul. *The Gospel Call and True Conversion.* Reformation Heritage Books, 2013.

Wayland, Francis. *The Elements of Moral Science.* American Baptist Publication Society, 1884.

Warfield, B.B. *The Inspiration and Authority of Scripture.* Presbyterian and Reformed Publishing Company, 1948.

White, James R., David F. Wright, and Michael J. Kruger. *Baptism: Three Views.* IVP Academic, 2009.

William G.T. Shedd. *The Perseverance of the Saints: A Study of the Doctrine of Eternal Security.* Banner of Truth Trust, 1978.

Wright, N.T. *The Resurrection of Jesus: A Theological Introduction.* Fortress Press, 2006.

www.ingramcontent.com/pod-product-compliance
Lightning Source LLC
Chambersburg PA
CBHW071132130626
46553CB00004B/1337